For my mother, and my father

SUDDENLY, WHILE ABROAD

HITLER'S IRISH SLAVES

NEW ISLAND

SUDDENLY, WHILE ABROAD
First published 2012
by New Island
2 Brookside
Dundrum Road
Dublin 14

www.newisland.ie

PRINT ISBN: 978-1-84840-200-3
EPUB ISBN: 978-1-84840-201-0
MOBI ISBN: 978-1-84840-202-7

Typeset by Mukesh Technologies, Private Limited, Puducherry, India.
Cover design by Mukesh Technologies, Private Limited, Puducherry, India.
Printed by TJ International Ltd, Padstow, Cornwall

New Island received financial assistance from The Arts Council
(An Comhairle Ealaíon), Dublin, Ireland

10 9 8 7 6 5 4 3 2 1

Contents

Acknowledgements

Whatever faults or errors this book contains are, of course, my own responsibility, but there are a number of people who have greatly helped me to write it. I should like to thank Maurice Earls, the editor of the *Dublin Review of Books,* who first suggested to me that I write an article for that journal about the 32 Irish merchant seamen who were imprisoned in the Farge camp. Maurice also provided an extremely helpful critique of some of the chapters in this book. I want to thank Tom Inglis, of University College, Dublin, who also read several chapters, and gave his usual perceptive commentary on them. I am grateful to my friend Robert Seidman, the writer and film producer, who brought an invaluable perspective to his reading of the book. I would like to thank both my daughters, Kirsty and Sarah, for the original research that they contributed – as well as their critical comments. I am sure that I tested the patience of their mother, Deborah Spillane, in talking to her about this book while it was being written, and I am deeply grateful for her tolerance and understanding of my preoccupation. My son Jamie was the first to read a complete draft of this book, and I am most appreciative of the many late-night discussions that we had about its contents, and for the shrewd historian's eye that be brought to bear on the final text. Jamie travelled with me when I visited the main concentration camp at Neuengamme, and the Valentin Bunker at Farge. His partner, Caoimhe Gallagher, also travelled with us to Germany: her fluency in German is much superior to my own, and helped me to obtain some key documents, as well as (literally) opening doors for us. I should like to thank our guide at the Valentin Bunker, Ms. Sandra Kern, who went to some trouble to facilitate our visit, and who was also most helpful in making archive photographs of the Bunker available to me. I am indebted to Dr. Reimer Möller, of the KZ-Gedenkstatte Neuengamme, for providing so much useful information about the trial of SS personnel in Hamburg in 1947. I am also grateful to Susan Hill, the Collection Access Officer, with Southampton City Council, for her assistance in obtaining the records of some of the Irish merchant seamen who were held captive in the Farge Camp. I must pay tribute to the pioneering work done by the Irish Seamen's Relatives Association in drawing public attention in Ireland to the fate of the Irish prisoners in Farge. I would also like to thank Harry Callan – the last Irish survivor of the Farge camp - for his hospitality and openness in talking to me about his experiences as a prisoner of the SS. Finally, I should like to thank my Editor at New Island, Eoin Purcell, who first approached me about the possibility of writing this book, and whose comments and suggestions - as well as his encouragement - have been of great assistance.

INTRODUCTION

Why do people have memories? It would be easier to die – anything to stop remembering.'

These words come from Vasily Grossman, a front-line Russian journalist who visited Nazi concentration camps in the immediate aftermath of World War Two. His comments reflect a response that was not uncommon among those who had been caught up in the horrors of that war. Others might argue that it is also time for the rest of us to forget. After all, the Second World War happened a long time ago, and since the vast majority of those who took part in it are now dead, perhaps it would be better to let them rest in peace.

I am more inclined to the view of Elie Weisel, who survived Auschwitz, and thought that to forget all that had happened there and in similar Nazi camps was simply 'to kill the victims twice'. I believe that we must continue to listen to the voices that emerged from that terrible conflict. The Second World War has cast far too long a shadow to be forgotten. It is a shadow that continues to fall beyond the children and grandchildren of those who fought in the war. Even if we wanted to forget the men and women who died or suffered in its cataclysm, their voices would still rise up, and insist on being heard.

Benedetto Croce once wrote that, "all history is contemporary history" – and his comment seems especially apt as far as Ireland is concerned. Ireland's role in World War Two is still able to generate heated controversy and division, and it is not hard to see why. On one hand, Ireland was one of just five European States who were able to remain neutral throughout the duration of the war. On the other hand, tens of thousands of Irish men and women volunteered to join the Allied armed forces, and to engage in the struggle against fascism. That apparent contradiction can still inform – or cloud – Irish perceptions of the war.

This book tells the story of 32 merchant seamen from Ireland who were held in conditions of great hardship in an SS slave labour camp from 1943-45 – and whose imprisonment there was not only illegal, but I believe, avoidable. The Irishmen who were imprisoned in this labour camp – near the village of Farge, in north-west Germany – may seem unlikely heroes of any story about the World War. They were all non-combatants, and none of them had volunteered for active service. The ships they served upon were not modern battleships, armed to the teeth with heavy guns, but were, for the most part, ageing freighters: slow, cumbersome, and without any adequate means of defence. Some of the Irish seamen were already in advanced middle-age when they were taken prisoner. Regardless of their age, they were sent to a labour camp by the Gestapo – where they were subjected to years of a brutal and degrading regime. Despite that – and unlike some other Irishmen – they steadfastly resisted all attempts by the SS to turn them into collaborators with the Third Reich.

When the camp at Farge was finally liberated in 1945, and 27 of the Irish seamen who had been imprisoned there were able to return to Ireland, they were largely ignored by the press, and soon disappeared from public view. Ironically, they are now acknowledged in Germany as a distinct group of victims of the Nazis. However, their suffering is still not properly recognised in their native country – even though the principal reason that they ended up working as slaves for the Nazis was their Irish nationality.

It is not only because of their suffering and endurance, or because they refused to collaborate with the Nazis, that I believe these men deserve to be remembered. It is also because a number of them chose to return to Germany after the war to give evidence in the trial for war crimes of some of their SS guards. This in itself required considerable nerve and commitment. Such trials were actively opposed by the Irish Government of the time, and no Irish representative was sent to provide practical or moral support for the Irish witnesses. Those who gave evidence before similar courts have spoken of the trauma that it caused them to relive their years of callous and inhuman treatment in the Nazis' camps.

As a result of the determination of these Irishmen to see justice done, a number of SS personnel from their labour camp were punished for their crimes, and sentenced to periods of imprisonment. But what was, perhaps, even more important was that the testimony of these Irish seamen asserted the fundamental principle that – even in a time of global hostilities – there remain certain boundaries to the ways in which any war should be conducted.

In a small but significant way, these Irishmen contributed to the proposition that war criminals – whether they operate in Germany or Rwanda, Bosnia or Syria – should continue to be held responsible and liable to be punished for any acts which deliberately victimise innocent civilians, or defenceless prisoners. For that alone, I believe that we continue to owe some debt of gratitude to the Irish seamen who were held in the slave labour camp at Bremen Farge.

1

SUDDENLY, WHILE ABROAD

My father began to plan his funeral about ten years before he died. He told me that he had already bought a plot in Dean's Grange Cemetery, in south County Dublin – close to his mother's grave. He said that he had intended to commit suicide some years previously and thought it would make sense to choose his final destination before he killed himself. To anyone who knew my father, this story was, simultaneously, highly implausible and all too likely to be true. He gave me a slip of paper on which he had scrawled all the relevant details – adding that he would not mind if I chose instead to put his body in a bin bag, and sling it in a rubbish tip.

My father's motives in telling me this weren't entirely clear: certainly, not to me and probably not to him either – perhaps, especially not to him. I was pretty sure that, at some level, it was bound up with the emotional mayhem that had been caused by his wartime experiences. Nonetheless, a few weeks later I was driving past Dean's Grange, with his slip of paper in my pocket, and I decided to pull in to see if I could find his plot. It didn't take long – although it turned out that the resting place my father had chosen for himself was a considerable distance from where his mother was buried. His choices may have been limited: the family vault was crammed full with an assortment of close and distant relatives. Pride of place on its weathered stone obelisk was given to my great-great-grandfather, Francis Blake Knox - the founder of this particular branch of the family. Although his name was carved on the grey stone, Francis was not buried in this cemetery, but in County Mayo, in the West of Ireland, where he was born and where he had died.

As I turned away from the vault, I stumbled upon another, slightly smaller grave, just a few yards away. Once again, the tombstone – which, this time, took the form of a large Celtic cross – bore the name of Francis Blake Knox. That didn't surprise me unduly: the name has been popular in my family for several generations, and was now attached to one of my own nephews. I was more perplexed by another of the inscriptions on this grave. It referred to 'Billie' – who had apparently died in Bremen in 1945. I had never heard of this relative, and there was no reference to the circumstances of his death.

When I next saw my father, I asked him who this person might be. Judging from the spelling on the tombstone, I had thought that 'Billie' might be a female relative, but my father told me that it referred to 'William Hutchinson

Knox', his cousin. 'What happened to him?' I asked. 'He was killed in Germany – just before the War in Europe ended.' I was curious to know why he wasn't called 'Blake Knox', but my father only muttered something about there being 'enough of us' in the world already. I knew from the tone of his voice that this was a subject he did not wish to discuss further. I also knew, from long experience, that the more I questioned him, the less I was likely to learn. It was only after my father's death that I learned what had happened to our lost cousin.

I had imagined that my father's unwillingness to talk about William was connected to his general reluctance to talk about the war in which he had fought. As a young man, my father had crossed the Border, from the State that was then known as 'Eire' into Northern Ireland soon after hostilities were declared in 1939, and enlisted in the British Army. Once again, his motives in doing so were not entirely clear to me – and, probably, not to him. My father was not greatly interested in politics, but he often expressed a visceral dislike of Hitler, and he connected - with some reason - the extreme nationalists of Nazi Germany to their contemporary equivalents in Ireland. We were not Jews, but my father held the Jewish people in high regard, and was revolted by their persecution. Perhaps, as a member of one religious minority – in his case, the Church of Ireland - he felt some sense of identification with another.

No doubt there were other factors in the mix besides his dislike of National Socialism – such as his simple desire for excitement – and there may also have been a sort of historical reflex that led him, his two brothers, and half-a-dozen cousins to volunteer for active service. His family had a tradition of serving in Irish regiments of the British army – for the most part, in the Connaught Rangers. They were by no means the only Irish family with that custom: from the time of the Peninsular campaign, at the start of the nineteenth century, soldiers from Ireland had helped to form the backbone of Britain's infantry divisions. The Irish Government did not go to great lengths to prevent such voluntary enlistment continuing during this war: they may even have welcomed its easing of the problem of chronic unemployment at home. One memorandum from the Ministry of Justice stated succinctly that, given the 'present economic circumstances', it was better for young Irish men to be in the British army 'than in our gaols'.

The Government proved to be much less tolerant – to say the least - of the 5,000 or so Irishmen who were already serving in the Irish Army, and chose to desert to join the Allied armed forces. General Dan McKenna – the Irish Chief-of-Staff – explained these desertions in what may seem like sympathetic terms: 'Those who have a natural taste for military life are more inclined to join the British Services', he wrote, 'where a more exciting career is expected.' The Irish Government did not share his understanding. In fact, they would later deny those soldiers who had deserted the Irish Army any access to public jobs and to state pensions when they returned home. This issue would fester for many years, and would generate much ill feeling and deep resentment.

My father ended up in Burma in 1942, with the First Battalion of the Inniskilling Fusiliers. Arriving outside Rangoon just a few days before the decision was taken to evacuate and burn that city. Rangoon was already in flames when my father joined the longest forced retreat in British military history. It lasted for more than three months, and covered over a thousand miles of unforgiving terrain. The retreating army was under constant and ferocious attack from elite Japanese divisions, as it fought its way to the Indian frontier. It suffered more than 10,000 casualties – one of whom was my father. He was hit by shrapnel from mortar fire, and his wounds turned gangrenous. Fortunately, an American missionary doctor had set up a field hospital under canvas. He operated on my father and saved his life.

General Slim described the men who limped out of Burma as 'utterly exhausted, and riddled with malaria and dysentery'. However, Slim could also recognise that 'they still carried their arms, and kept their ranks'. They may have 'looked like scarecrows', but Slim was proud that 'they looked like soldiers too.' It had taken a beating, but the Fourteenth Army was still an Army, and, a few years later, my father was lucky enough to be alive, and able to take part in the counter-offensive which drove the Japanese forces out of Burma.

He came back to live in Ireland in 1946, to a country that had remained politically neutral for the duration of the war. There were sound pragmatic reasons for the Irish Government following that policy: apart from the human casualties it would have involved, Irish participation in the war could have exacerbated serious internal divisions in a country that was still recovering both from a bitter civil war, and a deep economic depression. As a result of its neutrality, the Irish State had little direct involvement in the global conflict, and its resident citizens were even restricted in their knowledge of what had taken place. Martin Quigley, an agent in the OSS – the forerunner of the CIA – had visited Dublin for six months in 1943, and reported that for most Irish people the war in Burma and the Pacific 'seems as remote as if it were being fought on Mars.'

Stringent censorship had accompanied political neutrality – in what was officially known in Ireland as 'The Emergency'. In 1935, the Irish Government had set up an inter-departmental committee 'to prepare and submit proposals for the operation of censorship in time of war'. The report it had submitted was put into effect in August of 1939. Frank Aiken, who was appointed as Minister for the Co-Ordination of Defensive Measures at the outbreak of hostilities, claimed that its purpose was simply to prevent 'our people being oppressed by a barrage of propaganda'. However, as Clair Wills has noted, stripping reportage of the war of all editorial commentary produced 'its own kind of falsehood.'

This was perhaps most evident in Irish cinemas, where Joseph Connolly, the new Controller of Censorship, outlined what could – and could not – be shown to Irish audiences. His first principle was that that 'all news films' shown in Ireland 'must be free of war news'. He also insisted that there must be no sight, or mention of 'war preparations, parades, troop movements, naval and aircraft movements, defence preparations, pictures of shelters (or) sandbagging'. In addition, no comments – positive or negative – were to be permitted about 'any of the countries engaged as belligerents'. This was still a pre-television era, and newsreels were a primary source of information for audiences across Europe. The extraordinary constraints imposed by the Irish Government created immediate problems for Gaumont Pictures, who produced weekly newsreels for both Irish and British markets. They responded to the new situation by using quite different material for the two countries.

On 16th May, 1940, for example, the British version of the Gaumont newsreel covered the bombing of Rottterdam and the arrival in London of the entire Dutch government – which had fled the German *Blitzkrieg*. The Irish version featured the Pope proclaiming a new saint in Rome, and a festive carnival in Zurich. The next week, the British newsreel included the German bombing of Belgian towns, and dramatic footage of terrified refugees sheltering from machine-gun fire. The Irish version featured the King of Italy being received by Pope Pius XII, and the Kentucky Derby. In the years that followed, the newsreels shown in Ireland continued scrupulously to avoid screening any disturbing images of bloodshed and destruction. Instead, the patrons of Irish cinemas were kept well informed about international horse races, new arrivals in Dublin's Zoological Gardens, and, of course, the Pope's latest round of engagements. Eventually, in 1943, no further Irish editions of these newsreels were made or screened – apparently, to the great relief of Irish audiences.

Feature films were also subject to official censorship. Film distributors in Ireland were used to this, and apart from the objections to movies that featured the war, some of the other restrictions were based on traditional, moralistic grounds. There was a puritanical antipathy to what the Gaelic Athletic Association termed 'pictures extolling idleness, extravagance, superficiality and depravity of all kinds'. Such movies, it was claimed, carried a 'deadly, creeping poison' that threatened the spiritual health of the Irish nation. A similar attitude led the official censor to insist that the title of the Hollywood film *I Want a Divorce* – described in its publicity as 'a wise-cracking comedy' – be changed in Ireland to *The Tragedy of Divorce*. Some of the cuts demanded by the film censor defied any obvious explanation. In a report sent to the OSS in Washington, Martin Quigley cited the case of the RKO movie *Bombardier*, in which an instructor tells new recruits: 'There are three things a bombardier must remember – hit the target – hit the target – hit the target.' The censor insisted that the last two 'hit the targets' be cut. Quigley commented: 'Don't ask me why.'

Newspaper censorship may not have been quite as comprehensive, but the press was also strictly regulated by the Government. The details of Irish soldiers who had died while serving with Allied forces could not be reported directly in Irish papers: instead, those who were killed in action had died 'suddenly, while abroad'. When the British battleship, the *Prince of Wales,* was sunk by Japanese torpedo planes, in October 1942, with the loss of 327 lives, it was referred to in one Irish newspaper as a 'boating accident'.

12

Even the word 'Nazi' was not allowed to appear in print because the use of the word outside Germany was deemed to have 'an adverse connotation'. When Belfast was bombed in May 1941, with the loss of almost 1,000 lives in one night, the Irish press was instructed to avoid publishing any of the 'harrowing details'. All in all, the years of the Emergency saw what Ian Wood has described as 'an expanding bureaucracy,' working diligently to 'cocoon Irish people from the unsettling realities of a world at war.'

Meanwhile, the members of a ladies' knitting circle in Killarney were questioned by the Gardaí - who suspected them of making socks and gloves for Allied troops. Small wonder that Samuel Beckett later told Israel Shenker, with his usual mordant irony, that he preferred to live in 'France, at war, than Ireland, at peace.'

Censorship relaxed a little as the war entered its closing stages, but the most serious omission from Ireland's press coverage obtained until the very end. This related to its atrocities – and, in particular, to the systematic genocide being perpetrated against Europe's Jews. The position of the Censorship Board was stated clearly by T.J. Coyne, its Deputy Controller: 'The publication of atrocity stories', he wrote, 'whether true or false, can do this country no good'. In 1942, Coyne and Aiken informed the press censors that details of specific war crimes were not to be published in Irish newspapers. In December of the same year, the Allies issued a strongly worded resolution regarding the persecution of Jews, which gave accurate details of the mass deportations that had begun in Poland, and in other occupied countries.

In April of 1943, the Bermuda Conference also drew world attention to what was happening to the Jews of Europe.

Many years later, the Irish Cabinet Minister with special responsibility for censorship, Frank Aiken, admitted 'what was going on in the camps was pretty well known to us early on.' Despite that, there were no explicit references in the Irish press to the Holocaust until after the war was over. Even after Auschwitz, Belsen and Buchenwald had been liberated – and their horrors had been exposed – no recognition of the genocide came from official Irish sources. In that context, it is hardly surprising that the first newsreels which featured footage from the death camps were greeted with considerable scepticism by Irish audiences when they were shown in Irish cinemas. Indeed, one Irish newspaper even suggested that the British had used starving Indians to play the roles of concentration camp victims. The implication was that, whatever atrocities might have occurred, they were being cynically used to mask the real culprit, and that was the old enemy: British colonialism.

I remember, towards the end of his life, my father passing my son, Jamie, a faded photograph. It had been taken outside the Red Fort in New Delhi in 1941, and it showed eight young men. Six of them were sitting in a row of chairs. Two men stood directly behind them: I recognized one of these as my father. 'Who are they?' my son asked. 'My brothers', my father answered. Seven of the men were 2nd Lieutenants in my father's battalion: the eighth was their Commanding Officer. They had all recently arrived in India, after several months cooped up on a transport ship.

My father looked like one of the oldest in the group, and he was just twenty-three when the picture was taken. Under the feet of three of the men who were sitting down, he had marked a cross. Another cross had been drawn above the head of the man standing beside him in the back row. My father pointed to a good-looking young man with fair hair, who was seated in front of him: 'My best friend – Pat Kelly. He was the first we lost.' He took the photo from my son, and held it close to his eyes. 'We lost him the week after his birthday', he said, 'We had given him a bit of a party to celebrate. The next week he didn't come back from a night patrol. I found him two days later.' Kelly had been stripped, tied to a tree and disemboweled. My father sent a letter to my mother: 'I have seen a terrible thing', he wrote, 'and I don't think I will ever be the same again'.

Much later, I found out that Patrick William Kelly was the son of a Church of Ireland clergyman. He had been educated at Mountjoy School in Dublin (the school became Mount Temple Comprehensive in 1972, and its future pupils would include Bono and the rest of U2). Pat Kelly graduated from Trinity College, Dublin, shortly before the World War broke out. He travelled North with my father, and they enlisted and were commissioned in the same Irish regiment. They trained together in the Military Academy at Sandhurst, and they travelled to India on the same troop ship. Pat Kelly was killed less than a month after they arrived in Burma: he had just turned twenty-four. 'After that,' my father told me, 'I never minded killing Japs.'

The men and women who had spent the war years in Ireland might be forgiven for failing to understand the sort of lasting trauma – both physical and emotional – that Irishmen like my father had endured in Burma, and in the other operational theatres. And the lack of understanding could work in both directions. The Emergency had promoted a sense of national solidarity within Ireland, and generated a political consensus that had helped to heal some of the wounds left by a vicious Civil War. There was considerable national pride in the skill and determination with which the policy of neutrality had been pursued by the Irish Government, as well as great relief that the country had managed to avoid the appalling damage, and loss of life that had been inflicted throughout most of Europe. The Emergency had established many areas of shared experience – both ephemeral and profound – with little relevance to those who had served overseas in armed forces. Like many Irishmen who fought for the Allies, my father was broadly in favour of Irish neutrality: only bridling when any defence of that policy was couched in what he considered to be self-righteous terms. Nonetheless, I think it was sometimes hard for him to accept that the lives of those who had remained in Ireland during the war had been, in their own way, equally meaningful.

When my father died in 2008, he left a mass of papers. Sorting through them, I came across some old press cuttings. One of these, from the *Irish Times*, was dated 17th May, 1945. It described the homecoming of a small group of Irish merchant seamen, who had just been liberated from a Nazi concentration camp, where they had been part of a slave labour force. From the little that my father told me, I had assumed that our cousin, William Hutchinson Knox, was an Allied soldier killed during the invasion of Germany - like my uncle Lesley, who had survived the D-Day landings, but was shot dead by a sniper just a week before the war in Europe ended. Now, I discovered that William had been in the merchant navy, and that the conditions of his death were much darker than I had imagined.

By that time, I had learned a bit more about William and his place in our family. He was not my father's first cousin, as I had thought, but my grandfather's. In fact, William was over 30 years older than my father, and, while my father had been brought up in the West of Ireland, William had been raised in Dun Laoghaire, on the eastern coast. Their paths had seldom crossed and I believed that my father did not like to admit how little he knew about his relative. William also remained an elusive character to me, and there were aspects of his life that I found puzzling. Although a few members of my family had served in the Royal Navy, I knew of none, apart from him, who had joined the merchant marine. After more than thirty years of service, William Hutchinson Knox still held the relatively modest rank of Able Bodied Seaman. That was an honourable post, but it might be considered unusual at that time for someone like William, who came from a fairly privileged social background.

I did, however, discover in due course the reason why William was called 'Hutchinson'. Shortly before he was born, his paternal grandmother had died – my own great-great-grandmother - and William had been named after her father. Lieutenant William Hutchinson came from Kildare, a land-locked county, but had joined the Royal Navy as a Midshipman, and served in the Napoleonic wars while he was still a boy. In 1816, at the age of just 23, he was appointed as the first Master of the new harbour in the port of Dun Laoghaire. It took several decades to complete the construction of the two huge arms of that harbour, and William Hutchinson was the Master at Kingstown – as the port was re-named in 1821 - for almost 60 years. For several decades, Kingstown boasted the biggest artificial harbour in the world, and my cousin had grown up in an elegant Regency house that overlooked its sweeping granite piers.

Perhaps it was this family connection with the harbour that had first led William to consider a life at sea. That background provided one explanation for his choice of career, but I wondered if there were others. William's surname, for example, was both the same as his parents, his brothers, and other relatives – and yet also somewhat different. My father had explained this by saying there were 'enough of us' when William was born: did that suggest, in some way, that he was not one of 'us'? Perhaps, that also explained the differing path he had taken in life.

Many of the records of Irishmen in the British merchant fleet are kept in an extensive archive in the English port of Southampton. The RS2 Identity books that were issued to each seaman normally included a mug-shot photograph. William's photo is not dated, but was taken at some point in the inter-war years. I have looked intently at his image – trying to find some clues to his character. In his picture, William is staring straight ahead, but his expression seems downcast and cautious: his eyes are widened, as if he had been startled, or were afraid of something that the camera might reveal. His ears protrude to an alarming extent. His hair is combed neatly across the top of his head. There are certain physical similarities to photographs of his first cousin, my grandfather – but William seems to lack any of the latter's palpable self-confidence. When I showed the mug-shot to my son, he thought William looked like Nosferatu, in Murnau's vampire movie. There is also a form attached to the RS2 book that each seaman was supposed to complete. William did not fill in about half of the queries: there is no information, for example, about his height, his weight, or the colour of his eyes – and the space for details of his next-of-kin has also been left blank.

I understood that William had spent more than three decades working on long-distance sea routes: to North and South America, India, China, Australia and New Zealand. Clearly, he liked to keep on the move – which may explain, in part, why he never married. According to the *Irish Times*, he did not attend the funeral of his father: that may have been because he was thousands of miles away – or it may have been a deliberate absence. Perhaps, William was attracted by the democratic credentials of the merchant fleet. When he grew up in Kingstown, it was regarded as one of Dublin's most genteel and affluent suburbs: for James Joyce, it seemed to epitomise the stifling respectability of Ireland's bourgeoisie. But Kingstown was also a bustling port, and a popular seaside resort – where young couples went for romantic walks along its leafy promenades.

The merchant navy may have offered William a somewhat similar duality: on board ship, there was a hierarchy of command very similar of the Royal Navy – but the authority of merchant officers ended as soon as they stepped on shore. Unlike the Royal Navy, merchant seamen did not sign on for years of service, but only for individual voyages. The age restrictions were also a good deal looser: boys as young as 13 could serve in the merchant marine – and so could men who were well into their 70s. The merchant crews on long-haul voyages may have seemed rather exotic to someone like William, who had been raised in the strict conventions of late Victorian Ireland. British merchant ships were not the prototypes of liberal multi-culturalism, but they usually contained considerable ethnic diversity, and were often of mixed race. Once again, this was in marked contrast to the tight little world of Kingstown – where William's father, as a well-known surgeon, had played a prominent role.

Whatever the reasons, when war broke out in 1939, William was working above deck for the Anglo-Persian Oil Company. Anglo-Persian owned 92 merchant ships – almost twice the size, and with a great deal more tonnage, than the entire Irish merchant fleet. As soon as war was declared, the British Government requisitioned all of Anglo-Persian's ships. Their crews stayed in place, and their everyday work remained much the same. The only notable additions were the small guns installed on each of their sterns, which allowed the tankers to be classified as DEMS – 'Defensively Equipped

Merchant Ships'. It was considered unsafe to allow these low-angle weapons to be manned by untrained merchant seamen - so a few additional members of crew were usually recruited – mainly, from retired military personnel.

William's job may not have changed, but the context in which he worked certainly had. Instead of transporting cargo that was intended for domestic or industrial use, the Anglo-Persian tankers were now carrying oil to fuel the Allied armed forces. As such, they had become obvious – and soft - targets for German surface and submarine raiders. The Anglo-Persian fleet was to pay a high price for that change in its status: by the end of the war, almost half of its tankers had been sunk, and the lives of more than six hundred of its crewmen had been lost.

From another of my father's newspaper cuttings - this one from the *Times* of London – I learned that William was on board one of Anglo-Persian's ships, the SS *British Commander*, in August 1940. The entry of Italy into the war, as one of the Axis powers, had effectively closed the Mediterranean to Allied shipping, compelling them to round the Cape of Good Hope on their way to Asia and Australia. William's ship was carrying oil to India, when it was intercepted 300 miles south-west of the coast of Madagascar by a German surface raider called the *Pinguin*. The course of William's life as a merchant seaman had seemed fixed and irreversible – but then a world war intervened, and he was swept away in its bloody wake. William could not have known, but his future would become linked to that of a German naval officer called Ernst-Felix Krüder.

2

THE GERMAN RAIDER

On a bright summer morning in June, 1940, a nondescript ship, identified only by the code name of *HK 33*, sailed out of the port of Gotenhaven. Nowadays, Gotenhaven is known as Gdynia, and is part of Poland. Following the German invasion of September, 1939, it had been incorporated into the Third Reich. More than 50,000 ethnic Poles were forcibly expelled, and Gotenhaven was developed as an important German naval base. In appearance, *HK 33* seemed like a standard transport ship; painted a dull grey, and without any obvious armaments. In reality, she was one of the first wave of surface raiders whose purpose was to use deception and subterfuge in order to sink, capture or disrupt Allied merchant shipping. *HK 33* had originally been a freighter, the *Kandelfeis,* but had been requisitioned by the *Kriegsmarine* – the German Navy – in 1939, converted into a *Hilfskreuzer* – an armed auxiliary cruiser – and given a new identity. Conversion of the ship entailed the installation of weapons, ammunition stores, and accommodation for a large crew and a small number of prisoners.

The *Hilfskreuzers* wrought havoc on Allied ships in the early years of the war. Although there were less than a dozen of them, they sank almost a million tons of shipping. They did not attack merchant convoys that were escorted by warships, but there were not enough Allied escorts to protect every merchant vessel and the raiders preyed on those that were alone and vulnerable. The *Hilfskreuzers* used elaborate disguises to approach their targets, and usually revealed their true identity just before they opened fire on their victims. They used the cargos of their captured prizes to fuel and feed themselves – before they moved on to the next kill. At first, British naval command had no idea who these raiders might be or where they were operating. They were classified as 'mystery ships', and designated by letters of the alphabet.

When *HK 33* left Gotenhaven that June morning, she was escorted by the minesweeper, *Nautilus*, and the Wolf-class torpedo boat, *Falke*. *HK 33* was under the command of *Fregattenkäpitan* Ernst-Felix Krüder, an extremely capable, experienced and single-minded officer. Unusually for a German captain, Krüder had not attended Naval Academy. Instead, he had joined the Kriegsmarine when he was 15, and had worked his way up from the ranks. In the First World War, he took part in the naval engagement at Jutland, and also saw action off Sebastopol during the

Gallipoli campaign. For his services, he had been awarded the Iron Cross – both 1st and 2nd Classes. Shortly after the First World War ended, he led a Naval Assault Brigade against socialist revolutionaries in Berlin and Munich. His subsequent career had prospered under both the Weimar and Nazi regimes, and he was steadily promoted.

In the summer of 1940, Krüder was 42 years old, and at the height of his powers. According to those who served with him, he was imbued with unshakable self-belief, seemed utterly fearless, and possessed a steely determination to succeed. In all of this, he seemed to exemplify the so-called *Führerprinzip* – the Leader Principle beloved by the Nazis. According to the *Führerprinzip*, any problem could be resolved by bold and decisive leadership – of the sort supposedly provided at a national level by Hitler. In the year that followed, Krüder became just the type of charismatic commander whose men were prepared to follow anywhere. Tall, lean and athletic, he embodied the physical qualities that National Socialism revered, but which most of its leaders conspicuously lacked. He would achieve exceptional success, and public acclaim – which was all the more remarkable because *HK 33*'s crew was largely composed of untested naval reservists. But, eventually, the same characteristics that brought Krüder to triumph would also lead to his demise.

As the small convoy which he led moved into the North Sea on that summer day in 1940, it was supplied with Luftwaffe air cover, and reinforced by two more minesweepers. Together, they headed up the coast of

Occupied Norway, passing Bergen on the 20th of June. On the same day, the *Falke* peeled off to make her way back to Germany, while the remaining ships carried on northwards. Two days later, they pulled into the inlet of Sorguklenfjord – the longest and deepest fjord in Norway. In its seclusion and safety, *HK 33* changed identity: her grey hull was painted black, her guns remained camouflaged, and hammer and sickle markings were added. When *HK 33* emerged from the Norwegian fjord, it was as the Soviet cargo ship, the *Petschura*.

Krüder's ultimate destination was the Indian Ocean and Australian waters, but first his ship had to rendezvous with, and replenish a German submarine off Cape Verde in the North Atlantic. *HK 33* and her escorts continued to head north into Arctic waters, but she soon ran into heavy weather. The two minesweepers had turned back when Krüder spotted a British submarine that had surfaced close to his position. He headed further north to give the impression that *HK 33* was a Soviet cargo freighter bound for Murmansk. Then, on 28th of June, he changed tack again, and turned south – passing through the Denmark Strait into the choppy waters of the Atlantic on 1st of July. The following week, *HK 33* assumed a new identity – this time, as a Greek merchant ship, the *Kassos*. On 20th of July, the first part of her mission was fulfilled when she re-supplied a German U-boat, 700 miles south-west of Cape Verde.

In order to save fuel, Krüder towed the submarine south until she had reached the shipping lanes off Sierra Leone – at which point, the U-boat went on her own mission, and Krüder continued on his journey south. By now, he had decided to give his ship a proper name. He had been reading a book about whale fishing, and had liked its descriptions of Antarctic wild life. He suggested a name to *Seekriegsleitung* – German Naval Command – and it was approved: from then on, *HK 33* would be known as the *Pinguin*. On 31st July, 300 miles north-west of Ascension Island, she sighted a British freighter. It was the 5,000 ton *Domingo de Larringa*, on its way from Bahia Blanca, Argentina, to Newcastle in the north-east of England – carrying 7,000 tons of grain, and a crew of 36. The freighter had also spotted the *Pinguin*, and, fearing the worst, had turned sharply away, while sending a distress signal. The *Pinguin* gave chase: dropping its assumed identity, running up its battle flag, and opening fire with its heavy guns.

The bridge of the *Domingo de Larringa* received several direct hits: the ship caught fire, and slowed to a halt. A German boarding party found eight dead crewmen. Scuttling charges were placed in the freighter's engine room, but they failed to explode, and the *Domingo de Larringa* was finally dispatched with a torpedo. Meanwhile, the surviving crew had been taken aboard the German ship. This was the first 'blood' for the *Pinguin*, and the first prisoners she had taken. However, it would not be long before the crew of the *Domingo de Larringa* were joined by many other merchant seamen, and more Allied ships lay at the bottom of the ocean.

The day before the *Pinguin* sank the *Domingo*, the *British Commander* had left the Cornish port of Falmouth – with a crew that included my cousin, William Hutchinson Knox. *The Commander* was an aging freighter that had seen better days, and could now only manage, at best, a sluggish speed of around 10 knots – about half the speed of the *Pinguin*. She had been equipped with two small guns: both of which were located on her stern – which meant that they were only of practical use when the ship was in retreat. These weapons were supposed to be manned by the merchant crew – but their training in gunnery had only amounted to a rushed one-day course. The *Commander* left Falmouth as part of an escorted convoy that was bound for Gibraltar. For the first five days of her voyage, she risked attack from the German U-boats and bombers that were based in Occupied France, but there were no such incursions, and, at the Straits of Gibraltar, she separated from the other ships, and headed south alone.

The Captain of the *Commander*, John Thornton, had been warned that there was still a danger of attack from German raiders, but his ship reached Cape Town without incident. She arrived there on 19th of August, and the Captain and his crew spent that night on shore leave: I hope they made the most of that opportunity - because, for some of them, it would be their last chance to enjoy such freedom. The next morning, the *Commander* left port early on a southerly course, heading for the Cape of Good Hope – which she rounded twelve, or so, hours later. The ship then passed into the tranquil waters of the Indian Ocean, where the trade routes were still considered to be relatively safe. However, the Royal Navy's presence there was very limited: the Indian

Ocean covered more than 20 million square miles, and there were less than a dozen cruisers and destroyers in the entire India Squadron of ships. As a result most of the hundreds of Allied merchant tankers and freighters that crossed the Ocean were without any protection. For German raiders, such as the *Pinguin,* this meant that there were rich pickings to be had.

The *Pinguin* rounded the Cape of Good Hope on the same evening as the *Commander.* Six days later, Krüder launched one of his ship's seaplanes with fake RAF roundel markings. It soon located an Allied tanker, the *Filefjell* – a 7,000 ton Norwegian merchant ship, on her way to Cape Town, carrying 500 tons of oil, and 10,000 tons of aviation fuel. The German pilot dropped a weighted package, with a message written in English on the deck of the *Filefjell.* It purported to warn the ship of the presence of a German warship. The pilot was thoughtful enough to suggest a detailed escape route for the tanker: one that would lead her straight to the waiting *Pinguin.* When the *Filefjell's* Captain declined to follow his advice, the pilot strafed the Norwegian ship with canon and machine gun fire. Her Captain had no option but to surrender – since he and his crew were aboard what was virtually a floating bomb - and, an hour or so later, a crew from the *Penguin* boarded the tanker. It was decided to take her to a quiet stretch of water so that the cargo of oil could be transferred to the *Pinguin.* The two ships then sailed together further into the Indian Ocean.

Meanwhile, Thornton had set the *British Commander* on a course to the south of Madagascar. The shortest route to India lay in the Mozambique Channel – between Madagascar and the African mainland – but, since that narrow channel could easily be used for a naval ambush, all Allied ships had been instructed to take the longer, outside route. On the 26th August, the *Commander* was off Cape St. Mary – the southernmost point of Madagascar – when she picked up a distress signal from a Norwegian freighter that she was being stopped by a 'suspicious vessel'. No doubt, Captain Thorton was greatly relieved when the distress call proved to be a false alarm: the suspicious vessel had proved to be a British warship. At around one in the morning of 27th of August, the *Commander* was clear of Madagascar, and Thornton altered his course to pass west of the French island of Réunion. Once that had been done, he went to his cabin to catch up on some sleep.

A few hours after Thornton went below deck, his ship was spotted by the *Pinguin*. As a precaution, the *Commander* was sailing in the dark without any lights, and, for that very reason, Krüder suspected that she was an Allied tanker. After an hour of shadowing the tanker, Krüder was satisfied: he signalled the *Commander* to stop, and fired a warning shot across her bows. Thornton was woken, and rushed to the bridge of his ship. His first thought was that it was the same British warship that had stopped the Norwegian freighter the previous day: a second shell forced him to revise that opinion. Krüder signalled that the *Commander* was to 'STOP INSTANTLY. DO NOT USE YOUR WIRELESS.' But, the ship's radio officer was ordered by Thornton to transmit the code that meant his ship was being 'attacked by raider', and the message was immediately acknowledged by a South African operator. Thornton also proceeded to bring his tanker round to present her stern – and guns – to the enemy. Although neither Thornton nor his crew had any previous history of naval combat, the *Pinguin's* powerful searchlights revealed that the *Commander's* guns were being manned. Krüder at once ordered his own gunners to start shelling the tanker. My cousin and the rest of the crew then came under direct enemy fire – an experience for which none of them were prepared.

Thornton was clearly a man of some spirit: he later attempted unsuccessfully to seize control of a German transport ship, and managed to escape from a prison camp in Germany and make his way back to England. On this occasion, his gesture of defiance may have been admirable, but it was also futile: in reality, there was no contest between the firepower of the two ships. The *Pinguin's* main armament consisted of six 150 mm guns. She was also fitted with one 75 mm canon, one twin 37 mm mounting, four 20 mm anti-aircraft guns, and two single 53.3 cm torpedo tubes for 16 torpedoes. The only guns on board the Allied tanker were two small canons, manned by personnel who had never been properly trained. Within a few minutes, the *British Commander* had been badly hit, and was on fire. It was now clear to Thornton that armed resistance was pointless, but he instructed his radio officer to continue to send out distress signals. By this stage, the *Pinguin* was only about a mile off the *Commander's* port quarter. Krüder signalled that the crew had ten minutes to stop using its wireless, and abandon ship before he resumed shelling. Thornton gave the necessary orders, and his crew took to the ship's two lifeboats. The *Pinguin* then continued firing on the stricken ship until she sank – although it took a further 40 shells before the *Commander* finally slipped below the water.

None of the ship's crew had been killed, but some of them had been badly injured. Fortunately, my cousin was not one of them. The *Commander's* crew were all taken aboard the *Pinguin;* some to its well-equipped operating theatre. Others were herded down to join the prisoners from the *Filefjell* and the *Domingo de Larringa* below decks where they were to be kept for the following weeks in extremely cramped conditions.

According to survivors, Captain Thornton remained defiant when he arrived on board: informing Krüder that British cruisers were already on their way, and insisting that the *Pinguin* would not evade them for long. It was all a bluff: there were no such warships in the vicinity. Thornton later related that Krüder had been angry with him because he had put the lives of his merchant crew in danger: 'He told me that merchant seamen were not soldiers', Thorton reported, 'and that it would have been my responsibility had any of [them] been killed'. Krüder set his course further into the Indian Ocean, and, a few hours later, he spotted another Allied freighter, the *Morviken*, on her way to Calcutta: she became the third ship that Krüder sank or captured in less than 24 hours. In the same period, he took more than 100 merchant seamen prisoner: substantially more than his ship had been designed to hold.

By this stage, the activities of the *Pinguin* had become known to the Royal Navy – although the 'mystery ship' had only been identified as *Raider F.* In the days that followed the sinking of the *British Commander*, the *Pinguin* assumed a new disguise: the black of her hull was relieved by a continuous white stripe, and her funnel acquired two light blue bands. To a casual observer, she was now the *Trafalgar,* a Norwegian freighter in the Wilhelmsen Line. Krüder decided to make one more sweep towards Madagascar and on 12th of September, he came across another British freighter: the *Benavon* – which had sailed from Penang a few weeks earlier. On board was a crew that consisted mainly of Chinese deck hands and Shetland Island engineers. The *Pinguin* bore down rapidly on the *Benavon*, and, when they were less than a mile apart, Krüder raised his battle flag, and opened fire. The Captain of the *Benavon* seemed determined to fight: he ordered his ship to increase speed, and his crew to man the gun on her stern. By what can only have been a fluke, their first shot penetrated the *Pinguin's* hull, but the merchant seamen had not fused the shell properly and it failed to explode. The German gunners did not make the same elementary mistake. In returning fire, they hit the ammunition locker on the *Benavon's* poop, destroying the gun on her stern and killing all of the seamen who were manning it.

Having found the range, the *Pinguin's* gunners drove shell after shell into the Allied freighter. Within minutes, the ship was on fire, and her funnel and main mast had been brought down. The Captain gave the order to abandon ship, but before he could do so, another salvo struck the bridge: killing him and his entire complement of deck officers. All of the lifeboats had been destroyed in the German assault, so the survivors had to cling to a makeshift, wooden raft. They were in the water for over an hour before they were taken on board the *Pinguin*. Half of the *Benavon's* company had been killed, but a German boarding party found five men still alive inside the burning ship: three of them soon died of their wounds on board the German raider, and Krüder buried them at sea with full military honours. The remaining twenty five survivors joined the other Allied prisoners who were already below decks.

Four days later, the *Pinguin* came upon another easy victim, and, once again, it was a Norwegian freighter. The *Nordvard* offered no resistance to the German raider, and surrendered without a shot being fired. Krüder now had almost 200 Allied prisoners on board his ship. Before she was commissioned as a *Hilfskreuzer*, the *Pinguin* had been a merchant ship, and was manned by a crew of around 40 seamen. In her new role, she had to accommodate a ship's company of almost 400 – quite apart from the large number of Allied prisoners that she now held on board. Although Krüder's treatment of them was humane, the merchant seamen spent almost all of their days in hot and fetid conditions in the bowels of the ship. Apart from the space that they took up, and the food and water that they consumed, the large number of captives constituted a constant threat to the security of the *Pinguin*. Krüder, faced with this overcrowding, decided to send the *Nordvard* back to Europe with most of his prisoners – including my cousin William. Krüder informed *Seekriegsleitung* of his intentions, and the German Naval Command approved: the *Nordvard* sailed for Bordeaux, in Occupied France, in September of 1940.

It was not an easy voyage for the merchant seamen. As Gabe Thomas has noted, such journeys were characterised by 'grossly overcrowded living spaces, little or no sanitation, and minimal food'. The *Nordvard* was manned by a skeleton crew which was greatly outnumbered by the prisoners on board. The German sailors were acutely aware that their captives might use the force of numbers to try and seize the ship on its 20,000 mile journey. This was not a groundless fear. Irish seamen participated in several attempts to do just this on other German ships – at least one of which ended in bloodshed and death. This may explain why the merchant ratings were treated with considerable harshness on their way back to Europe: they were not allowed on deck for fresh air, and were kept under armed guard during any unavoidable contact with the crew. The prisoners had to endure more than two months of such captivity before the *Nordvard* docked in Bordeaux, in Occupied France, on 22nd of November, 1940.

In the months that followed the departure of their captives, the *Pinguin* was re-painted and re-named on numerous occasions as she made her way towards Australia. In October of 1940, she intercepted and captured the Norwegian motor-tanker, *Storstad*, off Christmas Island. Krüder decided to use the captured ship, first, as an auxiliary minelayer – and, then, to carry more prisoners back to France. By December of 1940, he had sunk or captured 11 merchant ships, and had taken more than 400 prisoners. But Krüder's most spectacular success came at the beginning of 1941 when the *Pinguin* came across a Norwegian whaling fleet off the coast of South Georgia in the Antarctic. With great tactical ingenuity, Krüder managed to capture their supply ship, eleven whalers, two factory ships, 20,000 tons of whale oil and 10,000 tons of fuel – all without having to fire a single shot.

By May of 1941, Krüder had sunk or captured 28 Allied ships, and a further four had been sunk by his mines. Under Krüder's leadership, the *Pinguin* had become the most effective auxiliary cruiser in the German fleet, and had accounted for more than 150,000 tons of Allied merchant shipping. Krüder had been awarded clasps to both his Iron Crosses, as well as the prestigious *Ritterkreuz* - the Knight's Cross - in recognition of his services to the Reich. He had also taken almost 250 new prisoners. But time was running out for Krüder, and for his ship.

On 8th May, the *Pinguin* torpedoed a small Allied tanker, the *British Emperor* – another ship in the Anglo-Persian fleet - to the north-west of the Seychelles. Before she sank, the tanker had been able to transmit a stream of SOS messages. These were picked up by the British cruiser, *HMS Cornwall*, and her Captain sent a Walrus spotter plane to investigate. The pilot reported that he had sighted what appeared to be a typical Allied freighter. The *Pinguin* was flying the Norwegian ensign, her crew were wearing merchant marine clothing, and the name *Tamerlane* was displayed on both sides of her bridge. However, the *Tamerlane* was not among the names of Allied shipping known to be in the area at that time. The pilot of the spotter plane also reported that he could see 'no coloured sailors' on deck – which was considered most unusual for an Allied merchant ship.

The *Cornwall* approached the *Penguin* at full speed, and ordered her to heave to. The *Penguin* responded by raising her battle ensign, and opening fire on the *Cornwall* with her heaviest guns. Before he did so, Krüder went below deck to dress in the full uniform of a Kriegsmarine officer. He also sent one last radio message to *Seekriegsleitung:* 'Am now engaging', the message read, 'with British heavy cruiser'. It was, in some respects, a reckless engagement, since Krüder's ship was clearly out-gunned by the British battleship. He had taken risks many times before on this mission, and they had always paid off. At first, it seemed that this one would too. The *Penguin's* opening salvo scored several direct hits – one of which temporarily put out the *Cornwall's* steering system out of action.

Despite that, the British cruiser was soon able to move out of range of the *Penguin's* guns. The German raider was not, however, out of the *Cornwall's* range, and now the Allied ship began to return fire. The first shell from the *Cornwall* brought down the *Penguin's* foremast. This was the first time in her mission that the *Penguin* had encountered any serious opposition: all of the merchant ships that Krüder had attacked in the course of the previous year had been virtually defenceless. He must have realised that his gamble had failed, because he gave an immediate order to abandon ship. His order came too late. Within minutes of the first impact, a further salvo from four of the *Cornwall's* guns had slammed into the *Pinguin*. One of these shells caused light damage to the fore of the ship. The second destroyed the bridge. The third exploded in the engine room. The fourth shell scored a direct hit to an ammunition magazine – where more than 100 mines were stored: then, in the words of the Captain of the *Cornwall*, 'the whole ship disappeared in a thick white cloud.' Three hundred and forty one of the German crew, and two hundred and thirteen of their prisoners were killed.

Among the dead was Ernst-Felix Krüder. After his death, he was promoted to *Kapitan zur See*, and was also awarded a posthumous *Ritterkreuz mit Eichenlaub* – Oak Leaves to add to his Knight's Cross. That was a rare distinction: out of the millions of Germans who saw military service in the World War, less than 1,000 received this decoration. Krüder was also mentioned by name in the *Wehrmachtbericht* – a daily radio bulletin run by Josef Goebbels, the Nazi Minister for Propaganda, which reported on the progress of the war. Krüder was praised as someone who had epitomised the *Führerprinzip*: a leader who had chosen to court death, rather than submit to the superior forces of the enemy. In fact, just before he died, Krüder had accepted the reality of his situation, and was in the process of surrendering when his ship exploded. The 553 men who died with him might have wished he had reached that decision a little sooner.

In his time as Krüder's prisoner, my cousin William had been present at more action that he could ever have expected when he joined the merchant marine. After the chronic overcrowding of prisoners on the *Pinguin* and the *Nordvard,* he and the other captured seamen must have felt some sense of relief to be back on dry land. As it turned out, William's real ordeal was only about to begin.

3

THE IRISH LEGATION

In the winter of 1940, when the *Norvard* docked in Bordeaux, the mood of Nazi Germany was buoyant – and with good reason. In the course of that year, France had fallen before the Wehrmacht's *Blitzkrieg* – and so too had the neutral states of Denmark, Norway, Belgium, the Netherlands and Luxembourg. Only Britain remained defiant – but the British Expeditionary Force in Europe had also suffered a humiliating defeat. The BEF had been compelled to jettison huge amounts of war materiel before evacuating the beaches of Dunkirk in northern France. Left behind were almost 900 field guns, 700 tanks and 45,000 motorised vehicles. This abandoned materiel could have equipped more than eight Army divisions, and there was barely enough left in Britain to provide for two. It was not surprising that the Irish Chargé d'Affaires in Berlin sent a personal cable to Dublin, on the day after the *Nordvard* docked, in which he reported that a 'successful invasion of Great Britain is now regarded as certain.'

My cousin might have hoped that the Charge d'Affaires would also report back to Dublin that an Irish citizen was being held captive by the Germans. He might have hoped that his Government's representative in Berlin would intervene to secure his safe repatriation to Ireland – or at least express some concern for his welfare. William was, after all, a non-combatant from a neutral country, and Ireland was one of the relatively few states to keep its diplomats in place across Europe throughout the duration of the war. In fact, William had a reasonable expectation of being sent home to Ireland. The majority of prisoners on the *Nordvard* had been Norwegian, and, within a few months, they were all safely back in Norway. But, if William hoped or expected that anyone would come to his aid, he was to be sorely disappointed. Given the history of Ireland's diplomatic presence in Nazi Germany, however, the lack of attention given to Irish prisoners captured on Allied merchant ships was not so surprising.

Soon after the Nazi regime gained power, Dublin had appointed Charles Bewley as the Irish Government's 'Minister Plenipotentiary and Envoy Extraordinary' in Berlin. Bewley was to remain in that position during the six critical years that followed – only being relieved of his post a matter of weeks before the outbreak of war. It is difficult to think of any Irish diplomat who would have brought a more partisan eye to the political situation in Germany. What is even more remarkable is that Bewley's virulent racial prejudices had been well known in Irish Government circles for many years. As far back as 1922, George Gavin Duffy, the acting Minister for External Affairs, had noted that Bewley was 'mad on the Jewish question', and recommended against sending him to Berlin on a diplomatic mission 'because his semitic [sic] convictions are so pronounced'.

Following Bewley's appointment in 1933, it soon became abundantly clear that his 'semitic convictions' had not changed. In the reports he sent back to Dublin, Bewley consistently minimised the danger to democracy that was posed by Hitler, and he repeatedly denied that the Nazis constituted any sort of threat to the safety of Germany's Jews. He considered that the racial laws introduced at Nuremberg – which deprived Jews of their civil rights as German citizens – had been caused by 'the provocative conduct of the Jews themselves.' He also reported that he could find no evidence of any 'deliberate cruelty on the part of the [German] Government towards the Jews.' One might conclude from Bewley's dispatches that a high proportion of Jews in Germany were employed as pornographers, or abortionists, or financial swindlers, or mixed up in the 'international white slave traffic'. In several reports, he even gave some credence to the grotesque medieval fantasy that Jews were engaged in the 'ritual murder' of Christian children whom they had abducted. In reality, of course, it proved to be Bewley's hosts in Nazi Germany who would murder Jewish children systematically, without compunction, and on an industrial scale.

In December of 1938, Bewley was asked by Joseph Walshe, the Secretary – or permanent head – of Ireland's

Department of External Affairs, to assess anti-Semitic feelings in Germany. In his lengthy reply, Bewley explicitly endorsed many racist opinions that were close – if not identical – to those held by the Nazis. He thought it was obvious that 'the Bolshevist movement was financed by the American-Jewish banking houses'. He claimed that, before the Nazis came to power in Germany, the 'press, theatre, cinema, stock exchange (and) banks were completely under Jewish control.' He argued that the mere presence of Jews invariably produced a 'demoralising effect' on any Christian community, and that Jews were properly regarded as 'an alien body in every state where they exist.' Bewley cautioned against anyone adopting 'an attitude of assumed moral superiority' to the Nazis – since it was impossible for anyone 'with any degree of reason' to believe that Jews 'should be treated like ordinary citizens'. He also suggested that the reason why more Irish people did not realise that Jews were 'anti-Christian, anti-patriotic and Communistic' was because they received too much of their information from the English press, whose control rested 'in Jewish hands'.

These were the views of the man who was largely responsible for processing the visa applications from Jews wishing to leave Nazi Germany for Ireland. Apart from Bewley, the only other member of the Irish Legation in Berlin during most of this period was his German secretary – whose attitude towards Jews proved to be markedly more tolerant than that of her boss. Bewley considered the few visas that Ireland offered to German Jews were evidence of a policy that was 'inordinately liberal', and there seems to be no doubt that he abused his consular responsibilities to delay and obstruct the issue of those visas. Ireland's economy may not have been robust enough to absorb a large number of Jewish immigrants. It may also be true that the full-blown terror of the Holocaust was not instigated until much later. However, none of this can excuse or justify the grudging Irish response to the flagrant persecution of Germany's Jews, or change the fact that less than 100 of them managed to negotiate the administrative hurdles, which Bewley had placed in their way, to find refuge in Ireland between 1933 and 1939 – and even those few who were favoured with Irish visas tended to be religious converts, or 'Christians with Jewish blood'.

The historian, Diarmaid Ferriter, has argued that Bewley was 'not representative of Irish diplomatic, political or public opinion' and that he was 'unpopular with colleagues in the department of External Affairs'. It is true that the crude and overt expression of anti-Semitism in which Bewley liked to indulge was most unusual in Irish diplomatic circles. It is also true that there was no equivalent in Ireland to the racial hatred of Jews that was articulated by mainstream political parties in some other European countries. Given his prickly sense of self-importance, it is entirely credible that Bewley was cordially disliked by many of his colleagues. However, it seems unlikely that he could have managed to stay in this crucial diplomatic position for six years if his views had been totally at variance with those held by all of Ireland's senior civil servants. In fact, as Clair Wills has commented, internal memos from the

Department of External Affairs and the Department of Justice, written from the mid-1930s, make 'depressing reading', and tend to confirm the existence of casual, but deep-seated racial and religious prejudice.

The apparent indifference of the Irish State to the fate of persecuted minorities in Europe was not confined to Jews. An international conference was held in July, 1938, to explore the plight of Jewish and other refugees, at Evian-les-Bains, in the south of France. It was attended by a small Irish delegation, led by Frank Cremins, the Irish envoy in Geneva. He informed the plenary session of the conference that Ireland was effectively closed to refugees, and could make 'no contribution' whatever to their settlement. Another Irish delegate expressed similar views less diplomatically: 'Didn't we suffer like this in the Penal Days', he asked, 'and nobody came to help us.' The evident lack of concern for the safety of European Jews contrasts sharply with the vigour with which the Irish Government and its diplomats later sought assurances that the religious monuments of Rome would not be damaged by Allied bombing.

Rome was of particular interest to Joseph P. Walshe, the Secretary of Ireland's Department of External Affairs throughout the war. According to Conor Cruise O'Brien, who worked under him in that Department, Walshe was 'an exceptionally devout Catholic, even by the exacting standards of the Ireland of the first half of the 20th century.' Mussolini was his special hero – 'both as an anti-communist champion and as a restorer of the glories of Rome'. O'Brien believed that Walshe hoped to see Ireland aligned, following a Nazi victory, with 'Franco's Spain, Salazar's Portugal and Mussolini's Italy' as part of Europe's 'New Order'. O'Brien cites a memo of Walshe's, written in June of 1940, which reveals him to be 'exhilarated by the victories of the Axis', and which implies that 'Irish neutrality should be revised in a pro-Axis sense'.

Charles Bewley was not the only Irish diplomat to pursue what may seem like incautious contacts with the Nazi regime on Walshe's watch – although, in one case at least, the reasons seem to have been less ideological than foolish or naive. In 1940, the Irish Minister in Madrid, Leopold Kerney, had arranged and paid for the 'escape' of a leading IRA figure, Frank Ryan, from a Spanish gaol. Kerney stayed in touch with Ryan after he had arrived in Berlin – at a time when Ryan was occupied in making plans with German Intelligence officers for subversive operations in Ireland. The Irish Minister was also in contact with Helmut Clissmann, whose Irish wife was already friendly with the Kerney family. Clissmann had lived in Ireland before the war, and had espoused extreme Irish Nationalist views. He was a member of the Nazi Party, and also of the *Deutscher Akademischer Anstauschdienst* – the German Academic Exchange Organisation – which, like all other German cultural organisations of that time, operated under Nazi control. During the war, Clissmann worked for German Military Intelligence - the *Abwehr* - and served as an important link between the *Abwehr* and the IRA. The latter had been identified by the Political Department of the Ministry of Foreign Affairs, in August 1940, as a 'natural ally of Germany'. Clissmann was also involved in various attempts to recruit Irish prisoners of war to join an 'Irish Brigade' that would fight in the war on the same side as the Nazis.

In 1942, Clissmann flew to Madrid to arrange a meeting between Kerney and Dr. Edmund Veesenmayer – an SS *Brigadeführer*, who advised Joachim von Ribbentrop, the Nazi Foreign Minister, on Irish affairs. Dr. Veesenmayer specialised, as Eunan O'Halpin has noted, 'in the manipulation of nationalist movements [in Europe] for German policy ends'. Veesenmayer was also a dedicated Nazi, and would be convicted as a war criminal for the role he played in the murder of hundreds of thousands of Croatian, Serbian and Hungarian Jews. In 1942, Irish Military Intelligence reported that he was concocting a plan 'for the landing of parachutists and airborne troops' in Ireland. It seems Veesenmayer was confident that Russia would soon be knocked out of the war, and that Germany could then address the delayed invasion of Britain. In that context, he still believed that Ireland would be of strategic value to the Nazi cause. Some controversy surrounds the precise role that Kerney played in his talks with Dr. Veesenmayer, and whether these had been properly authorised by the Government in Dublin: at all events, although his judgement was questioned, Kerney remained as Ireland's representative in fascist Spain for the rest of the war.

In the *Nestor* episode of Joyce's *Ulysses*, Mr. Deasy, a schoolmaster, asks Stephen Dedelus why he thinks that Ireland 'has the honour of being the only country which never persecuted the Jews'. When Stephen cannot give the correct answer, Deasy informs him this is simply because Ireland 'never let them in'. In fact, several thousand Jews were living in Ireland in 1904, the year in which *Ulysses* is set – substantially more than their current numbers. Even though the Jewish population in Ireland was still relatively small in the first half of the twentieth century, anti-Semitism was not unknown – as Joyce reveals, with corruscating effect, elsewhere in his novel. In the war years, anti-Semitic prejudice found predictable expression through the IRA and other extreme Nationalist groupings, but it could also surface from time to time in mainstream political parties, and even within Dáil Éireann.

In 1943, Oliver J. Flanagan, a newly-elected Deputy, reminded the Dáil that the Jews had 'crucified Our Saviour nineteen hundred years ago'. Flanagan believed that the descendants of the Christ-killers were still 'crucifying us every day of the week'. He praised Hitler for 'routing the Jews out of Germany', and recommended that the same policy be followed in Ireland. 'Where the bees are, there is honey', he concluded, "and where the Jews are, there is money.' Flanagan continued in much the same vein even after the war was over, but he was elected to Dáil Éireann without interruption for the next 43 years – eventually becoming the Father of the House. It would be a mistake to over-estimate the significance of what Flanagan represented in Irish politics. He was originally elected as an Independent Deputy, and was often seen as a marginal – and even rather absurd - figure: once famously claiming that there had been 'no sex in Ireland' until the advent of television. Nonetheless, he still managed to serve a term as the Irish Minister for Defence, and was also awarded a Knighthood – of the Order of St. Gregory the Great – by the Pope.

In 1935, the Fianna Fáil Government had introduced an Aliens Act that was ostensibly designed to prevent so-called 'suspect elements' from entering the Irish State. In practice, the Act was applied in an extremely restrictive manner. It is clear that the notion of 'suspect elements' was interpreted to mean anyone who might pose a threat to a supposedly homogeneous Irish society – and that included Jews in flight from Nazi Germany. As Clair Wills has observed, such Jews were more likely to be treated as 'potentially troublesome aliens rather than people suffering from persecution.' There was also an underlying assumption that they were, in some sense, the authors of their own misfortunes. In 1945, the Secretary of the Department of Justice, A.S. Roche, could still write: 'The immigration of Jews is generally discouraged.' He believed that Jewish immigrants to Ireland would form a 'colony of a world-wide Jewish community' that would soon become an 'irritant in the body politic'. Roche also dismissed attempts to assimilate Jews in other countries: a policy which he believed had led to 'disastrous results.'

Even when Irish Jews wished to join their country's defence forces, it was still a cause of official concern. G2 – Irish Military Intelligence – advised caution when dealing with would-be Jewish recruits to the Irish army. One memorandum spelled out the alleged problem in unambiguous terms: 'The fundamental characteristic of the Jewish people', it stated, '[is] that they have no national allegiance'. The same memorandum recommended that Protestant recruits should also be scrutinised carefully – since some of them were 'unreconstructed bastions of pro-British sentiment'. After the war, the suspicion and prejudice lingered: in 1948, there was a proposal to bring some orphaned Jewish children to Ireland, and the Department of Justice re-affirmed its customary opposition to such immigration – even when, as in this case, it was a temporary measure. 'It has always been the policy', an internal memorandum stated, 'to restrict the admission of Jewish aliens'. The reason given was that an increase in Ireland's Jewish population 'might give rise to an anti-Semitic problem': a circular form of logic which would surely have appealed to Joyce's schoolmaster, Mr. Deasy.

Whatever his faults may have been, Eamon de Valera – Ireland's Taoiseach throughout the war - was not an anti-Semite. In August, 1939, he finally pressurised his Government's representative in Berlin into resigning. Charles Bewley left his job discredited, and, as he complained, 'without even the consolation of a pension'. Soon after his dismissal, Bewley gained new employment in Germany which he may have found more congenial: working for Dr. Josef Goebbels, the Propaganda Minister in the Nazi regime. Bewley remained convinced that National Socialism was 'the strongest, perhaps the only, force which [could] prevent the spread of the Communist Empire.' He continued to offer the Nazis political advice on Irish matters during the course of the war: in particular, he tried – without success – to convince them that it would be in German interests to help 'eliminate' de Valera by supporting an IRA-led coup. Bewley's attempts to join the *Sicherheitsdienst* – the security branch of the SS – also proved unsuccessful: he may have admired the Nazis, but the feeling was not reciprocated. The SS believed that he was 'too lazy' to be of much use to them as an agent. They did not even regard him as trustworthy. His brother, Thomas, worked for the British Embassy in Washington, and the SS – mistakenly - thought this cast 'reasonable doubt' on the Anglophobic bona fides of Bewley himself.

After the war was over, Bewley spent the rest of his life in Rome, where he re-wrote his own history in a self-serving autobiography that could not find a publisher while he was alive. Bewley had described Hitler as the 'finest orator' he had ever heard, in a confidential report sent to Dublin in 1933. However, in his posthumous *Memoirs of a Wild Goose*, he claimed to have recognised from the outset that Hitler was merely 'a commonplace figure mouthing commonplace sentiments with the self-sufficiency of the half-educated'. It should, perhaps, be noted that Bewley was not the only Irishman drastically to revise his opinions of Nazi Germany, following its downfall.

De Valera had intended to replace Bewley with Dr. Thomas Kiernan, a former Director of Radio Éireann. However, his accreditation was complicated by constitutional issues. At that time, senior diplomatic appointments, such as Kiernan's, needed to be approved by King George VI – which was clearly impossible while

Britain was at war with Germany. Instead, the First Secretary of the Legation in Berlin, William Warnock, was promoted to the post of Charge d'Affaires. Warnock did not share Bewley's noxious anti-Semitism, or his overweening sense of self-regard. Warnock was, by instinct and inclination, a more conventional career diplomat and rather more guarded than Bewley in expressing his personal opinions. However, in 1940, he held pronounced anti-British views that were similar to those of his predecessor. In a breach of protocol, he had risen to give Hitler's triumphant Reichstag speech, of July, 1940, a standing ovation. In a dispatch sent to Dublin the same year, he predicted that the Luftwaffe's blitz of London would soon have a 'shattering effect on the morale of the self-centred and self-satisfied British.' In May of 1940, Dr. Ernst Woermann, an SS *Obersturmführer* and Director of the Political Department of the German Foreign Ministry, reported that Warnock had suggested to him that Ireland was only waiting for the right moment to join in 'the war against England'.

Warnock may have been influenced in his view of the Nazi regime – and the likely outcome of the war - by his former senior colleague, Charles Bewley. In 1942, Warnock visited Rome and the Irish Minister there, Michael MacWhite, reported back to Irish Military Intelligence that 'the first call he had made on his arrival' was to Bewley. In the same year, Warnock advised against seeking the release of James Joyce's Jewish friend, Paul Léon, from Auschwitz. Léon had spent the summer of 1941 correcting misprints in *Finnegans Wake*, and had taken a great personal risk by returning to Paris in September of that year. He had gone back to rescue an important section of Joyce's library and archive from the family apartment on the Rue des Vignes: the remainder he bought at an illegal auction which had been held by Joyce's landlord. On 20th August, 1941, he told Samuel Beckett that he was leaving the following day. Before he could do so, he was arrested by the Gestapo, and taken to Drancy concentration camp.

James Joyce had recently died in Switzerland, and the Society of Swiss Writers in Zurich appealed to the Irish Government to intercede on behalf of his friend, Léon. Dublin advised Warnock: 'in case there is danger than Léon be shot please intervene with foreign office on his behalf.' Warnock replied that such intervention would be 'received very badly' by the Nazi regime. In his opinion, the attempt to save Léon's life would be regarded as 'interfering in internal German affairs,' and ran the danger of damaging Ireland's 'good relations' with Nazi Germany. Dublin deferred to his judgement, and Léon was executed in a Silesian concentration camp on 4th April, 1942. Léon had been able to rescue many of Joyce's original manuscripts from his Paris apartment - including the only known drafts of the *Ithica*, *Scylla and Charybdis* and *Penelope* episodes of Joyce's great novel *Ulysses*. In 1942, the Irish Government chose not to try and prevent Léon's execution, but - sixty years later - another Irish Government paid €11 million to acquire those same manuscripts from his family. It was the largest amount ever paid by the Irish State for any cultural artefact – and, in my opinion, represents one of the relatively few worthwhile investments made by the Irish Government during the years of the Celtic Tiger economic boom.

In most of his reports from Berlin, Warnock tended to put a positive gloss on events from the German perspective – usually quoting from a variety of sources that seemed to confirm his own assessments. In February, 1941, for example, he drew Dublin's attention to a report from the *New York Post* which claimed that 'England is not fighting for democracy, [but] carrying on an Imperialist war.' Writing a few days after the German invasion of the Soviet Union, Warnock reported that there was 'great confidence that [a] decision in favour of Germany will be reached within six weeks'. Later that month, he made disparaging references to the 'savage methods' of the Soviet Army, and claimed that the majority of Russian prisoners taken by the Germans had proved to be 'committed communists'. It has been suggested that Warnock's reports were simply designed 'to reflect his interlocutor's views uncritically', and that they do not represent his personal opinions. However, there are enough instances when he explicitly presents his own views to reveal Warnock's fundamental sympathies.

In January of 1943, for example, Warnock described, with obvious approval, the beneficial effects that he believed German Occupation had brought to Eastern European agriculture: 'The remnant of the former Poland', he wrote, had now 'reached (a) self- supporting stage after three years of intensive work and organisation under German supervision.' His comments suggest very considerable naivety, or woeful ignorance. The increased output in Polish agriculture had only been achieved through brutal coercion, and the extensive use of slave labour. Its purpose was not to feed the Polish population – but to export food to Germany. The previous year, *Reichsmarshall* Hermann Göring had spelled out that goal with unvarnished clarity: reminding a group of senior Nazis that they were not in Poland 'to work for the welfare of the people in your charge, but to get the utmost out of them so that the German people can live.'

In 1942, Hitler had told Hans Frank, the SS *Obergruppenführer* who ran the German administration in Poland, that his goal was to turn that country into one 'great labour camp'. His ultimate intention was to replace '12 million Poles, with 3 to 4 million Germans', and make it an ethnic German province of the Reich. Two months after Warnock sent his dispatch to Dublin, the decision was taken to stop feeding any Jews who were still left in Occupied Poland. Severe penalties were also introduced for any of those Jews who tried to obtain food on the black market. In a speech delivered at Berlin University in 1941, Hans Frank had described Jews as a people who 'wallowed in dirt and filth'. The following year, he began to organise the mass deportation of hundreds of thousands of Polish Jews to the death camps at Auschwitz, Treblinka, and Chelmo. As the end of 1943 approached – and as a result of what Warnock had politely termed 'German supervision' – the only Jews known to be left alive in 'the remnant of the former Poland' were there as slave workers. In November of that year, even those Jews were executed by the SS in *Aktion Emtefest*: Operation 'Harvest Festival'.

By then, the balance of the war had already shifted in favour of the Allies. In the face of Germany's first serious setbacks and defeats, Goebbels, the Nazi Minister for Propaganda, made a famous speech on 18th February, 1943, at the Berlin *Sportpalast,* in which he declared 'Total War' on the Allies. For several hours, he ranted in front of a carefully selected and highly responsive audience – which he later described to *Reichsminister* Albert Speer as 'the best-trained' to be found in the whole of Germany. In the course of his speech, he described 'international Jewry' as a 'contagious infection'; as the 'incarnation of evil'; as the 'plastic demon of decay'; and as the agent of 'culture-destroying chaos'. He whipped his audience into a state of frenzy as he conjured up an apocalyptic vision of Asiatic hordes, led by 'Jewish liquidation commandoes', sweeping in from the East, and bringing with them the spectre of 'hunger, misery and forced labour'.

The dreadful consequences of a Soviet victory, he told his audience, would not be confined to Germany, but would lay waste 'the entire continent' of Europe – leading to 'the liquidation of our entire intelligentsia', and 'the descent of our workers into Bolshevist-Jewish slavery.' In reality, the dire future that Goebbels envisaged bore a striking resemblance to what already existed in those Eastern European countries that Nazi Germany had occupied. Towards the end of this incendiary speech, Goebbels asked his audience a series of ten rhetorical questions. The fourth of these was: 'Do you want a war that is more total and radical than anything we can imagine today?' His ecstatic listeners roared back their assent. Goebbels had boasted to Speer of the cynical ease with which he could manipulate an audience. Viewed from that perspective, he had given a virtuoso performance at the *Sportpalast:* 'If I'd told those people to jump from the third floor', he gloated in his diary, 'they would have done it!'

Goebbels' speech was broadcast throughout the Reich – on radio, and public address systems - and was widely publicised, but it failed in one of its primary objectives: to resolve the critical shortage of labour in Germany's war economy from within its own population reserves. At the time of the *Sportpalast* speech, there were virtually no German men in their twenties who had not already been conscripted. The shrinking work force was particularly critical in armaments factories – from which, in the first half of 1942, the *Wehrmacht* had drafted more than 200,000 men. Goebbels had hoped his speech would encourage more German women to take their places. By their own estimates, however, the most that Nazi officials hoped to recruit was less than 700,000 additional females. As Adam Tooze has pointed out, at this stage of the war Germany required 'not hundreds of thousands but millions of additional workers.' The only places to find such vast numbers were in the countries which Nazi Germany occupied - and in their POW and concentration camps. As some Irish merchant seamen would soon discover to their cost, the principal impact of Goebbels' speech was to accelerate the drive for slave workers needed to maintain production in the Third Reich's war industries.

When he reported to Dublin a few weeks after the *Sportpalast* speech, Warnock did not mention its rabid anti-Semitism, or provide any analysis of its underlying purpose. Instead, his considered opinion was that Goebbels had '(handled) the situation with great skill'. Later in 1943, Warnock even echoed some of the major themes expounded by the Nazi Minister in the *Sportpalast* - when Goebbels had portrayed Bolshevism as a creed that intended to enslave Europe, and destroy its fundamental values. In a confidential dispatch sent to Dublin on 23rd October, Warnock clearly stated his personal conviction that 'nobody who had enjoyed the benefits of European civilisation' could possibly welcome a German defeat, because this would 'cause the disappearance of the last vestiges of individual freedom, and the extermination of religion and culture as Europe knows them'.

In October of 1943, as his period as Chargé d'Affaires in Berlin was drawing to a close, Warnock reported, with evident excitement, that a 'secret weapon' had apparently been developed by the Germans, which was 'so phenomenal that it will change the whole course of the war.' He was, once again, drawing upon the inflated rhetoric of Dr. Goebbels: referring, this time, to the production of the V-1 missile – an indiscriminate flying bomb that was later used to terrorise the civilian population of southern England. Goebbels had promised that the superior technology of the Nazis' 'miracle weapons' would win the war for Germany. In fact, the cumulative explosive tonnage, carried by the 10,000 or so V-1 rockets that were launched, was less than half of what Allied bombers could drop in a single day – and far more slave workers died manufacturing these rockets in Germany than were ever killed by them on English soil.

Warnock's last dispatch from Berlin, written in January 1944, was in response to a request from Dublin to see if it were possible to help some 'named Jews' escape the Nazi regime. In contrast to the warm empathy which he had frequently expressed for the 'magnificent discipline' of the beleaguered German nation, Warnock's response to this request was brusque and dismissive. 'The German authorities', he wrote, 'are inclined to regard (such) action by other countries as indirect criticism of their Jewish policy.' This was, more or less, the same advice Warnock had given in 1942, when asked to intervene on behalf of Paul Leon. Clearly, in his eyes, even indirect criticism of Nazi Germany, and its barbaric treatment of innocent civilians had remained unacceptable.

Many years later, Warnock conceded that he 'might have expressed anti-British sentiments' during his period as Chargé d'Affaires, but claimed that he had always regarded Nazi Germany as 'objectionable' – about as mild a criticism of that genocidal State as might be conceived. He also refuted suggestions that he had tried to curry favour with the Germans, but acknowledged that, when he entertained Nazi officials, he felt it was his 'duty' as Ireland's representative to make sure that they had 'a good meal'.

Against this background – of overt sympathy, or tacit accommodation with the Nazi regime – it may not seem surprising that Warnock appears to have made little or no attempt to intervene on behalf of any Irish citizens who were in the crews of Allied merchant ships that had been sunk, or captured. Those seamen later claimed to have written a number of letters to him – seeking his assistance. It is not known for certain if he ever received their letters, but it is seems likely that he knew they were being held prisoner. When they were captured, all prisoners of war or internees were obliged to fill out a *Kriegsgefangenen Postkarte* – a captured POW postcard – which was then sent, through the agency of the Red Cross, back to their Governments and their families. The postcards filled in by Irish merchant seamen – which are dated and stamped by the British censor in June, July, and September of 1942 – establish that the relevant authorities all had documentary proof that Irish nationals were being held prisoner in German POW camps.

Apart from this documentation, there is proof that the families of Irish prisoners were able to receive letters and postcards from their imprisoned relatives in 1942 – and that Irish politicians were aware of this correspondence. What is more, one of the *Kommandants* of the labour camp, in which Irish merchant seamen were later held, testified before a British military court in 1947 that their full details – along with individual photographs – were sent to the Irish Legation in Berlin in July, 1943. Soon after that, *Kommandant* Walhorn stated, the Irish Legation was destroyed by Allied bombs – so the details had to be re-sent, and the seamen 'had to be photographed all over again'. Walhorn's testimony was never questioned – either by the Irish prisoners, or the Irish authorities. His awareness that the Irish Legation had been destroyed by bombs in 1943, and that the details and photographs of the Irish prisoners needed to be re-supplied, adds further credence to his account. Given this amount of evidence, the contention that the Irish Legation in Berlin was not aware that Irish merchant seamen were being held captive in Germany in the early years of the war seems unsustainable.

It may well be that Warnock felt he was too busy with the everyday demands of his Legation, – where all the work had to be divided between himself and Eileen Walsh, his Irish secretary – to become involved with the plight of Irish prisoners. But it is clear from his dispatches to Dublin that the Irish community in Berlin was very small, and he still found time – in the early years of the war, at least – to organise St. Patrick's Day parties, to play regular rounds of golf, to travel abroad, and to dine with senior figures from the Nazi administration. As far as those serving in the Allied armed forces were concerned, he may well have felt that their incarceration was part of the risk that they knew they were taking when they joined a belligerent army. For Irishmen like my father, who chose to volunteer, there was clearly an implicit acceptance of the possibility of imprisonment, serious injury or violent death. However, the situation was very different, and, in some respects, a good deal more complex for my father's cousin.

When William and many other Irishmen entered the merchant marine, Ireland was still part of the United Kingdom. For the majority of those Irishmen who wanted to go to sea, but did not want to enlist in the Royal Navy, the British merchant fleet was an obvious choice – unless they were happy to spend their lives ferrying coal and cattle across the Irish Sea, or carrying supplies to some of the lighthouses dotted around Ireland's coastline. They could not have reckoned that they would ever become drawn into a global military conflict – or be held for years as prisoners. As it turned out, the first casualty of the Second World War was the merchant ship *Athenia:* sunk off the west coast of Ireland on 3rd September, 1939, just a few hours after war had been declared. In the years that followed, more than 30,000 merchant seamen on British ships were to die as a result of action by the Axis powers: a higher proportion of fatalities than in any branch of the Allied armed services – including the Royal Navy, and the US Marines. Only the merchant officers wore uniforms, and it was not unusual for the ratings to be abused in the streets of Britain as 'shirkers', but their sacrifices proved crucial in the defeat of Nazi Germany – and in the survival of the Irish State.

In 1939, Ireland did not have its own naval service – even in name – while its merchant marine had been neglected by successive Irish Governments, and allowed to fall into a dramatic decline since Irish Independence. By 1939, the Irish merchant fleet could scarecely muster more than 50 ships – and none of these were ocean-going. Britain, on the other hand, could still claim the largest mercantile fleet in the world, with more than 5,000 vessels, and the most extensive global reach. Small as it was, Ireland's own merchant ships were not immune to attack from German submarines and surface craft. In the course of the war, sixteen Irish-registered ships were lost at sea – a small number, but a high proportion of the total Irish fleet. Due to the shortage of its own marine, Irish trade remained heavily dependent throughout the war on the support of Allied merchant ships, and the protection of the Royal Navy. Ireland was in the middle of a blockaded area, and, despite some determined attempts to become self-sufficient, food and fuel supplies were still reliant on the convoys of merchant ships that crossed the North Atlantic.

In 1938, the Irish Government had calculated that barely 5% of the tonnage entering Irish ports was Irish-owned. During the six years of hostilities that followed, Ireland continued to depend on foreign shipping: even the basic ingredients for bread had to be imported from Canada. The Atlantic convoys sailed at very considerable risk to the lives of their crews, and Ireland's neutrality increased the danger – since it meant that Allied ships were denied access to southern Irish ports. As Martin Quigley – the OSS agent in Ireland – pointed out in 1943, 'use of the great harbour at Cork, for example, would shorten lines of communication, bringing Allied sea power hundreds of miles closer to major Nazi submarine operational areas.'

In the first three years of the war, more than 3,000 Allied merchant ships were sunk in the Battle of the Atlantic – some within sight of the Irish coast - and the bodies of hundreds of dead seamen were washed up on Ireland's western seaboard. One Fine Gael Deputy drove home the grim implications of this human flotsam: 'We are living', he told the Dáil, 'on the lives of men who have taken risk in order to feed us.' The Northern Irish writer, Louis

MacNeice, expressed a similar sentiment in more lurid and accusatory terms in a poem addressed to the citizens of Eire. 'To the West off your own shores', he wrote, 'the Mackerel are fat'. They had feasted, he suggested, 'on the flesh of your kin'; the merchant seamen who had died bringing essential supplies to Ireland. In fact, many Irish citizens would not have been aware of the debt they owed to those seamen: in 1941, the press censors were instructed by the Irish Government to suppress all future references to shipping between Ireland and Britain.

There was another factor at work for many of the Irishmen who served in Britain's merchant marine. After years of service, Irish seamen often felt a powerful bond of loyalty to that fleet. This was certainly the case as far as my cousin William was concerned. I learned that he later expressed that simple code of honour in effective terms to an SS officer, who was trying to persuade him and other Irish seamen to join the German war effort. They had all refused, and, in exasperation, the officer turned to William and said, 'You work for the British – why won't you work for us?' Harry Callan was a young Irish seaman who was present on that day - and who survived the camp. Almost seventy years later, he told me that William had replied: 'Why would I bite the hand that has fed me?'

Ireland's Charge d'Affaires, William Warnock, was described by one of his former colleagues as a 'mild-mannered' individual. Perhaps, he was too mild – and too ready to avoid confrontation – to be of much value to some of those Irish citizens who were imprisoned in Germany, and needed his assistance. Warnock may not have concerned himself about the future of Irishmen like my cousin, but the Germans did. Most of the Irish seamen brought to France at the end of 1940, and the beginning of 1941 were sent on to be questioned at an unfinished housing estate just outside Paris. The concentration camp at Drancy was later to become infamous as the place where thousands of Jews in France – such as Paul Léon - were held before they were transported to Auschwitz. But the Irish prisoners who arrived there in 1941 were of special interest to *Abwehr II* – the section of German Military Intelligence that dealt with Europe's national minorities. At that stage of the war, it was still believed that Ireland could be of strategic value to Nazi Germany, and the *Abwehr* officers believed that they could convince the Irish seamen that they shared a common enemy in England.

4

WITH A POP GUN

In his account written after the war, Captain Theodor Detmers recalled that 29th of January, 1941, was 'a broiling hot day', with 'a haze over the water'. Detmers was, at 37, the youngest man to command one of the eight surface raiders that were launched in Germany in 1940. His ship, the *Kormoran*, was the largest of the *Hilfskreuzer*s. Like the *Pinguin*, she had set sail from the port of Gotenhaven, and was provisioned for a twelve-month voyage. The *Kormoran* was, however, much better armed than the *Pinguin*, with her heavy guns concealed behind false hull plates, and fake cargo hatches. The *Kormoran* had left Gotenhaven on 3rd December, 1940, and, once clear of German waters, had disguised herself as a Soviet freighter, the *Vyacheslav Molotov*. Late on the evening of 12th December, under cover of a heavy storm, she had slipped into the icy waters of the North Atlantic.

Detmer's mission was almost the same as that of Ernst-Felix Krüder: to seek out and destroy Allied shipping in the Atlantic, before moving to the Indian Ocean, with orders to lay mines off the Australian coast. During the first two weeks of her voyage, the *Kormoran* encountered only merchant ships from the United States, which she was forbidden to attack since the USA was not yet at war with Germany. On 6th January, 1941, however, she sighted and sank a Greek freighter, the *Antonis*. The following week, the German raider sank a 7,000 ton oil tanker, the *British Union* – part of the Anglo-Persian Oil Company fleet - and took 28 merchant seamen as prisoners. The sinking of the *Union* attracted the attention of an Allied cruiser, the HMS *Arawa*. However, she failed to locate the *Kormoran*, or to determine her true identity. From then on, she was referred to by the Royal Navy as *Raider G*.

By mid-day, on 29th January, 1941, Detmers recalled, it was so hot that the 'horizon was hardly visible at all.' He was in his cabin after lunch when the alarm bells sounded. Detmers rushed to the bridge, and managed to spot 'the light streak of a ship's wake' in the distance. Some minutes later, he could make out its 'vague shape'. It was impossible to determine the ship's nationality, so Detmers increased speed and turned the *Kormoran* towards her. He expected to see some sign that his manoeuvre had been noticed, but there was none. He moved closer until the *Kormoran* was near enough to the freighter 'for reasonable shooting'. By this stage, Detmers could see the small gun that the ship was carrying in her stern, and knew that she must be an enemy freighter. Suddenly, the ship turned two or three points away from the *Kormoran*, and, as she did so, Detmers could see that this was a big Allied tanker of 'at least 10,000 tons'.

The ship that Detmers was preparing to attack was the 12,000 ton *Afric Star* – a refrigerator ship that was carrying meat and butter to England. On board were two Irishmen: William English – a veteran seaman from Arklow in County Wicklow - and Harry Callan, an assistant cook, from Derry City in Northern Ireland. At the time of his encounter with the *Kormoran*, Harry was just seventeen years of age. I met him more than 70 years later – in December, 2011. He was then living in the quiet suburb of Santry, on the northside of Dublin. When I rang the bell on the front door of his house, I noticed that a plaque with the crest of the Merchant Navy was mounted inside the porch. Harry greeted me with a firm handshake. He was dressed immaculately, and his house conveyed an immediate impression that there was a place for everything, and everything was in its place; a characteristic often found in seamen of all nationalities and descriptions.

Harry had been just 16 when he had started working as a galley boy in the autumn of 1939. 'They would take anyone at that time', he told me, 'It didn't matter what age you were.' He had joined the *Afric Star* at the beginning of 1941, working as an assistant cook on a voyage to the West Indies. Seventy years later, he could still recall vividly what had happened on that sweltering afternoon when he first became a prisoner. 'We saw this ship flying the Russian flag', he remembered, 'it was around one o'clock, and we were just about to have our dinner. I went out on the deck to have a look at her. The next thing, she was going round behind us. We thought she was just letting us go ahead, and not getting in our way.' But that was not Detmers' objective. Once the *Afric Star* was well within the range of his guns, he 'gave the order to drop camouflage, and run up the war flag'. At the same time, he fired a shot across the freighter's bows, and signalled her to stop. Harry's ship had a gun on her stern, which was intended as a means of defence: 'It was a 'pop gun' – that's what we used to call it", Harry explained. 'We had a Royal Navy man with us – a Navy gunner. He had trained us to use the gun. My job was to pass up the ammunition. When we first fired it in training, there was a big bang, and then a big crack. There was a tear on the side of the ship – the vibration from the bloody gun had split it.' They decided that the gun would be of no use to them, and never used it again.

Detmers' first priority was to sever the radio aerial on the *Afric Star*: 'He was trying to stop us sending any distress signal', Harry told me, 'but we managed to get a message out anyway.' When Detmers realised that a radio signal was being sent, he ordered his gunners to resume firing on the *Star*: as he later commented, 'shooting at that distance was child's play to them'. Within a few minutes, Detmers recalled, the freighter's Captain had seen 'the uselessness of further resistance'. 'Some shells hit the bridge', Harry told me, 'and the skipper told us to abandon ship.' The *Kormoran* continued firing as the crew boarded two lifeboats: 'It was terrible', Harry remembered, 'I was scared stiff. I jumped down into our boat, and lay flat because of the firing. When I looked up, I saw that the whole bulkhead had gone. The German ship was pounding the *Star*, but she couldn't sink her. She was stuffed full of meat, and that was keeping her afloat.'

Apart from the shelling, there were other dangers for the crew: 'The lifeboats had been riddled with shrapnel, and were taking in water,' Harry remembered, 'We thought, 'if the Germans don't pick us up soon, we'll all drown - or the sharks will get us'.' Detmers ordered the lifeboats to put into the side of the *Kormoran,* and come aboard. 'It was just as well, she picked us up', Harry told me, 'because both our lifeboats quickly sank, and we'd all have died if we had been left in them.'

Detmers had taken 75 prisoners – including three civilian passengers. Two of these were women, still dressed in their bathing costumes, who had been taking coffee on deck when their ship was attacked. Detmers also captured code books and other vital documents, which were soon to prove of practical value to the German raider. Detmers decided that the *Afric Star* was too badly damaged to keep as a prize, and felt 'reluctantly compelled to sink her'. The explosives officer in his boarding party fixed charges in her engine room, but they failed to scuttle the ship. Detmers ordered his torpedo officer to sink her, and the *Star* went down less than three hours after she had first been sighted. The *Kormoran's* boarding party had come back with the *Afric Star's* brass bell, and gave it to their Captain. Detmers found it 'a place of honour' in his cabin, where it served to remind him of 'the biggest of all the ships we sank.' A bottle of champagne was opened, and one of the ship's crew was instructed to paint the names of all the ships that the *Kormoran* had sunk on the ward-room wall. So far, that only amounted to three, but, as Detmers observed, 'there was plenty of room on the wall for more'.

As it turned out, Detmers did not have to wait long before a new name could be added. Later that same night, another merchant ship was spotted by the *Kormoran's* officer of the watch. She was sailing in the dark without lights – which suggested to Detmers that she was probably an enemy freighter. He closed on her, gave a warning and opened fire. Once again, the enemy ship was soon in flames, and its crew had begun to abandon ship. The code books that had been taken from the *Star* revealed that this was a 5,000 ton British freighter, the *Eurolychus,* with a cargo of bomber planes bound for what was then a British colony: the Gold Coast, in West Africa. Detmers ordered the sinking of the stricken ship, and she was dispatched with a single torpedo – just a few hours after he had done the same to the *Afric Star*. The distress calls of the *Eurolychus* had been picked up by two British warships, the *Norfolk* and the *Devonshire* – who pursued the *Kormoran*, but without success. Once again, the Royal Navy was unable to identify the ship responsible for the sinking of Allied merchant freighters.

The *Kormoran* now headed south-west for the Cape Verde Islands. There were no sightings of enemy ships for the next few weeks, and Detmers recorded in the ship's log that the only life he saw in that time were 'flying fish, or an occasional school of dolphins'. The Kormoran was due to rendezvous with the supply ship *Nordmark* to the west of the Ascension Islands. On 7th of February, the *Nordmark* was sighted at the arranged rendezvous point. Like the *Kormoran*, she was camouflaged – in her case, as the American ship *Dixie* – but, as Detmers noted with approval, her guns could be in action 'in an extraordinarily short space of time.' There was another ship steaming alongside the *Nordmark*: the *Duquesa* - a captured refrigerator ship, which was loaded with foodstuffs. Detmer made sure to supplement his own ship's stores from the freighter's 'inexhaustible riches' of prime Argentine beef – before sending her 'to the bottom of the Atlantic.'

When supplies had been taken on board, Detmers handed his prisoners – including Callan and English – over to the *Nordmark* to be taken back to Europe. Before they left his ship, he called the captains of the three Allied freighters to his cabin, where they 'drank a friendly glass of beer' together. Detmers told them that he hoped they 'would not look back with too much resentment on their involuntary stay as prisoners on board a German warship.' In fact, the Allied seamen had been treated well by the crew of the *Kormoran*, and they were to speak of Detmers with a degree of affectionate nostalgia in the years that lay ahead. Detmers believed that they were also relieved to be on board a ship like the *Nordmark* which – unlike the *Kormoran* – 'would not go around looking for trouble'. The merchant seamen might not have agreed with his assessment. Altogether, there were almost 600 merchant sailors on board the *Nordmark* – from ten different ships - and they were all crowded into the ship's No. 5 storage tank. To say the least, the living conditions that the prisoners endured on the *Nordmark* were constricted – similar to those experienced by my cousin and his shipmates on the *Nordvard*. However, 320 prisoners – including Callan and English – were subsequently transferred to another German ship: the blockade-runner *Portland*. Their time on the *Kormoran* and the *Nordmark* had been uncomfortable, but uneventful for most of the merchant seamen. The same could not be said for the next stage of their voyage.

Once on board the *Portland*, the prisoners were accommodated below deck in Nos. 2 and 3 holds. No. 1 hold was empty, apart from several hundred empty sacks – some of which were given to the prisoners as bedding. No.s 1 and 4 holds were then sealed off to prevent any access by the seamen. The German crew was far outnumbered by their prisoners, and, as the *Portland* drew closer to Bordeaux, some of the seamen saw this as a last opportunity to win their freedom. On 10th of March, 1941, the first attempt to seize control of the ship was botched when their plans were discovered by their guards, but a new strategy was soon formulated. Over the next few days, the prisoners secretly managed to break into the No. 4 hold, and spread sacking around the oxygen cylinders they found there. On the evening of 13th of March, the seamen made their next move, and set fire to the ship's cargo. They hoped that a fire at night would attract the attention of any British aircraft or warships in the area. At first, the German crew seemed able to control the fire, and the prisoners believed their attempt to escape had been another failure.

The next morning, however, the flames re-ignited, and the seamen were compelled at gun point to fight the fire they had started. When the Chief Officer of Harry's ship, the *Afric Star*, protested at this, he was publicly whipped: another seaman who went to his aid was also subjected to a brutal beating. When all the burning sacks had been thrown overboard, the German crew set up a gauntlet of whips and clubs, through which they forced their prisoners to run to the point of exhaustion. That was only a foretaste of what was to come. Later the same afternoon, armed guards entered the holds in which the seamen were kept. Then, in the words of Harry Callan, 'all hell broke loose'. The guards turned out the lights, and opened fire without warning in the darkness. When the lights were switched back on a few minutes later, it was clear that several prisoners had been shot. Two of them were seriously injured: Arthur Freeman and Frank Evans. Evans had been standing beside Harry Callan when he was hit. He and Freeman both died from their wounds, and were buried in Bordeaux. Soon after the *Portland* anchored, seven of the Allied merchant seamen were formally charged with the crime of 'mutiny at sea': a charge that implicitly recognises that the seamen were not combatants. Those charged were tried later that year in Hamburg, and found guilty. In the years that followed, these seamen were treated with a special degree of physical brutality – which left some of them permanently disabled.

Frank Evans was one of the three civilian passengers who had been on board the *Afric Star*. He was also the husband of Joan Evans: one of the two women who had been taken prisoner by the *Kormoran*. When the *Portland* docked in Bordeaux, both of these women were sent to a succession of camps – before being interned at Liebenau, near Ravensberg. This prison had previously been used as a mental asylum and close to 700 inmates had been murdered by the SS to make room for the new arrivals. Soon after she arrived at Liebenau, Joan Evans realised that she was pregnant. She gave birth to a daughter – named Francis, after her husband – inside the prison walls. After the war, the German sailors who had served on the *Portland* were tried in Hamburg. 'The British kicked up a big fuss about Frank being shot', Harry told me, 'but the way things were then, no-one ever served any time for killing him.'

The *Portland* docked in Bordeaux on 14th of March, 1941. Meanwhile, the *Kormoran* had been ordered to make another rendezvous: this time with Ernst-Felix Krüder and the *Pinguin*. Both German crews were delighted to see each other: Detmers was particularly pleased to meet Krüder, whose formidable reputation had preceded him. According to Detmers. Krüder told him that the previous months of 'hunting' in the Indian Ocean had been exhilarating. In recent weeks, however, he said that the Allies had become more cautious, and 'game' had become much harder to track down. Krüder advised Detmers that some targets could still be found off the coast of Southern Africa – where he had sunk the *British Commander*. They arranged a second meeting to take place north of the Seychelles, on 1st of June. Three weeks before that meeting could take place, Detmers learned that the *Pinguin* had been sunk, and Krüder was dead. 'That was a fate', Detmers later wrote, 'which, we were well aware, threatened us too.' He concluded that, in any war, it was 'sheer luck' whether or not death ever 'caught up with you.'

In the next few months, luck seemed firmly on Detmers' side, and the *Kormoran* sank another six Allied merchant ships. These were all undefended vessels, but Detmers was also to encounter a well-armed Australian cruiser. On 19th November, 1941, the *Kormoran* was steaming off the coast of Western Australia, disguised as a Dutch merchant ship, the *Stratt Malakka*. It was, Detmers later recalled, a day of 'warm sunshine'. It was also the *Kormoran's* last day afloat. By mid-afternoon, Detmers was relaxing in the officers' mess, enjoying a cup of coffee. Then, the alarm bells began to ring, and a runner came to tell him that a ship had been sighted. When Detmer returned to the bridge, all he could see was, 'a small light spot', on the distant horizon, that was drawing closer. It was the *Sydney* - an Australian light cruiser.

Detmers quickly realised that 'evasion was out of the question'. His only option was to play a waiting game in the hope that the Allied cruiser would come within the range of his guns. When the *Sydney* asked the *Kormoran* to identify herself, Detmers sent confusing messages back and pretended not to understand those he received in return. When the *Sydney* was less than 3,000 metres away, Detmers considered that she had come within 'a beautiful shooting range'. The *Kormoran* abandoned its Dutch camouflage, ran up its battle flag and opened fire. There should have been no contest between these two ships, but the German raider had the advantage of surprise and was able to inflict serious damage on the Australian cruiser before the *Sydney* could reply.

By the end of the engagement, the *Kormoran* had also been badly damaged, and within a few hours, Detmer had taken the decision to abandon and scuttle his ship. He watched from a lifeboat as the *Kormoran* 'lifted her bows into the air and slipped under the surface'. Almost all of the German crew were later rescued, but the *Sydney* went down with all 645 of her company. Detmers regretted their deaths but was delighted that a brand new cruiser had been sunk by a 're-fitted passenger ship'. German Naval Command was also jubilant, and Detmers soon learned that he had been awarded the *Ritterkreuz* – the Knight's Cross - for his services to the Reich. Detmers remained a prisoner of war in Australia until 1947, when he was allowed to return to Germany, and begin a new life as a civilian.

He later praised the treatment which he and his crew had received in their POW camp. A photograph taken in the camp shows Detmers and his brother officers from the *Kormoran*. They are clean-shaven, and their hair has clearly been brushed. Their white shirts are clean and crisp, and their uniforms have been pressed. They seem healthy, relaxed and well-fed. Sadly, by that stage, the same would not be said the Irish seamen – such as Harry Callan - whom Detmers had sent back to Europe.

5

THE MINING TOWN

It had not taken German Military Intelligence long to realise that none of the Irish merchant seamen they had questioned at Drancy was prepared to join the German war effort. Within a few months, they had all been moved to a Prisoner of War camp in Germany. For anyone who grew up watching Second World War movies on TV every Christmas, the image of an Allied POW camp has a certain familiar and endearing quality. The Allied prisoners seemed decent, brave and clever chaps - effortlessly out-foxing the dim-witted German 'goons' who guarded them. In 1941, the majority of Irish merchant seamen were taken from Drancy, outside Paris, to a POW camp about 60 kilometres west of Hamburg – and, to say the least, Stalag X B did not conform to any such re-assuring stereotype. It was located near Sandbostel, and had been built on a swamp. For much of the year, the climate was cold, damp and a breeding ground for all sorts of disease and infection. Its first prisoners were several thousand Poles, but from early 1941 the camp also received substantial numbers of merchant seamen.

Stalag X B soon became one of the most notorious of POW camps. Maurice Archer was just 18 years old, and serving on the merchant freighter, *Wendover*, when she was attacked and sunk by the German raider, *Thor*. The first thing he noticed when he arrived in Sandbostel was the heavy 'stench of death'. When new prisoners arrived, they were normally stripped and hosed down with disinfectant. In the bitter winter of 1941, dozens of Russian prisoners died of exposure when they were forced to stand naked in the freezing cold for hours – waiting to be issued with uniforms. Almost half of the POWs lived a semi-subterranean existence in turf-roofed huts. The toilets in the camp were open pits, with bare boards laid above them on which the prisoners had to squat while they relieved themselves.

With the exception of the Officers and NCOs over the rank of sergeant, every Allied POW was forced to work. They were regarded as the property of the German Reich, and could be loaned or hired out as suited their masters. Prisoners could not expect to be treated with any degree of leniency by their captors. German regulations specified that the camp guards were entitled to ensure their orders were obeyed, 'by force of arms' if necessary. Indeed, the same regulations advised that guards who failed to take such action would themselves be held responsible and punished.

The type of work that Allied POWs were expected to do was both varied and extensive. They included the mining of coal, salt, iron, graphite and potassium. Prisoners were used to build roads, to lay sewage pipes and quarry stone. They unloaded goods wagons, collected rubbish, and levelled ground. They put down railway tracks, repaired bridges and dug gravel pits. In breach of the Geneva Convention, they were also used to manufacture armaments that would be used against their own countries. Before the war had ended, Allied POWs were used to make bombs, build army trucks, construct runways for German bombers and manufacture engine parts for tanks and planes.

Many thousands of POWs passed through Stalag X B; the number of those who died is not known, but it seems certain that tens of thousands of prisoners perished from hunger, illness and murder. The treatment that was meted out to Soviet prisoners was, by policy and design, especially harsh. In 1943 – when the camp regime is supposed to have improved somewhat – W.A. Jones, a merchant seaman from Australia, was briefly held in Sandbostel, and he witnessed the desperate plight of the Russian prisoners. 'Never in my born life', he wrote, 'have I seen human beings so stupefied and stunned by suffering. There was hardly a man among them who did not look like a dog about to be whipped.'

The extreme severity with which these prisoners were treated was entirely in keeping with the Nazi ideology as articulated by the SS *Reichsführer*, Heinrich Himmler. 'Russian prisoners', he believed, 'do everything *en masse* and so this mass must be trampled down and slaughtered to the last man.' He advised that the conditions of their imprisonment should be intentionally brutal: 'like cutting a pig's throat, and letting it gradually bleed to death.' Himmler's subordinates in the SS made sure that their master's wishes were met, but his attitude to the suffering of Soviet prisoners was not confined to dedicated Nazis. Soon after the war ended, the Soviet military administration built a monument to the Russian POWs who had died in Sandbostel. However, in 1956, that monument was blown up on the orders of Saxony's Ministry of the Interior. Inscribed on the monument was a claim that more than 50,000 Soviet prisoners had died in the camp, and the local German authorities were enraged by that figure – insisting that the Russian dead did not number more than 20,000.

Harry Callan was one of the Irish seamen who arrived in Sandbostel in 1941. My cousin William was already in the camp when he arrived, though Harry could not recollect meeting him there. Harry was to spend almost eight months in Sandbostel, and remembered it as 'very rough'. Fortunately, there were protests from Switzerland – the Protecting Power under the Geneva Convention – about the treatment that the merchant sailors had received. The growing number of naval prisoners also encouraged the Kriegsmarine to build its own camp. During the Spring and Summer of 1942, about 50 of the Irish seamen were moved again. This time, they were marched to Milag Nord at Westertimke – a new internment centre that had been built for the merchant seamen. In fact, there were two camps at Westertimke: Marlag and Milag Nord. Marlag was for the Royal Navy, and was divided into two compounds: one for officers, and the other for petty officers and ratings. Milag Nord was exclusively for merchant seamen, and was located a few hundred yards away from the Marlag camp. 'We couldn't see the Royal Navy men', Harry Callan told me, 'because there were a lot of trees between them and us'. It wasn't only trees that separated the two groups of sailors. Although the merchant camp was smaller, it contained many more prisoners. Merchant officers and crews were held together, and their living conditions were of a markedly lower standard.

Like military POWs, merchant naval officers were not expected to work, but petty officers and ordinary ratings were employed in factories, quarries and farms. On occasions, ratings who refused to work were kept on morning roll call until they capitulated. Several such incidents took place in the winter of 1942/43, when for several months no Red Cross parcels were distributed at Milag, and the starving seamen refused to work. The deputy *Kommandant* was prepared to keep the ratings standing for hours in 20 degrees of frost until they finally abandoned their protest. On another occasion, the morning roll call was surrounded by soldiers armed with cocked machine guns, and the ratings were given a 15 minute deadline to start work – which they wisely decided to accept. There were, however, some more serious incidents.

On the night of 13th, of May 1942, a young English seaman called Walter Skeet was killed in the Milag camp. According to his file in the British National Archives at

Kew, Skeet was 23 years old at the time of his death. He had been working as a radio operator on the *British Petrol* – another tanker in Anglo-Persian's fleet – when she was attacked, and he was taken prisoner by the surface raider, *Widder*. It appears that he had arranged to meet one of the Kriegsmarine guards on the night he died in order to trade cigarettes for food. When he arrived for their meeting, Skeet ran into a different guard. According to some witnesses, this guard panicked, and opened fire without warning. The first shot knocked Skeet to the ground: as he staggered to his feet, he was shot for a second time at point-blank range. The dying man was carried by John Whyte – one of my cousin's shipmates on the *British Commander* – to a nearby hut, where he was attended by a medical officer from the *Afric Star*. Skeet's wounds were too grave, however, and he died soon after reaching the hut. What is, perhaps, most revealing about Skeet's death is its aftermath; the doggedness with which his killer was pursued by the British, and the deliberate obstruction of that lawful pursuit by the German authorities – even after the war was over.

The other merchant seamen in the Milag camp believed that Skeet had been murdered. His death was immediately reported to the Swiss Embassy, the Protecting Power, for transmission to the British Government. Detailed statements were made by half-a-dozen other prisoners, and these were sent by the Swiss on to the British War Office. Skeet's family was contacted, and the circumstances of his death explained to them. The guard who had shot Skeet was moved out of the Milag camp the next day, and his name and identity were concealed by the Kreigsmarine. Nonetheless, for the remainder of the war, the British authorities made strenuous efforts to identify him.

These efforts persisted after the war was over: witnesses to the killing were sought in Norway, Canada and Australia – as well as in Britain – and their affidavits were collected and assessed. It was not until 1948 that the British reluctantly conceded that – without full co-operation from the Germans – Skeet's killer would never be found, or prosecuted. The file kept in the British National Archives on this single case runs close to 150 pages: it reveals a concern for the fate of one young man that stands in marked contrast to the apparent indifference shown by the Irish authorities to those citizens of Ireland, who were being held at that time in the same camp as Skeet.

Despite all of its hardships, it must be acknowledged that Milag Nord was regarded by most merchant seamen as a distinct improvement on Sandbostel. The new camp soon filled up with prisoners. One of these was a cadet officer from Tramore in County Waterford, named Christopher Ryan. He had followed in the footsteps of his father, and joined the Merchant Navy shortly before the outbreak of war. On the night of 31st of January, 1941, just one month after his 21st birthday, Ryan had been on board the cargo vessel, *Speybank*. The merchant ship on which he was serving had been en route from Cochin, on the west coast of India, to New York, with a cargo of tea, manganese ore and teakwood. Despite the value of her cargo, the *Speybank* had not been part of a convoy; the Royal Navy simply did not have enough cruisers to offer her protection. The *Speybank* was alone in a vast expanse of ocean when she was attacked by the raider *Atlantis* – known only to the Royal Navy as *Raider C*. Like the other *Hilfskreuzers*, the *Atlantis* was capable of radical alteration in her appearance. She carried a dummy funnel, variable-height masts, a fake crane and deckhouse – as well as ample supplies of paint and canvas – which allowed her to assume no less than 26 different silhouettes.

The *Atlantis* was commanded by one of the most remarkable and capable officers in the German Navy. *Kapitan zur See* Bernhard Rogge was a so-called *Mischlinge*, and had been forced to apply for a *Deutschblütkeitserklärung* – a German Blood Certificate – since he was partly Jewish. *Grossadmiral* Karl Dönitz, when he was later on trial for war crimes at Nuremberg, cited his support for Rogge as proof that he was not motivated by anti-Semitic prejudice. Rogge became one of the most successful of raider commanders – winning not only the *Ritterkreuz mir Eichenlaub*, but a further decoration that was created specially for him, and was presented personally by Hitler. In the 1960s, a Hollywood movie was even made about his exploits at sea. Rogge was one of the few German officers of Flag – or senior – rank who was not arrested and tried by the Allies after the war and this was largely due to his humane treatment of his prisoners.

There had been no casualties on the *Speybank*, and Rogge noted in the ship's log that he had taken 'seventeen white prisoners' on board the *Atlantis*. The non-white crew were kept in place to man the freighter because Rogge had immediately realised the value of the *Speybank's* cargo, and decided not to sink the ship, but to keep it as a prize. He saw that the freighter had a full store of supplies and sufficient fuel to be able to reach France. He also realised that the *Speybank* could be used to Germany's further advantage. The ship was not only intact, but had not managed to send out a distress signal. She was part of the Bank Line merchant fleet, and her shape and fittings were standard for all the other sixteen ships in that line – which meant she was already equipped with an highly adaptable disguise. Rogge requested that the *Tannenfels*, a blockade runner at anchor in Italian Somaliland, be ordered to rendezvous with the *Atlantis*. When she arrived, all of the *Speybank's* crew was transferred to the *Tannenfels*. Rogge put the ship under the command of one of his junior officers, and sent both ships back to Europe – where the *Tannenhels* arrived at the end of April.

According to the Irish cadet, Christopher Ryan, the prisoners were 'exhausted, hungry and freezing', after spending the previous two months confined in the ship's hull. Soon after they disembarked, they were 'herded onto a cattle train', and, five days later, they arrived in Hamburg. The *Speybank* docked in Bordeaux a few weeks later. Her arrival was kept secret, and she was soon re-commissioned in the German navy as the raider, *Doggerbank*. At the beginning of 1942, she left port again - to lay mines off the coast of South Africa. The following year, the *Doggerbank* was west of the Canaries when she was sunk by a German submarine: her disguise had proved all too effective, and she had been mistaken for a genuine Allied freighter. There was just one survivor.

Ryan and the other prisoners taken by Rogge were first sent to Sandbostel, and then moved to Milag Nord – where there were already several thousand merchant seamen in the camp complex. As an officer, Ryan was not compelled to work, and he found conditions in the camp to be, 'tolerable', with a 'loose adherence' to the protocols of the Geneva Convention. But the camp was becoming over-crowded with the regular influx of new prisoners. One of them was an English engineering officer called John Woods. He had been brought ashore at the French port of Brest – along with the remainder of the crew of the *Silver Fir,* a merchant freighter that had been sunk on its way to New York by the German battleship *Scharnhorst.* The Captain of the *Silver Fir* had ordered his one antiquated gun into action, but the German warship blew it off the poop deck before it could fire a single shot. John Woods watched three seamen clamber into a boat on the port side, minutes before a shell smashed into it, killing all of them. In his own lifeboat, an Irish seaman called Jim Hughes had been hit by shrapnel in the neck. 'We fished him out of the water', Woods recalled, 'but he died later on board the *Scharnhorst*'. According to Woods, the prisoners from the *Silver Fir* were 'shoved into the bowels of the ship under a gun-turret' – where they could hear the *Scharnhorst* firing on other Allied ships.

One of the ships attacked on the same day as the *Silver Fir* was the freighter *Athelfoam*, and on board that ship were two Irish seamen who would later die in German prison camps; Patrick Breen, from Blackwater in County Wexford, and James Byrne, from Arklow in County Wicklow. Jack Matthews was serving on the same ship as a cadet officer. The *Athelfoam* had received reports that German warships were in the vicinity. These turned out to be the *Scharnhorst,* and her sister ship, the *Gneisenau*. 'The convoy had broken apart', Matthews remembered, 'and these two battleships were zig-zagging, coming in from both sides and picking us off'. On the morning that the *Athelfoam* left Swansea, in South Wales, a Bofors gun had been installed on her stern. According to Matthews, the *Athelfoam* was the first merchant ship to be fitted with this type of weapon. Just before she left port, six soldiers also came on board. They had volunteered just a few hours earlier for an undisclosed mission – it proved to be a dangerous assignment.

When the *Athelfoam* was attacked, Matthews ran to his action station: 'There, astern of us, was the *Scharnhorst*. She was coming up at a rate of knots. I could see her battle ensign, and she was a much bigger ship than I had expected. She signalled us to 'stop – do not use your radio'. But we kept on sending distress signals, so that our monitoring stations could get a fix on us. Then the *Scharnhorst* opened up'. The first shot went across the *Athelfoam's* bows, but the merchant ship did not reduce speed. A few minutes later, anti-personnel shells burst overhead: the *Scharnhorst's* gunners were trying to cut the *Athelfoam's* radio aerial. According to Matthews, 'we kept signalling, and they kept firing'. Before long, the *Athelfoam* was on fire, and the crew had begun to abandon ship. Matthews tried to guide the Bofors' gunners onto a boat: 'They wouldn't go at first. They were petrified by what was happening. Eventually, I got in the boat, and they followed me'. They were about to cast off, when another shell exploded. The next thing Matthews knew, he was 'hanging upside down, and the boat had tipped to one side.'

There were some axes stored close to the boat. Matthews managed to reach one of them, and hacked at the supporting line, but, to his dismay, 'the boat took a dive, her nose went under, and she levelled out full of water.' Matthews managed to scramble back on board, and started to bail: 'We had lost two men', he remembered, 'a soldier and our bosun. It was shrapnel in the bosun's case. He had come down off the deck, when he was hit. The back of his head was gone. The soldier was in the boat when she tipped. He was thrown out, and when she came down, it was on top of him, and he was crushed. It was terrible to see. There was blood everywhere. There was no point in bringing the bodies with us, so we left them in the water.'

This was the last lifeboat from the *Athelfoam* to reach the German warship. Once its mission had been completed the *Scharnhorst* made for the nearest French port. On the way back to Occupied France, there were funerals for two merchant seamen who had died on board the German warship. 'They had a marine band', Matthews later recalled, 'and a firing squad, and it was very, very impressive. There was no animosity between us and the German crew. They appeared to be just as upset at the funerals as we were. There were some SS or Gestapo people on board, but they never had much to do with us.' Matthews had been one of the last to climb aboard the *Scharnhorst*: 'one of the ship's officers said to me: 'Why did you not want to come aboard? Did you think that we would machine gun you? Believe me – we Germans are not like that'.'

There were also two young Irishmen from the *Silver Fir* came on board the *Scharnhorst*; William Kelly, from Waterford, and Owen Corr, from Rush, near Dublin. Along with the rest of the prisoners, they were brought ashore at Brest, on the French Atlantic coast. After a few days, they were marched down to the local railway station to be put on cattle trucks. As they waited to board the trucks, Kelly came up with a cunning plan; he suggested that all the seamen from the *Silver Fir* should pretend they were Irish. The reason, according to Woods – the engineering officer – was Ireland's neutrality: 'We thought that we'd be repatriated if they thought we were Irish'. Once again, that was not an unreasonable expectation for merchant seamen from a netural country. However, the *Silver Fir* seamen were unable to fool their guards for long, and the pretence at playing Irish was soon exposed. Looking back, Woods had no regrets about that discovery, since the Irish seamen 'ended up being treated worse than we were.'

By 1942, the camp at Milag Nord had become, in the words of Lieutenant David James, a Royal Navy officer, 'a small township with a population of between three and four thousand men of all colours and nationalities'. At that time, it was unusual for any crew on a British merchant ship not to contain some Caribbean, Chinese or Indian seamen. British spotter planes were even advised to treat with suspicion any ship that claimed to be British where there was no evidence of a mixed race crew. As a result, German raiders sometimes used dark make-up to disguise their sailors when they were on deck. The diverse mix of races and nationalities in the Milag camp included Brazilians and Egyptians, Javanese and West Africans, Icelanders and Sudanese – which may explain why the camp reminded Lieutenant James of 'some mining town of the 1890s'.

Milag was also a camp where James considered the black market to be 'extensive, and well-organised'. There were rival football teams whose stars, James noted, 'could command high transfer fees'. One Irish prisoner carved himself a hurley stick, and practised for hours on his own. There was also a gambling den, run by the 'Milag Jockey Club', where poker schools were in constant session. Milag Nord could even boast a full professional orchestra – which had been on board the troopship *Orama* when she was captured off Narvik in 1941. With no Naval Discipline Act to guide them, and 'no common Service tie of loyalty' to support them, Lieutenant James believed that it was extremely difficult for merchant officers to impose order on their ratings. He thought the Milag camp was a place where conventional social values had been, 'completely reversed'. In James's view, the Marlag Royal Navy camp was very different: apart from its strict disciplinary code, he identified the chief distinctions as its 'smaller size and the absence of the coloured element'.

The German *Kommandant* of both camps was *Kapitan zur See* Schuur. According to James, he was a 'nasty little

Prussian martinet' whose 'only merit was that he was doing his best to drink himself to death.' However, at the end of the war, neither Schuur, nor his successor Schmidt, nor most of the other German guards in Milag Nord were charged with any criminal offence. The sole exception was the security officer – an *Oberleutnant* in the Gestapo called Schoop. He had shed his SS uniform, grown a beard, and was carrying a case filled with money and jewellery when he was apprehended by Allied troops, quickly tried by a military court and executed.

There was a small, but steady input of Irish seamen to the rich and unique mix of ethnicities held in the Milag camp. One of those to arrive at the start of 1942 was a radio officer from Ballina, County Mayo, called Gerald O'Hara. Gerald was the son of a shoe maker, and the youngest of eleven children. According to his son, Eamon, the family were 'of a strong republican tradition' – though 'totally opposed to violence in any shape or form.' Gerald attended primary and secondary schools in Ballina – and then headed for Atlantic College in Dublin, where he took a course in wireless telegraphy. He went on to work on many transport and passenger ships – and spent the next twenty years travelling the world. In 1932, he married a local Ballina girl, and, when war broke out in 1939, they had two sons. In 1940, Gerald was part of a merchant convoy that was attacked by German submarines in the Mediterranean, but his ship managed to survive intact. Soon after that, he joined the crew of the SS *Devon*.

On 19th of August, 1941, the German raider *Komet* spotted a slow moving coal-burning vessel, close to the

Galapagos Islands: it was the 9,000 ton *Devon*. Shots were fired across her bows; the *Devon* quickly surrendered, and all of her crew were taken on board the *Komet*. The *Devon's* cargo of miscellaneous goods was deemed to be not worth saving, and the ship was soon dispatched with gunfire. This was the ninth and last ship that the *Komet* sank on her maiden voyage. The following month, she rendezvoused with her sister *Hilfskreuzer*, the *Atlantis*, and a supply ship, east of New Zealand. The *Komet* was given enough fuel to reach Europe, and arrived in Hamburg with her prisoners on 30th of November, 1941.

At that point, Gerald O'Hara's family, back in Ballina, had not heard from him for many months, and his wife was growing desperate. She had contacted the International Red Cross, the Papal Nuncio in Dublin and the German Embassy, seeking news of her husband. According to their son, she also tried to make contact with Irish politicians to see if they could assist her, but found them 'very unhelpful', and was 'disappointed and hurt by their lack of response.' Eventually, postcards from her husband began to arrive from Milag Nord – which re-assured his family. In one postcard, written on 19th of June, 1942, Gerald informed his family that 'we have plenty of shows, games, etc., so [as to] make the most of camp life.'

Unlike the Allies, each branch of the German armed forces ran their own POW camps. Both Marlag and Milag Nord were under the control of the Kreigsmarine. In general, this tended to work to the advantage of the prisoners – and this may have been particularly true in the case of naval camps. According to Lieutenant David James, there was 'a strong link between men of the sea.' He believed that even if 'they have to fight in the course of war', they still shared a common enemy: 'the elements'. This view was also held by Jack Matthews: 'we were treated', he claimed, 'as one seaman would treat another seaman.' Such consideration may have been of special significance to those veterans who had spent many years at sea. My cousin William was one of those, and so was another Irish sailor – Thomas Murphy from Dublin.

By 1941, Murphy had served for more than 30 years in the merchant marine. Most of that time had been spent on routes in the southern hemisphere, but he was captured by the Germans on the other side of the world. Soon after Hitler launched Operation *Barbarossa*, Churchill had offered aid and munitions to the Soviet Union – as it reeled under the devastating impact of the German invasion. Churchill's naval advisors had recommended him not to send supplies to Russia by the Arctic route – since they believed that their surface forces would be open to a high risk of attack from Luftwaffe units based in Occupied Norway. However, Churchill proved implacable, and the first merchant convoy left for the port of Archangel in August, 1941. The first sixteen convoys were completed with few incidents, and it seemed that Churchill's resolution had been thoroughly vindicated.

On 27th of June, 1942, the seventeenth Atlantic convoy left Hvalfjörður in Iceland. PQ17 consisted of 35 merchant ships. One of these was the SS *Earlston* – and Able Bodied

Seaman Thomas Murphy was in its crew. The convoy was first sighted five days later by a Focke-Wulf reconnaissance plane. The next day, the convoy was attacked by German torpedoes and bombers but managed to escape unscathed. Sustained attacks were resumed on the following day, but still the convoy managed to avoid serious damage. Then, on the 5th of July, new orders came from the British Admiralty that the merchant ships were to scatter. The orders were inexplicable – since it meant the convoy lost the protection of the destroyers escorting it, and the merchant freighters became easy prey for German U-boats and aircraft. Twelve Allied ships were sunk on that first day – and a further 12 were lost in the next 48 hours.

Thomas Murphy's ship was hit by bombs from a German plane on the morning of 5th of July. Later that day, his ship was torpedoed by the German submarine U-334 – and, again, attacked by German aircraft. One bomb fell into a hold of the *Earlston* that contained ammunition, and a huge explosion ripped the ship apart. 30 of her crew were killed instantly, but Murphy was one of those taken alive by the U-boat from the freezing water, and brought to Germany. He was more lucky to be rescued than he may have imagined. Earlier that year, *Grossadmiral* Karl Dönitz had issued an instruction to all U-boats; in future, they were informed, 'all attempts to rescue crews of ships sunk, even picking up swimmers and taking them aboard lifeboats, the righting of capsized lifeboats, and the issuing of food and water must cease.' So far as Donitz was concerned, all such aid went 'against the most basic requirement of warfare', which was 'to destroy enemy ships and their crews.' He advised all U-boat Commanders that seamen were only to be picked up 'if they have information important for U-boats'.

Thomas Murphy was not only lucky to have survived, he was also relatively fortunate to be sent to a camp where the conditions were not unduly harsh. Sadly, that was not to last. In early 1943, with the tide of war starting to run against him, Hitler adopted a more aggressive policy towards the use of foreign workers and POWs for forced labour. By this stage, there were simply not enough workers left in Germany to maintain its war economy. From then on, all political prisoners and POWs from Germany's Eastern front, including Russians, Poles, Jews and Slavs, were sent to construction and armaments work camps, where in the words of the Irish cadet officer, Christopher Ryan, many of them were 'worked to death for the Nazi war machine.' Thomas Murphy and Gerald O'Hara and thirty other Irish seamen would also become victims of this change in Hitler's policy.

6

THE *ABWEHR'S* IRISH FRIENDS

Not all of the Irish men and women that were to be found behind German lines during World War Two were there as prisoners. Some had deliberately chosen to spend the war in Nazi Germany. One of these was the Irish novelist, Francis Stuart. In 1940, he had decided to take up employment as a lecturer in English Literature at Berlin University: a rather unusual appointment within the context of German academia, since Stuart had no previous teaching experience – or any formal qualifications, for that matter. This was, of course, a post from which all Jews had been excluded since 1938, by the Nuremburg racial laws. That provision would, no doubt, have given Stuart something of an advantage in any open competition, but, in this instance, it was unnecessary. Stuart's academic appointment had been discreetly arranged by several influential members of the Nazi Party – including Helmut

Clissmann, of the *Deutscher Akademischer Austauschdienst*, with whom Stuart had become friendly in Dublin.

Stuart arrived in Germany in 1940 as an emissary of the IRA, and delivered a message to German Military Intelligence from James O'Donovan, a senior IRA figure who combined that role with his day job in Ireland's State-run Electricity Supply Board. O'Donovan had visited Germany three times in the previous year – attempting to forge stronger links between the IRA and the *Abwehr*. After his last visit, he wrote that he had come away convinced that, if Germany won the impending war, then Ireland, 'at last would become a place worth living in and living for'. Stuart's mission the following year was to build upon O'Donovan's contacts.

Although he had left the IRA some years previously, Stuart had remained close to some of its members. As his subsequent radio broadcasts make clear, he had also remained sympathetic to its political objectives, and when Stuart made the decision to travel to Germany, the IRA was openly in favour of a Nazi victory in the war.

For the previous two years, the IRA's Chief of Staff had been Seán Russell. Under his leadership, the organisation had turned its back on the anti-fascist position that it had adopted in the late 1920s and early 1930s. For Russell, the left-wing rhetoric of that time had only been a tiresome distraction from what really mattered: armed struggle with Britain. In the years immediately preceding the World War, Russell had helped James O'Donovan draw up the so-called 'S' Plan': the code name for a bombing campaign that the

IRA hoped to launch in a number of British cities. Their objective was to paralyse British transport systems, and power supplies. On 12th of January, 1939, a formal ultimatum had been delivered to the British Foreign Secretary, Lord Halifax, demanding the complete withdrawal of British armed forces and civilian representatives from every part of Ireland. Three days later, the IRA issued a formal declaration of war, and, over the next few months, there were several dozen explosions in London, Manchester, Birmingham, and Liverpool. Then, in August, 1939 – a few days before the outbreak of war – an IRA bomb, concealed in the basket of a bicycle, exploded without warning in Coventry. Its victims were an 82 year old man, a schoolboy, two shop assistants, and a road sweeper. As David O'Donoghue has observed, O'Donovan had returned from Germany just three days before the Coventry bomb exploded, and was able to follow its aftermath 'from the safety of his ESB office'.

The Irish Government, at first, believed that the IRA's 'England Campaign' was a covert operation by extreme Unionists in Northern Ireland – intended to scupper any negotiations between Dublin and London about the possible ending of Ireland's partition. According to Tom Barry – a former IRA Chief of Staff – the squalid campaign had actually been financed by the Nazis and the money had been channelled by Joseph McGarrity, head of Clann na nGael and the IRA's chief fund-raiser in the USA.

In fact, the IRA had been seeking a closer connection with Nazi Germany since 1937. The relationship between the IRA and the Nazi regime was clearly meant to be of mutual advantage: in July of 1940, the IRA leadership issued a statement assuring the Irish people that if 'German forces should land in Ireland, they will land as friends and liberators.' The Irish public was also informed by the IRA that Nazi Germany desired neither 'territory nor economic penetration' of Ireland. Even when German bombs fell on Dun Laoghaire in 1941, the *War News*, the IRA's main propaganda sheet of that time, claimed it was clearly a British plot, and concrete evidence of black propaganda. For the IRA, the fact that the bombs were found to be German merely proved it was the British who had dropped them: 'in order to make the Irish people think that the Germans are their enemies'.

In 1940, the *War News* expressed satisfaction that the 'cleansing fire' of the Wehrmacht was driving the Jews out of Europe, and condemned the arrival in Ireland of any 'so-called Jewish refugees.' According to the *War News*, the Northern regime was already in the hands of 'international Jewry', while de Valera's Government in Dublin was dominated by 'Jews and Freemasons'. The *War News* advised its readers that Jews were 'like the English': 'when they are strong they bully and rule.' As an historian of the IRA, Brian Hanley, has pointed out, a variety of ethnic and nationalist groups across Europe collaborated with the Nazis in order to further their own agendas – even if that led to their subsequent involvement in the persecution of Jews, and the imprisonment of their political opponents. It appears that the IRA was only too eager to play a similar role in Ireland.

Seán Russell had travelled to the USA in April 1939, to establish himself in the eyes of Irish-America as the undisputed leader of militant Republicanism. Franz Fromme, an *Abwehr* agent, arranged for him to travel to Genoa the following month. From there, he went with Fromme to Berlin. While in that city, Russell enjoyed 'all the privileges of a diplomat', spending the summer in a large villa outside Berlin, with a car, chauffeur and translator at his disposal. Soon after his arrival, Russell was given access to the high-security Brandenburg military camp, where he was trained by the *Abwehr* in the use of explosive ordnance. On 4th August, 1940, Russell attended a high-level meeting in Berlin with von Ribbentrop, the German Foregin Minister; Admiral Wilhelm Canaris, the Head of the *Abwehr*; Erwin von Lahousen, his deputy; and Dr. Edmund Veesenmayer, Ribbentrop's advisor on Irish Affairs. Three days later, Canaris sanctioned the transport of Russell and Frank Ryan – the IRA leader that Ireland's Minister in Spain had helped set free – to Ireland on a German U-boat for the purpose of sabotage. Russell became ill during the voyage, and died en route to Galway. He was buried at sea and the plan which was code-named *Unternehmen Taube* – 'Operation Dove' - was aborted, and Ryan returned to Germany.

At the infamous Wannsee Conference of 29th of January, 1942, fifteen leading figures from a range of Nazi and State organisations met in a villa just outside Berlin to discuss the 'preparations for the final solution of the Jewish question in Europe'. The conference was chaired by Reinhard Heydrich, the *Reichprotektor* of Bohemia-Moravia, and those present included Gestapo members, senior civil servants, and the SS *Obersturmbannführer*, Adolf Eichmann – who was Heydrich's advisor on Jewish affairs, and who kept the minutes of the meeting. Eichmann recorded that Heydrich reported that there were 4,000 Jews currently residing in Ireland. Heydrich also made it clear just what was planned for them – and for all the rest of Europe's Jews. 'In the course of the practical execution of the final solution', he stated, 'Europe will be combed from West to East.' All able-bodied Jews would then be allocated for 'appropriate labour'. It was reasonable to suppose, Heydrich added, that a large portion of those would be 'eliminated by natural causes'. The 'final remnant', he suggested, could not be permitted to 'act as the seed of a new Jewish revival', and should be 'treated accordingly'.

The same year as the conference at Wannsee, the IRA leader, James O'Donovan, wrote an substantial manuscript that he titled 'Germany and Small Racial Groups'. O'Donovan had been interned the previous year by de Valera's Government in Dublin for IRA activities, but remained optimistic about the political future of Ireland – based on his 'hypothesis of [England's] defeat' in the war. In his confidential document, he identified both England and the USA as 'centres of Freemasonry, international financial control and Jewry', and called for closer ties between Ireland and Nazi Germany – which he predicted would win the war, and emerge as the dominant power in Europe. There seems no reason to doubt the fate of several thousand Irish Jews if his wishes had come true and Nazi Germany had launched a successful invasion of Ireland. But in 1941 and 1942, the Nazis hoped that they would be helped in their genocidal undertaking not only by IRA activists like O'Donovan, but also by some of the Irish prisoners whom they held in POW camps.

The majority of such prisoners had been serving in the Allied armed forces. The British Expeditionary Force, that had been forced to evacuate at Dunkirk, had contained a sizeable number of Irish soldiers, and many others had been captured since then. The *Abwehr* hoped that these men could form the nucleus of an 'Irish Brigade', which could be deployed on the side of Nazi Germany. As the war progressed, the recruitment of non-German troops – including Muslims, Slavs and Indians - became a particular priority of the SS: ironically so, given that organisation's self-proclaimed mission to preserve Aryan racial purity. However, their attempts to entice Allied POWs to join their ranks produced mixed results. There was some success in establishing a 'Free India Legion' – even though Hitler remained dubious about its value – but similar attempts to set up a British 'Free Corps' proved a dismal failure.

In July of 1940, Francis Stuart visited Irish prisoners in POW camps in Germany. Later in that year, he toured those camps again to interview Irish prisoners who might be interested becoming attached to the Waffen SS. The Irish POWs were promised that their 'brigade' would only be committed to 'a national war for the liberation of Ireland'. Stuart was not the first Irishman to embark on such a project:

during the First World War, Roger Casement had tried – with very limited success – to raise a similar unit. Stuart was well aware of his predecessor's history: like Casement, Stuart's family roots were in County Antrim; like Casement, he had grown up in a Protestant and Unionist environment; and like Casement, he brought something of the zeal of the convert to his embrace of Irish Nationalism.

Earlier that year, Stuart had sought permission to translate W.J. Maloney's book, *The Forged Casement Diaries*, into German. As the title indicates, Maloney had sought to prove that the so-called 'Black Diaries' of Roger Casement – which revealed his active homosexuality – had been forged by British Intelligence officers in order to discredit him. Maloney's book certainly presented an overwhelming case for Casement's 'innocence' – but only because its author rigorously suppressed any evidence to the contrary. For reasons that are not clear, Maloney refused permission for the translation, so Stuart wrote his own account of Casement's life – *Der Fall Casement* – which also argued that the diaries were fake. The book ends with extravagant praise for the 'New Germany' that Hitler had created – although Stuart claimed, after the war, that he not written those passages.

It may have seemed fitting that Stuart was accompanied on his mission to the POW camps by Franz Fromme. After the war, Fromme would describe himself as a 'modest interpreter and translator'. There seems little doubt, however that, in 1940, he was both an *Abwehr* agent and an ardent Nazi. He was also someone who had met Casement during the First World War, and had even translated some of his essays into German. Fromme and Stuart had first become acquainted in Dublin in 1939, and Fromme had vouched for Stuart when he presented himself to the *Abwehr* in Berlin in January, 1940. Fromme had also acted as Seán Russell's interpreter in his negotiations with the Germans.

In April of 1940, Fromme had introduced Stuart to the *Abwehr* agent Hermann Görtz – who, it was intended, would co-ordinate German espionage in Ireland - shortly before Görtz parachuted into County Meath. Stuart had given Görtz his wife's address in County Wicklow as a safe house from where he could commence his espionage work and Görtz had stayed there soon after he had arrived in Ireland. Stuart does not seem to have enjoyed his visits to the POW camps. While there, he had apparently seen prisoners being beaten viciously by guards, and the reception that he received from the Irish prisoners that he met was far from sympathetic. It would appear that Stuart was disturbed by the whole experience: at any rate, he pleaded his commitments in the English faculty of Berlin University to avoid any further visits.

Eventually, some prisoners were selected by *Abwehr* II as possible recruits for the Irish 'Brigade', and more than 100 of them were sent to a secret training camp; Stalag XX A (301) – which was also known as Camp Friesack. Soon afterwards, an *Abwehr* agent, Joseph 'Jupp' Hoven, went to Rome to request that a Catholic priest be sent to the camp to minister to the spiritual needs of the Irish prisoners. Hoven had first visited Ireland in 1937, to conduct anthropological research, and had become friendly with Helmut Clissmann and with the veteran IRA leader Tom Barry. At that time, Barry was Chief of Staff of the IRA, and he met frequently with Hoven with the intention of fostering links between that organisation and Nazi Germany. Barry had travelled to Germany in 1937, in the company of Hoven, to develop the relationship. In 1942, Hoven was convinced that the only reason Irishmen were serving in the British forces was because they had been 'economically forced' to do so.

Following Hoven's trip to Rome, an Irish priest, Fr. Thomas O'Shaughnessy, travelled to the Friesack camp. Soon after his visit, the priest returned to Ireland, and gave an account of what he had observed to Irish Military Intelligence. According to Fr. O'Shaughnessy, the Germans appeared willing to make 'all sorts of concessions' to any Irish prisoners who were prepared to join them. Fr. O'Shaughnessy reported that a few Irish prisoners had 'pretended to fall in wholeheartedly with [the Germans'] designs', but he believed that this was done simply in order to receive better treatment. The priest was convinced that none of the Irish prisoners had 'any serious intention' of fighting alongside the Wehrmacht or the Waffen-SS: they simply wanted to be sent home to Ireland. While he was there, O'Shaughnessy also reported that Helmut Clissmann had visited the camp – hoping to convince the Irish prisoners to become part of the German war effort.

Some of those who had arrived at Friesack had expressed overt hostility to Stuart's recruiting efforts but had been sent there by mistake. In fact, several of the Irish officers in the camp were actually working for MI9 – the section of British Military Intelligence that communicated with Allied POWs – and had been instructed by MI9 to volunteer. Most of the prisoners in Friesack came from the British Army, but a small number of merchant seamen from Milag Nord were also included. Jack Matthews could recall that one of the crew on the *Silver Fir* was sent to Friesack. This was Owen Corr, from Rush, in County Dublin. Matthews remembered that Corr was 'whipped away' from Milag Nord, along with some other Irish seamen to another camp. 'They were away for a couple of months', he recalled, 'and when they came back, they said that they had been pressured to join the German forces, or to go back to Ireland to spy for them. But, to a man, they refused.'

To encourage the Irish prisoners to accept their offer, the Germans offered them what Fr. O'Shaughnessy had rightly identified as an extraordinary degree of freedom. Some of the prisoners in the Freisack camp were allowed to move into flats outside the camp, and even to strike up romantic relationships with German women. Corr was one of those allowed a taste of liberty, and, when news of this was fed back to Dublin, it appears that it led Irish Military Intelligence to identify him as a possible Nazi sympathizer. In fact, it was not long before Corr had asked to be returned to the camp at Milag Nord. He told Jack Matthews that the Irish prisoners in Freisack had been treated well, 'in the beginning', but, when they proved uncooperative with the Germans, they were put on short rations. Life soon became intolerable for them and nine of them managed to escape from the camp, via a tunnel they had dug.

There was a suspicion that this break-out had been faked as a form of protection for the few Irishmen that were prepared to work for the Nazis. In any event, the Friesack camp was subsequently broken up as a 'hopeless effort'. It would seem that only two Irishmen – out of all the Irish POWs held in Germany – were eventually prepared to join the Waffen-SS, and Corr was not one of them. According to Matthews, he was ill when he was brought back to Milag Nord: 'He was very thin, with sores on his head, and it took some time before it all cleared up.' Corr may have felt some relief to be back in the confines of Milag Nord, but, if he did, his relief was not to last for long.

Even though the war had begun to turn against Germany, there was still a stubborn belief that the Irish merchant seamen could be persuaded to work for the Third Reich. Throughout their captivity in Sandbostel and Milag Nord, the Irish prisoners had consistently refused to sign a contractual agreement to become *freie arbeiter* – voluntary workers – for Nazi Germany. This refusal had become a matter of principle both for the men involved – and for the Gestapo. The latter had not given up on this objective, and further attempts were made to secure the Irishmen's agreement to sign work contracts. In January of 1943, thirty-one of them were moved out of the Milag camp. It is not known on quite what basis these men were chosen: there were, at least, eight other Irish-born seamen who were left behind in Milag Nord – and some of the thirty-two who were sent to Bremen had not lived in Ireland for many years. Almost all of those who were taken from Milag

Nord had been born in southern Ireland – including my cousin, William. The sole exception was Harry Callan, who had been born in Northern Ireland. Harry believed that he might have been included with the others because the Germans knew that he came from an Irish Nationalist family background. According to Harry, the Irish seamen were led to believe that they were about to be repatriated. That was a cruel deception; instead, they were brought by Gestapo officers on a train to the Labour Office in Bremen – where, once again, they were induced to sign a contract to work as *freie Arbeiter* for the Germans.

The Irishmen spent a week there: 'They tried to get us to work in the Messerschmitt factory', Harry remembered, 'but we wouldn't do it.' The Gestapo had decided to offer the Irish seamen a tantalising amount of personal freedom: 'While we were in Bremen', Harry recalled, 'they gave us the free run of the city. Maybe they thought it would soften us up. We spent most of the day about the town – just walking around, and looking at the shops.' At night, they slept in beds that belonged to French workers in the Messerschmitt factory: 'they were working on the night shift, so the beds were empty.' Once it became clear that the Irish seamen were not going to agree to work in the aircraft plant, they were moved again – this time to Hamburg: 'They tried to get us to agree to work on merchant ships', Harry remembered. There was fresh bait to tempt them from the Gestapo: 'They said that we would only be used on neutral ships. It was as much as to say to us, 'If you agree to go on a Swedish ship, then you can always get off when it docks in Sweden, and make your own way home'.' The Irish prisoners were sceptical of the offer: 'We weren't having any of it', Harry recalled, 'We just didn't believe them.'

Christopher Ryan had been in the Milag hospital when the Irish seamen were taken to Bremen, but he was later given the same ultimatum: work freely for the Germans or be sent to a labour camp. Ryan refused 'point-blank' to cooperate. As a result, he was locked up in a Gestapo prison – where he spent the next six weeks. 'Conditions were bad', he later recalled, 'I was kept in a cell the whole time and kicked about'.

Until this point, the Gestapo had tried to tempt the Irish seamen to work voluntarily for the Nazi regime. From here on, the Germans seem to have accepted that those tactics were not going to succeed and they were abandoned for good. On 6th of February, 1943, thirty-one Irish prisoners were taken to another camp – where they would soon be joined by Christopher Ryan. It was situated close to the village of Farge, near Bremen, and it would make all their previous hardships and suffering seem mild in comparison. Their imprisonment at Milag Nord had been under the control of the Kriegsmarine, and living conditions there had been, for the most part, bearable. Now, the Irish seamen were being taken to a very different type of camp, and their future would no longer be controlled by the Kriegsmarine – but by the *Schutzstaffel*: the SS.

7

THE SS AND CO.

The SS is sometimes considered solely as a military force, but, from an early stage in its history, it had also become involved in a wide range of commercial enterprises. In the autumn of 1934, Heinrich Himmler – the SS *Reichsführer* – had launched the first SS 'corporate venture', when he founded a publishing house. At first, such ventures had an explicitly cultural dimension. The SS soon established a photographic agency, and also had invested in the manufacture of fine porcelain. These enterprises were not set up on a strictly commercial basis – or were even intended to be profitable. Indeed, the lack of any financial motive was initially viewed by the SS as a cause for racial pride – since it was imagined that this lack of concern for profits provided evidence of the National Socialists' high-minded goals, and contrasted with the sordid avarice that they attributed to Jewish bankers and financiers.

However, as the losses on their various enterprises mounted, it did not take the SS long to seek to compromise with the marketplace, and a concerted attempt was begun to make their ventures economically productive. By 1938, there seemed to be one area where they could fulfil their new financial goals without undermining their ideological integrity – by supplying both the raw materials and the workers that were needed for the grandiose construction projects of Hitler and his favourite architect, Albert Speer. Since both workers and building material were in relatively short supply, the obvious solution for Himmler was to force concentration camp prisoners to quarry stone and produce bricks, cement and other essential components. In April of 1938, the SS established *Deutsche Erd und Steinwerke* – the German Earth and Stone Works - for that very purpose. As *Generalbauinspektor für die Reichshauptstadt* - General Construction Inspector for the Reich Capital - Albert Speer was able to make a large amount of funding immediately available to the new company.

In 1934, Hitler had given the SS control of Germany's concentration camps, and it was to prove one of Himmler's most crucial power bases. However, *Konzentrationslager* were by no means the only camps to be established in the Third Reich. In fact, there was an astonishing number and variety of them in Hitler's Germany – and to begin with, the vast majority of these were not intended for punitive reasons. There were, for example, Party camps run by the National Socialists for the *Deutsche Arbeitsfront* – the Nazi Trade Union; for Nazi Youth organisations – such as the *Hitler*

Jugend and the *Bund Deutscher Mädel*; and for members of
the Nazis' various military and paramilitary formations –
such as the *Sturmabteilung* and the SS. Apart from these,
there were many other camps organised by state and state-
sponsored agencies. As Caplan and Wachsmann have
observed, most of these camps were designed to 'foster the
positive ideals of the Nazi state', and they proved extremely
popular with many ordinary Germans. The Nazis also
created, in tandem with these educational and recreational
camps, their pernicious equivalents – penal colonies where
real or imagined enemies of the Reich were held captive
often in atrocious conditions. Eventually, there would also
be a very large number and range of these camps – from
extermination centres to labour colonies - but they would
all share a common underlying objective: to terrorise their
inmates and intimidate the wider population.

In the summer of 1935 – after a year of SS control –
there were still only five concentration camps operating in
the whole of Germany. Together, these held approximately
4,000 prisoners. In September of the following year, the SS
opened the first of its new 'model' camps at Sachsenhausen,
and in time this would become the specialist training centre
for SS camp personnel. As the number of populations
subject to German control increased rapidly during the
early years of the war, so did the number of concentration
camps – and the volume of prisoners that they held. By
the end of 1940, the amount of prisoners held in such
camps had risen to more than 50,000, and the numbers
continued to rise dramatically throughout the remainder

of the war. Before long, the large camps were supported by an expanding network of smaller sub-camps. These were usually administered by the main or "mother" camps, which also supplied their guards, the *Totenkopfverbände* – or Death's Head Units – the professional corps of SS jailers. By 1943, the majority of prisoners were not held in large camps, but in their smaller satellites. In 1942, the SS had set up 186 of these sub-camps: by January 1945, there were almost 700, and more than 80% of all concentration camp inmates were imprisoned in them.

Forced labour by prisoners had initially been used by the Nazis as a penal and educative instrument, and competition with private German companies was restrained because of the depressed state of the external economy. The SS had subjected prisoners to hard labour as a form of punishment. This often involved pointless work – such as digging ditches, and then filling them back in, time after time. At first, this labour was simply designed to add to the burden and misery of the prisoners' lives. As the years passed, however, the SS realised that better use could be made of their captives. From 1938, however, the growing demand for workers resulted in an increasing use of camp labour, and this allowed the enterprises run by the SS to take full advantage of the regime's new construction projects. About half of the satellite camps set up after 1942 were established at existing armaments companies. The other half were organised around construction projects: mainly, at underground production facilities. Himmler had stated, in May 1942, that "it needs to be emphasised (that) the aim of re-educating the re-educable [remains] unchanged. Otherwise, the notion might arise that we are arresting people, or keeping those already arrested in custody, in order to have workers.' That claim was already unsustainable in 1942, but, as Jens-Christian Wagner has noted, there was one constant factor in the operation of all the Nazi camps: 'terror remained a constitutive element of prisoner work until the end.'

The camp at Farge, where the Irish merchant seamen would be taken in February of 1943, was one of the satellites attached to the large concentration camp at Neuengamme, near Hamburg. The main camp had been established by the SS in 1938. A brickworks had been opened, and the SS had signed a commercial contract with the city of Hamburg to supply material for its construction projects. By the end of that year, there were around 100 prisoners in Neuengamme, all of whom had been transferred from the camp at Sachsenhausen. In January of 1940, the Neuengamme camp was visited by Himmler, who decided on its radical expansion. After brief negotiations, the extension of Neuengamme into a fully-fledged concentration camp was put into effect, and a new contract was drawn up between the *Deutsche Erd und Steinwerke* and Hamburg's civic authorities. The city agreed to finance the extension of the brickworks with the provision of credit, and received, in return, the rights to the bulk of its annual production. Beside the delivery of bricks, the free use of prisoners for work on dykes and canals was also part of the deal. Within a few months, there were more than 1,000 additional prisoners employed in the camp, and workers had begun to be rented out to external factories that were sometimes owned and controlled by the SS, and sometimes by private companies.

The SS clearly benefited from this arrangement – but that was certainly not the case as far the prisoners were concerned. By the end of 1940, there were around 3,000 prisoners working at Neuengamme – and more than 400 inmates had already died. The following year, several thousand Jewish prisoners arrived from Auschwitz. Many of these were still in their teens, and they had been selected because of their youth and health – which would be ruthlessly broken in the months ahead. By the end of 1941, there were around 5,000 prisoners in Neuengamme, and more than 1,000 had died. A major expansion of the entire camp system took place following the German invasion of the USSR in June 1941. Whole armies of prisoners arrived in Germany: as Wachsmann has pointed out, these could be numbered 'not in tens but hundreds of thousands'. However, the plan to maximise the exploitation of Soviet POWs as slave workers was undermined by the lethal consequences of the Nazis' own political ideology. Instead of creating gigantic labour bases, the work camps became graveyards for Soviet prisoners – and Neuengamme was no exception to that general rule. The first 1,000 Soviet prisoners arrived there in April, 1942. By the end of June, 700 of them were already dead.

By 1942, Himmler had decided to extend the Nazis' euthanasia and medical experiment programmes to many of his concentration camps. Working together, SS officials and roaming teams of doctors selected prisoners whom they thought were no longer able to work. In June, 1942, 220 sick prisoners were moved from Neuengamme to a facility at Bernburg, where they were gassed on arrival. Experiments on prisoners also began at this time: on 27th of September, 1942, 197 Soviet prisoners in the main camp were gassed by the new compound Zyklon B, and another 251 prisoners were killed in the same way a few months later. Such criminal activities continued throughout the remaining years of the war – up to and including its final weeks. However, even before Goebbels proclaimed 'Total War' in his *Sportpalast* speech, more pragmatic economic considerations had begun to gain traction – although the underlying ideological aims, and their murderous consequences, were not abandoned and did not disappear.

From 1943, the official commitment to force POWs into Germany's war industries began to make a serious impact, and soon a dense network of satellite camps – attached to existing ones – stretched across Germany. These new camps were set up in old schools, restaurants, disused military barracks, or factory buildings, and – unlike previous concentration camps – they were no longer situated on the outskirts of towns. There were so many new camps that they could not all be operated by the SS on its own: Instead, the camps were often run as joint enterprises by the SS and representatives of local towns or companies. In this context, the number of individuals involved with the camps also expanded exponentially: construction firms could provide land and buildings; SS guards could be supplemented by local assistants; civilian administrators could organise the deployment of the prisoners; civilian foremen could supervise the work brigades; local businesses could supply the camps with a range of services; local doctors were often called to attend to the prisoners – and to select those who were no longer capable of work, and could be safely murdered.

Neuengamme would eventually become the hub of 87 sub-camps, and one of the first of these was the so-called *Arbeitserziehungslager* – 'Education through Work' camp - at Farge, a small village in north-west Germany. There were around 200 *Arbeitsziebungslager* in Germany, and their ostensible purpose was to punish those voluntary workers who were deemed to have infringed the terms of their contracts with the SS. The punishment consisted of subjecting them to an exceptionally harsh work regime in order to 'educate' them in the value and purpose of labour. In theory, the prisoners who were sent to any *Arbeitserziehunslager* were only supposed to remain there for a maximum of three months. In reality, they were often kept there for a good deal longer – if they were able to survive – but none were kept in the Farge sub-camp for as long as a group of Irish merchant seamen.

The Irish seamen who were sent to the Farge camp came from all over Ireland. They came from Dublin and Cork, Blackwater and Ballina, Waterford and Wicklow, Tralee and Clifden, Kinsale and Rush, Ringsend and Tramore, Galway and Carlingford, Bray and Dun Laoghaire, Clogher

Head, Rosses Point and Passage West. By the time they were sent to Farge, most of these seamen had been held captive in German camps for several years, and their health had suffered as a consequence. Bad as their previous living conditions may have been, they were about to get a great deal worse.

The ethos of the slave labour camps was concisely expressed by Albert Speer's colleague, Fritz Sauckel, the *Generalbevollmächtiger für den Arbeitseinsatz* – the General Plenipotentiary for Labour Deployment – who stated in emphatic terms that the Nazis' goal was to exploit their workers, 'to the highest possible extent at the lowest conceivable degree of expenditure'. The Irish seamen would soon be joined at the Valentin bunker by thousands of Soviet, Jewish and Polish prisoners. According to Christopher Ryan, British and American POWs were not included in Germany's slave labour policy, 'because Hitler feared perpetrating such obvious war crimes against them.' The *Kommandant* of the main camp at Neuengamme had overall control of the sub-camps: between 1942 and 1945, that position was held by the SS *Obersturmbannführer* Max Pauly. As the prison complex at Neuengamme grew rapidly, so did the death rate among its prisoners: by the start of 1943, there were almost 10,000 prisoners in Neuengamme and its satellite camps. In that year alone, almost 4,000 of those inmates would die there.

Harry Callan had just turned nineteen when he arrived in Bremen Farge. The Irish seamen were still in Hamburg when they had been woken up unexpectedly in the middle of the night by SS guards. 'They rounded us on to two lorries', Harry recalled, 'and we headed off.' None of the Irish prisoners had any idea where they were going, but they could sense that their situation had changed. 'They had been offering us inducements to work for them', Harry told me, 'but now they knew we weren't interested in taking them.' The merchant seamen arrived at their new camp early in the morning, and were brought to a spartan, make-shift dormitory. According to Harry Callan, there was 'a cement floor, an old mattress, and one blanket', for each prisoner. The Irish prisoners were told to sleep on the floor, and left alone. But their sleep was soon interrupted. 'About an hour later', Harry told me, 'we were bedded down when the door flew open, and a group of SS guards rushed in. That's when the rubber hoses came out, and the beating started.' This was the first lesson that the Irish seamen were to be given in what Harry Callan later described as 'the meaning of terror'. From then on, he recalled, 'we didn't know what the next day would bring. There was just the hope that at least one of us would survive.'

According to Harry's former shipmate, William English, the seamen were informed by the SS that they should no longer consider themselves under the protection of the Geneva Convention. They were also told that they would receive no further parcels from the International Red Cross. The loss of Red Cross parcels represented a serious degree of deprivation – even by the standards of a Nazi POW camp. Such parcels often meant the difference between life and death for prisoners. Although the contents of the parcels varied, they were intended to contain enough basic provisions – such as jam, condensed milk, and corned beef - to maintain each prisoner for one week. The parcels also formed a tangible link with the outside world. Instead, the Irish seamen were told, they would have no contact with that world. Instead, they would live entirely at the mercy of the SS. The vicious beatings administered on that first night in Farge lasted for over an hour – as if to drive home to the prisoners the helplessness of their situation. Their heads were shaved, they were deloused and all their personal possessions were removed. 'Then, we were taken outside', Harry remembered, 'and given a bowl of soup'.

It was not yet four in the morning, but the day was about to start for the Irish prisoners. After the soup, they were lined up by their guards, and marched out into the darkness, as slaves. Red Cross visitors were not allowed to see them for almost two years: when they were finally permitted into the camp, they reported that the Irish seamen lived in a state of 'constant fear', under the supervision of SS Guards who were prepared to 'shoot them under the least provocation'.

The Irish prisoners did not know it when they arrived at Farge, but they had been brought there to work on what was viewed as the most important project of the Kreigsmarine. 'Project Valentin' was the codename for an immense fortified bunker, where *Reichsminister* Albert Speer planned to construct submarines on an assembly line in pre-fabricated sections. Speer's ambition was to build a new U-boat every 56 hours, and, in order to achieve that goal, the Germans were prepared to work their labour force to the point of death. In a sense, Valentin also proved to be the last throw of the dice for the Kreigsmarine. In July and August of 1943, the Allies would launch 'Operation Gomorrah' - a series of devastating air raids which had catastrophic consequences for the shipyards of northern Germany. It became quite clear that there was only the chance of a few more *Endkampfs* – or final struggles – and that is why the completion of the Valentin bunker became such an imperative for both the Kriegsmarine, and the Nazi leadership.

In order to meet their goal, thirty-two Irish merchant seamen were kept for the next two years in conditions that were aptly described by Christopher Ryan as 'sheer hell'. Farge became a camp where, as Ryan also observed, 'death was permanently in the air'. Winter was the worst time, he believed: 'It was always freezing, and people were dying all around us from disease, starvation and exhaustion. Some were shot dead on the spot, others were beaten to death.' The detention of the Irish seamen was illegal because, as civilians, they should have been repatriated under the Geneva Convention. The Nazis gave them POW numbers, but their civilian status was never formally contested by their captors. This recognition of their status became critically important when the war was over - because the compensation fund set up by the German Government was not open to POWs. In any case, even if they were regarded as full prisoners of war, the detention of the Irish seamen in Farge would still have violated the terms of the Geneva

Convention – which stipulated that POWs should not be compelled to work on military projects for their country's enemies.

There seems very little doubt that the Irish Government was aware that some of Ireland's citizens had been forcibly removed by the Gestapo from the camp at Milag Nord, and had become part of the slave labour force at Farge as an illegal punishment for them refusing to volunteer to work for Germany. These seamen had written on several occasions to their country's representative in Berlin – and, as it happens, so had their captors. The prisoners' relatives in Ireland had advised Irish politicians of their captivity, and the International Red Cross had passed the relevant information on to the proper authorities. Despite all of this, Irish politicians and diplomats did nothing to help these Irish citizens for well over a year.

8

THE BUNKER

By the second half of the World War, the military strength of the Allies had begun to assert itself. The Luftwaffe had lost control of the skies, and there had been calamitous reversals for the Wehrmacht on the Eastern front. In North Africa, the *Afrika Korps* had been decisively defeated at El Alamein – even though William Warnock, in a dispatch to Dublin, expressed a faint hope that 'Rommel may still establish himself on [a] firm footing.' As far as the naval war was concerned, the turning point had come towards the end of 1942, when the threat to Allied shipping from German U-boats had begun to be neutralised. Improved weaponry, better air support and advances in radar technology all played a role in this development, but the crucial breakthrough took place in mid 1941.

On 8th of May, 1941, U-110 – the submarine that had sunk the merchant ship *Athenia* off the Irish coast – had been captured and boarded by the Royal Navy. In the stern of the U-boat, the British found a machine that would decisively affect the outcome of the war. The eventual decryption of this 'Enigma' machine by the code-breakers at Bletchley Park, provided the Allies with the key to understanding the movements of Germany's submarine 'wolf-packs', and enabled them greatly to reduce the damage these could inflict on Allied merchant convoys. As a result of this critical breakthrough, in May of 1943 alone the Kriegsmarine lost 43 of its 110 submarines.

The Germans responded to this crisis by developing a new type of submarine – the XXI – which was larger, faster and which could dive deeper than its predecessors. This new U-boat represented a revolutionary breakthrough in submarine design – being the first that had been intended primarily to operate while it was submerged. Until then, submarines had operated as surface ships that had the capacity to submerge in order to escape detection, or to launch covert attacks. The radical innovations of the XXI - which was also known as the *Electroboot* – changed that underlying concept, and seemed to offer the prospect of Germany regaining the upper hand in the Atlantic.

But first the new U-boats had to be built, and Germany's capacity to produce them had been drastically reduced by Allied bombing – which had been able to target submarine pens with growing precision. Karl Dönitz - the *Oberbefehlshaber* of the German Navy – had advised Hitler that the first Type XXI U-boats would only be available for deployment at the end of 1944. Not surprisingly, this timeframe was unacceptable to Hitler and he immediately ordered Albert Speer to ensure that the date was brought forward. For that to happen, a radical solution was required: Speer began to plan the construction of the largest fortified site in Germany as the final assembly place for the new submarines. In many respects, this project was of a kind that was likely to appeal to Speer as an architect. From the outset, the bunker at Farge was conceived on the same monumental scale as those buildings which Speer had designed over much of the previous decade.

In January of 1934, the first anniversary of the Nazis' seizure of power, Speer had taken over the *Schonheit der Arbeit* - 'Beauty of Work' - office, which Hitler had given the task of introducing better hygienic and aesthetic conditions to the German workplace. Given Speer's later history, it seems bitterly ironic that in this capacity, he had sought to bring daylight into workshops, improve industrial safety and open up showers, rest rooms and sports facilities for Germany's work force. Speer had only joined the Nazi Party in 1931, but he had soon become such a favourite of his Führer that there was speculation that the two might even have enjoyed an erotic relationship. They certainly shared an appetite for colossal building projects that bordered on the obsessional. This was an appetite that was not only pursued by architects in totalitarian regimes, such as Nazi Germany and the Soviet Union: it was also embraced by many of the Modernists that the Nazis claimed to despise. The skyscrapers that define the city profiles of New York and Chicago are testimony that Speer was not alone in aiming at breathtaking and overwhelming effects. For Speer, there seems to have been an inner compulsion that drove him constantly to reach for the gigantic dimensions that characterise so much of his work.

It was a preoccupation that he held in common with his Führer: 'Even the pyramids', Hitler had declared in the autumn of 1938, 'will pale against the masses of concrete and stone colossi that I am erecting.' Like the Pharaohs, whose work he so admired, the monuments of Hitler's Reich would depend on the expendable lives of multitudes of slave workers. Years after the war, Speer's own brother reminded him that he had once drawn a similar parallel to Hitler. In 1938, Speer had asked Himmler to set up brickworks at Oranenburg concentration camp to supply him with material to re-build Berlin. According to Speer's brother, the *Reichsminister* had requisitioned these slave workers, 'with the [same] cold-bloodedness with which you dealt with moral problems'. He reminded Speer of the cynical and dismissive comment that he had made then: 'Even in Ancient Egypt', Speer had remarked, 'the enslaved Yids had made bricks'. In fact, as Eugen Kogon has pointed out, slaves were more highly valued in Ancient Egypt than in Nazi Germany. The former had been, at least, 'properly fed' by their masters - whereas, the Nazis 'could simply afford to draft in new slave contingents when the old ones had been used up'.

The Nazi labour policy involved the underfeeding and overworking of foreign workers, and in that process, those workers were subjected to every form of degradation and brutality. It was a policy that was built on slavery and murder: one that marked a flagrant violation – not only of the conventions of war, but also those of basic humanity. Two men - Albert Speer, and his deputy, Fritz Sauckel - were central to the formulation of this policy. Speer bears a particular responsibility for its execution. He decided on the number of foreign slaves required by the German war industry; he determined that it was necessary to recruit those workers by force; and he was prepared to accept – and at times encourage - the vicious abuse of slave labour in the manufacture of war materiel, and in the construction of German fortifications, such as the Valentin Bunker.

By the summer of 1943, the total number of foreign workers in Germany had reached close to 7 million and around 1.5 million of these were drawn from POW camps. There was a particular dependence on foreign labour in armaments factories and on construction sites. Ironically, in its final years, the Third Reich – for all its commitment to racial purity - played host to at least as many foreigners as the multi-cultural German society of today. There were other blatant contradictions in the Nazis' foreign labour policy. On one hand, the Nazis made strenuous attempts to mobilise millions of workers for employment in the Reich. At the same time, the SS and the Wehrmacht were deliberately murdering millions of people who could have worked productively for the German war economy.

By 1943, when the Irish seamen arrived at the Farge camp, the use of forced labour in Nazi Germany had already begun on a massive scale. The concentration camp system may have been born out of the vindictive desire to torture and torment the Nazis' political opponents, but, by 1943, the camps had also become the means through which the social, economic and racial policies of the Nazi State could be enforced. The growth of the work camps was clearly related to the regime's frantic hunt for new sources of labour – leading to a huge expansion of prisoners working in armaments production. When the Irish prisoners arrived at Farge, that slave labour force made up almost 20% of all workers in German industry: the vast majority of these were POWs, or internees, Jews or other civilians who were compelled to work for the German war industry under extreme duress.

In fact, the use of slave workers had been planned long before Germany went to war and was designed to continue long after it was over. Konrad Meyer, one of Himmler's favoured architects, estimated that a huge slave labour force - close to a million strong - would have to be kept in place for at least twenty-five years after the war in order to complete the work that was envisaged for Europe's 'New Order'. During the war, this policy was intended to achieve two purposes. The primary goal was to satisfy the urgent requirements of the Nazis' war machine – which, in Speer's chilling words, needed 'oiling with blood.' The secondary purpose was to eliminate those people who were deemed either to be racially inferior, or hostile to the Nazis.

The scale of the mass killings that occurred in the Nazi camps confounds the human imagination. There were almost 2 million Soviet prisoners employed in Germany after 1941: less than half of them survived the war. A further

2 million Soviet prisoners are believed to have starved to death over the winter of 1941-42. In the final years of the war, it is estimated that several million more prisoners died in these Nazi camps. When the numbers of Jewish workers who died in labour and POW camps – excluding the death camps – are also considered, it seems likely that around 7 million slave workers died in places like Farge: of ill-treatment, exhaustion, disease, starvation, or deliberate murder.

By 1943, Albert Speer had accumulated so much power that his protégé, Karl Dönitz, could fairly describe him as the, 'economic dictator of Europe'. In February 1942, Speer had been given responsibility for the production of armaments and ammunition. He had proved highly effective – so that when his brief was extended to include the production of all war materiel, he was regarded by many Germans as their best hope for final victory. He had increased production for the Army: now, Speer turned his attention to the German Navy. From the start of 1943, top priority was to be given to building U-boats rather than surface craft. In fact, this had been identified much earlier in the war by Donitz as crucial to any German victory.

Speer's goal was to build at least three new U-boats every week, and he believed that he could achieve this by adapting the assembly line production techniques that had been pioneered in the USA by Henry Ford. As it transpired, this proved to be a serious strategic error on Speer's part, compelling him to commission different sections of the submarines from companies which had little or no experience of ship-building – leading in turn, to constant problems of quality control.

It could be argued, in any case, that launching a major U-boat building programme was pointless at this stage of the war. From a military perspective, the huge quantities of steel that were required for the Valentin Bunker might have been better used to build thousands of tanks. However, by that stage Hitler was not the only one who was desperate for a solution to Germany's growing difficulties. Donitz and the Naval High Command had also come to identify the Valentin Bunker as just the sort of ambitious project that could renew the prestige and power of the Kriegsmarine. In a sense, then, the Bunker can also be understood as an expression of Nazi ideology – an enormous and lasting monument to its self-delusion. It is believed that the Allies delayed bombing the Bunker because they preferred to see Germany's shrinking resources being wasted on what they considered from the start to be a doomed enterprise.

Work on Speer's lethal fantasy persisted up to the final weeks of the war, and involved using thousands of slave workers to dig excavations, lay railway tracks, haul bags of cement, mix concrete and move steel beams. Once the work had begun, it continued relentlessly, day and night without pause – for the next two years. From the beginning, Project Valentin involved both small and large private contractors – the Thyssen group, for example – but the Bunker remained primarily a Naval project. The SS may have guarded the prisoners while they were in the Farge camp, but at work, the guards came from the Kriegsmarine – which clearly implicates the German Navy in any war crimes that were committed there.

The foundations for the Valentin Bunker were laid more than fifty feet deep, and they needed to be. The design plans had made provision for huge stores of timber and sheet metal across four separate levels. There were large workshops for plumbers, carpenters, metal workers and electricians. There was further space for quality control units, boiler rooms, medical supplies and dispatch bases. In addition, there were offices for the numerous construction and business managers who would work on the site – as well as room for radio operators and telegraphists. The roof of the Bunker was built out of dozens of massive steel arches – manufactured on site and lifted into place. Concrete was then poured over this framework to provide immense structural strength. When it was finished, the roof was almost 25 feet thick, and had used more than 500,000 cubic metres of concrete. 'I was asked once how they got that amount of concrete up to the roof', Harry Callan told me, 'I said, 'By conveyor belts'. The man who asked me laughed. He said, 'They had no conveyor belts that could do that in them days'. I said, 'They had no cranes that were big enough either – but I saw two of them on that site in 1943'.'

By any standards, the scale of the Valentin building could not fail to impress: 'The first thing you did when you walked into the bunker was to look up', Harry recalled, 'and that was when you realised the size of it. It was four hundred and thirty metres long, and forty-five metres high.' Each section of the Type XXI submarines was to be built separately, and that work was subcontracted to various firms throughout Germany. The pre-fabricated sections were then to be carried to the Valentin complex – either overland, or by barge – and brought into the bunker through a lock gate that opened into the River Weser. The building was designed to house thirteen successive assembly bays. The last of these could be flooded, so that when a large door opened in its west wall a completed submarine could enter the Weser directly. 'The bunker had to be that size', Harry told me, 'because the new submarines they were building were such big ones.'

By any standards, the Valentin Bunker was at the cutting edge of technological innovation when it was conceived and built. It had been designed by a brilliant young engineer called Erich Lackner. He is now considered to be one of the most important civil engineers of the twentieth century, and the biennial awards which are named after him are counted among the most prestigious that any young scientist can win.

As soon as full-scale construction of the submarine pens was under way, the prisoners assigned to Project Valentin worked in two shifts – each of which lasted for a minimum of 12 hours. 'We got a bowl of soup after we got up at four in the morning', Harry recalled. Christopher Ryan described each morning in the Farge camp beginning in 'an atmosphere of terror. Nobody was allowed to speak. Prisoners were beaten right, left and centre. Roll call lasted for an hour, and prisoners had to stand at attention the whole time.' After roll call, the work detail was marched to the bunker: 'It was about 3 or 4 miles away', Harry remembered, 'We got down there for a six o'clock start, and we started work as soon as we arrived.'

The Irish prisoners began by laying the rail tracks that were needed for the preliminary construction of the Valentin bunker: 'We started off bringing the railway lines down to the bunker', Harry recalled, 'Then, we dug the dykes on both sides.' At first, they worked alongside a contingent of young Jewish women, who had been brought to Farge from Eastern Europe. The prisoners had to work in their shirt sleeves and thin jackets in a region of northern Germany where it is not unusual for winter temperatures to fall below minus 20 degrees and there was never any reduction in the working hours, no matter how cold it became. Prisoners tried to protect themselves against the weather by wearing empty bags, pieces of blankets, or other strips of fabric under their work clothes. This was strictly forbidden, and inmates who were caught doing so were beaten or shot. Instead of socks, prisoners were usually given rags to wrap around their feet. Christopher Ryan saw many workers collapse from exposure or exhaustion, 'and be run over by trucks'.

Around noon, there was a half-hour meal break: 'We got two slices of black bread and half a cup of ersatz coffee', Harry told me, 'Then it was back to the job until around six.' The rations that the prisoners were given were the bare minimum that had been calculated were necessary to keep them alive. After work, they were marched back to the camp at Farge. 'We usually got there a little after seven', Harry remembered. When they returned to the camp they were made to wait for as long as two hours in silence until they got a final bowl of watery turnip soup. They were put to bed for the night at nine o'clock – unless there was an air raid: 'Then we had to get up, and sit around, waiting for it to stop.'

Some of the prisoners were detailed to work in the cement detachments at the bunker. This involved lifting, carrying and emptying 50 kilo bags of cement. The prisoners would inevitably inhale some of the dust during the day, and hack it up in wet balls during the night. Even worse than the cement detachments were those that involved transporting the huge iron and steel girders. Accidents were frequent, and life expectancy was so low that these detachments were known to the prisoners as 'suicide squads'. Not all of the Irish prisoners were capable of the hardest work: 'Thomas Murphy wasn't able for it', Harry told me, 'Neither was O'Hara – because he was asthmatic.'

But even those who were spared the most exacting details didn't escape the climate of terror. Behind the crushing burden of work was the constant threat of serious physical violence. According to Harry Callan, 'We got thumped around everywhere. The SS treated us as if we were animals.' All of the prisoners at Farge were expected to subsist and work to the point of exhaustion on what was clearly a grossly inadequate diet. Given the lack of food, it is hardly surprising that prisoners died from starvation in Farge every week.

Labour camps like Farge did not exist in isolation from the towns and villages that were close to where they operated. The growth of satellite camps meant that hundreds of thousands of prisoners were employed throughout

Germany, and, in the final years of the war, as Michael Thad Allen has observed, there was 'hardly a single locale with any factory of note [that] lacked a contingent of prisoners'. Allen has also noted that their work was not hidden from the general public: 'Every morning columns of sombre workers, starving and bruised, could be seen marching from fenced enclosures down the streets of ordinary German towns.'

The camp at Farge was no exception: it was a relatively short distance from Bremen, and all of the grinding labour took place a few hundred yards from where the civilian population of Farge lived. 'We were working near houses in the village', Harry recalled, 'We could see them while we were working – so they must have been able to see us.' In fact, the SS took no steps to conceal the camp at Farge - or any of the other sub-camps that were based around Neuengamme: a local photographer was even allowed to enter the camps at Farge.

By and large, the local German population seemed to accept that the camps had a worthwhile purpose to fulfil, and the sight of slave workers close to their private residences did not seem to shake or undermine that belief. While it can be assumed that there was limited knowledge of the concentration camp system before the war, it is indisputable that there was greater awareness among the German public in the last years of the war. As Joachim Fest has commented: 'The concrete visibility of the victims attained a level that went far beyond what the population had been able to see, read, or hear about in the early years of National Socialism. The population could not fail to see the wretched columns driven from stations to the camps.' Their apparent lack of sympathy – or even interest – in the fate of the men and women that they could see trudging to work every day and night, may perhaps be linked to the brutalising impact of the years of war. It may also be that the use of forced labour had come to be tolerated in a society that could also accept the concept of 'total war'.

The Irish seamen were among the first inmates to arrive at the new Farge camp, but they were soon joined on Project Valentin by many others. They came from nearly every country in Europe, but the largest groups were Jews, Russians and Poles. Before long, the Bunker had become the largest construction work site – not only in the Neuengamme complex - but in the whole of Germany. In the course of the war more than 100,000 prisoners would pass through the Neuengamme complex. When the war in Europe ended in May, 1945, more than half of them were dead: one of those who died was my cousin William.

9

HEART OF DARKNESS

In the words of the cadet officer, Christopher Ryan, the labour camp at Farge was 'a God-forsaken place'. It was located in a disused Navy fuel depot, and the first accommodation provided for the Irish seamen was an empty fuel tank buried underground, beneath several metres of solid concrete. The circular tank was 50 feet wide and 25 feet high and its cover was camouflaged with sand. Eventually, the seamen were given their own hut - a flimsy structure above ground - and slept in what Ryan described as 'three tier rickety wooden bunks'. They were soon joined in the camp by other nationalities: 'There were Jews, Russians, Poles, and all sorts of political prisoners', Ryan recalled. The latter included 'some German Communists and trade unionists that the Nazis wanted rid of'.

Not all of the political prisoners proved to be sympathetic to the other inmates. The SS liked to structure their camps on a hierarchical basis in order to stimulate competition and division between their captives. They deliberately involved certain prisoners as functionaries in the management of the camps so that a system of collaboration and reward could be developed. The top positions in the Farge camp were given to the German prisoners. These functionaries – known as '*Kapos*' – were granted certain privileges and in return, were expected to drive and beat the other prisoners to ensure that they worked hard enough. By all accounts, most of the German *Kapos* went about their business with considerable vigour, and, in some instances, a marked degree of sadism. One of these Kapos was called Ludwig Zehnter. He was not a political prisoner, but had been sent to Farge, in May 1944, for the criminal offence of impersonating an SS officer. He later summed up his attitude as follows: 'If I did not beat the prisoners severely enough, I was myself beaten. I did not like being beaten, so I made sure that I was not beaten often.' Not surprisingly, Zehtner was greatly feared by the other inmates. 'Sometimes he had a reason for the punishments he inflicted – sometimes not', one German prisoner later testified. 'Zehnter's brutality was necessary', he concluded, 'to make the camp system work.'

The critical role that *Kapos* played in that system was also described by Leopold Falkensammer, the *Kommandant* of the camp at Altengamme – another of Neuengamme's sub-camps. In a lengthy statement made after the war he admitted that 'naturally' he despised the prisoners who were in his charge for being 'obstacles in the way of Germany's aspirations'. He also acknowledged 'a feeling of disgust that the prisoners' behaviour necessitated our harsh treatment'. Fortunately for Falkensammer's sensibilities, there was a solution at hand: 'We reduced this problem by handing over the internal administration of the camps to nominated prisoners called *Kapo*s. These were given slightly better rations and accommodation, and in return they organised the prison population'. Falkensammer was relieved that 'towards the end of the war, we had very little direct contact with the inmates. It was all left to the *Kapos*.' In fact, according to Falkensammer, it was the *Kapos* who had 'organised' many of the dreadful 'cruelties and atrocities' for which he, a senior and honourable officer in the SS, had been falsely accused.

These fastidious sentiments did not prevent Falkensammer from initiating a series of medical experiments at Altengamme, in which the penises of healthy Russian prisoners were amputated to see if they could be transplanted on to other prisoners whose penises had also been surgically removed. There was one small difficulty, which Falkensammer confessed had been 'unforeseen' by him - 'the negative attitude of the prisoners towards our experiments'. Indeed, he noted that many of the Russians tried to commit suicide, and "one or two succeeded'. Since they 'could not afford to lose prisoners once the experiments had started', Falkensammer devised a straightforward solution, he 'shackled the prisoners with handcuffs to their beds.' The mutilated Russians then tried to starve themselves to death, but, once again, Falkensammer was able to come up with a simple expedient; he assigned two male nurses to each patient, and warned them that they would both have their own penises cut off if the patient died. Falkensammer believed that this proved to be a 'wise precaution' and no more prisoners were able to kill themselves. Instead, they were all murdered by the SS when the experiments were complete. Falkensammer was proud that these hideous operations were his own idea, and finished his account of the medical procedures with the claim that all of the surgery took place under 'proper operating theatre conditions', and that 'there was no cruelty involved.'

The sister camp at Farge also treated its captives as if they were sub-human. A military court, sitting in Hamburg in 1947, heard graphic evidence of how the prisoners had been subjected to extreme levels of physical violence: they had been severely whipped, battered with wooden poles and slats, had their teeth knocked out, and been shot, drowned, strangled, clubbed and beaten to death. Although a number of SS personnel at the camp were tried for these and other war crimes, none were executed – unlike Falkensammer, who was hanged by the British. All of the *Kapos* at Farge also managed to survive – including Erich Meissner, the Head *Kapo*. He was described by one of the prisoners who suffered at his hands as 'a brutal madman.' Meissner had been an active figure in the KPD – the German Communist Party – before his captivity, and after the war was able to resume his political activities in what had become the German Democratic Republic. In that system, his status as a former prisoner of the Nazis earned him great respect. He went on to serve as the Mayor of Leipzig, and was treated for the rest of his life as an honoured member of East German society.

Unlike many of the POWs in the Farge camp, a high proportion of the Irish merchant seamen – including my cousin, William – were already middle-aged when they were captured. They were ill-prepared for the type of gruelling labour that they were now obliged to perform. Many of them were already suffering from the effects of years of confinement and deprivation. There was scant respite for such men – they had been assigned to a work regime that would further drain them of their mental and physical resources in the years that lay ahead.

At first, some of the Irishmen found it hard to believe that they had been sent to a so-called 'Labour Education' camp, whose ostensible purpose was to punish those *freie Arbeiter* who had signed contracts with the SS, and were alleged to have broken their conditions of employment by being 'work-shy'. Franz Xavier Sauer was one of the SS Guards in the camp. He was an Austrian, who had served in the elite *Liebstandarte Adolf Hitler* division of the Waffen-SS before he was transferred to Farge. In 1947, he told a military court in Hamburg that he could remember one of the Irish seamen approaching him soon after they had arrived at the camp: 'He said, 'Why have we been brought here? We are merchant seamen, not labourers. Don't you know that?' But [the Gestapo] told us to employ them in exactly the same way as all the others and to make sure that they didn't escape'.

According to Christopher Ryan, it was a 'rule of the camp that no one could be allowed to rest, but must be kept on the move.' He thought it was a 'grim joke' on the part of the camp guards to make the prisoners run around the camp at night, when most of them could hardly stand. Each guard carried a length of weighted hose pipe. 'Prisoners were just slashed at random,' Ryan remembered, 'Sometimes, they used wires or whips – sometimes just their boots and fists.' There were also a number of Alsatian guard dogs, which could be set upon the prisoners. The SS personnel at Farge would sometimes amuse themselves by staging boxing matches between their captives: the winner would gain an extra ration of bread – and the starving men fought each other with a passion born of hunger and despair. At other times, one of the camp's *Kommandants*, Karl Walhorn, would arm himself with a hunting rifle. He would place a small piece of potato or turnip on a rubbish tip and then hide in one of the huts until a prisoner ran out to retrieve it – at which point he would open fire.

Kommandant Walhorn had joined the SS in Bremen in 1934. Two years later, he was transferred to the *Totenkopfverbände* – the Death's Head units in charge of concentration camps. He justified his setting of traps and shooting of prisoners by claiming that he 'had to make an example': 'There was a death penalty for those disobeying economic decrees in Germany', he told a military court, 'and I was told that I should pay for it with my head if all the potatoes were not accounted for.' He claimed that he was entitled to shoot 'because I had issued an order expressly forbidding potato stealing.' Walhorn may well have informed the camp's inmates that the penalty for stealing food was death, but it speaks volumes that the prisoners were so desperate that they would risk being shot for a piece of raw potato. He conceded that his actions 'might be thought to be going too far'. Nonetheless, he maintained later that shooting the starving prisoners had 'certainly achieved its objective, and potato stealing stopped.' The rations allocated to the camp were meagre enough but Walhorn did not even issue all of them to its inmates, telling one *Kapo* that he preferred to return food so that it could be used to, 'feed Germans.'

There was an unusually high turnover of camp *Kommandants* at Farge. Between 1943 and 1945, there were six of them: *Oberscharführer* Karl Walhorn, *Politische Oberwachtmann* Sebastian Schipper, *Untersturmführer* Georg Adolph, *Sturmscharführer* Heinrich Schauwacker, *Hauptscharführer* Erich Voss and *Untersturmführer* Hemlmut Schrader. Their individual regimes varied – in relative terms – in severity and also in each *Kommandant's* particular targets. One Kapo later summed up the difference between two of them: 'Schipper hated Jews, and Schauwacker hated Russians.' Schauwacker was generally considered to have been the most unstable, and the most violent of all the *Kommandants*. He had joined the Nazis' original paramilitary force, the *Sturmabteilung*, in 1927 when he was still a teenager. In later years, he liked to boast that he was an *Alten Kampfer* – an 'Old Fighter' – a term used to describe the earliest members of the Nazi

Party. He claimed to have taken part in numerous attacks on Jews and Jewish property in Bremen throughout the 1930s. In 1939, Schauwacker joined the Gestapo, and two years later he volunteered for the *Einsatzgruppen*: SS death squads that operated on the Eastern front, and the first Nazi units to commence the mass murder of Jews as a systematic policy. Schauwacker was promoted to the rank of SS *Strumsharführer* in *Einsatzgruppen B* – which operated in Belarus and is believed to have murdered more than 300,000 civilians.

The last *Aktion* in which Schauwacker participated was just outside the Belarussian town of Minsk – where he helped to execute more than 6,000 Jews between 28th and 30th of June, 1944. Before they were shot, Schauwacker had made the victims dig their own graves. Three days later, the Red Army liberated Minsk, but by then Schauwacker was on his way back to Germany. Four months after that, he was appointed *Kommandant* of the camp at Farge. It had the reputation of being one of the hardest labour camps in the whole Nuengamme complex: a reputation that Schauwacker seemed determined to uphold.

One of the SS Guards at Farge later described Schauwacker as *'einen Teufel in menschen Gestalt'* - 'a devil in human form'. One of the *Kapos* told the military court in Hamburg that Schauwacker 'got on well enough with the prisoners one minute, and wanted to kill them the next.' That was not a figure of speech. An SS guard described one instance of Schauwacker's homicidal fury: 'One night, we walked past a shed in which dead bodies were stored', he recalled, 'Schauwacker went to the corner of the shed to relieve himself. He must have seen something – because he suddenly went into the shed. He came back out with a small Russian prisoner. He took him over to the sewage pit. He lifted the lid, and rammed the man head first into the pit. The prisoner struggled, but Schauwacker was stronger. Ten minutes later, when he pulled the man out, he was dead.' The Irish seaman, William English, testified that Schauwacker went on a murderous rampage during his last weeks in the camp, shooting and beating some prisoners to death – choking and suffocating others. According to English, Shauwacker said that he knew he would be hanged by the Allies, and was determined to 'take as many [prisoners] with him as he could'.

Schauwacker's unrestrained violence towards the prisoners began to affect the work schedule at the Valentin Bunker. As a result, the Gestapo in Bremen relieved him of his command, and held him briefly in police detention. Schauwacker was outraged at being detained, and wrote directly to Goebbels, assuring him of his continuing devotion to the cause of National Socialism. He also cited some of the services that he believed he had rendered to the Third Reich. Among these, he numbered the thousands of 'men, women and children', that he had murdered in Belarus. The Bremen Gestapo held a trial for Schauwacker – much of which seems to have focused on the technicality of whether or not he was still a fully paid-up member of the Nazi Party. Within a few weeks, he was set free, and soon became involved in setting up some local units of the so-called *Werwolf* organisation – a guerrilla force that was intended to operate behind enemy lines should Germany lose the war, but which, fortunately, proved to be largely ineffectual in the face of the Allied forces.

After the Allies captured Bremen, they found copies of Schauwacker's correspondence with Goebbels, and tried to arrest him for the mass-murders that he had boasted about in his letters. Schauwacker was consistently able to evade capture, and despite several sightings he was never apprehended. In 1953, his wife applied for a pension as the widow of a German soldier – which she was duly granted. However, it is believed that Schauwacker was not dead, but had succeeded in escaping to South Africa, where he managed to live comfortably under the Apartheid regime.

It was in the Farge camp that Harry Callan first got to know my relative, William. 'I was only nineteen when I was sent to Farge', Harry told me, 'and to me it seemed like he was an old man.' By this stage, Harry had learned to speak some German: 'The first two words I learned in German were '*schnell*', [fast], and, '*raus*' [out]', he told me, 'because they were the two words that were used constantly to all of us.' There were other advantages in learning the language: 'You could talk a bit to the guards and the more German you knew, the easier it went for you.' In some respects, the Irish seamen were fortunate that they had been among the first to arrive at Farge. Given the racist nature of Nazi ideology, it may seem surprising that the hierarchy of prisoners in the camp was not entirely based on their ethnic origin. Instead, survival rates tended to favour those who had been

Patrick Breen from County Wexford. Taken prisoner in 1941, when his ship, the *Athelfoam*, was attacked in the North Atlantic by the German battleship *Scharnhorst*. Breen was the first Irish prisoner to die – in May 1943 – in the labour camp at Farge.

The radio officer Gerald O'Hara from Ballina, in County Mayo. He was taken prisoner when his ship, the *Devon*, was attacked off the Galapagos Islands, by the German surface raider, *Komet*. O'Hara died in the Farge labour camp in March of 1944.

William Knott from Ringsend in Dublin. Knott survived his years as a slave worker in the Farge camp, and gave evidence against his SS captors in Hamburg in 1947.

William Hutchinson Knox, from Dun Laoghaire in County Dublin. He was the first of the Irish prisoners in Farge to be captured by the Germans, and the last to die in the camp.

The picturesque north German village of Farge – where thousands of slave workers were once forced to build the Valentin Bunker.

Early days in the contraction of the Valentin Bunker. The foundations were laid at a depth of fifty feet.

Above and below: The Valentin Bunker became the biggest construction site in Germany – employing up to 12,000 slave workers in two 12-hour shifts. It is believed that somewhere between 4,000 – 6,000 slave workers died while building the Bunker. The identities of most of them remain unknown. Courtesy of Sammlung Schmidt, Staatsarchive Landeszentrale für politische Bildung, Bremen.

Courtesy of Sammlung Schmidt, Staatsarchive Landeszentrale für politische Bildung, Bremen

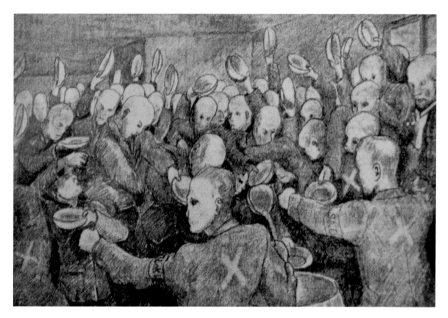

A drawing by one prisoner of the serving of soup at the Farge camp. Courtesy of Sammlung Schmidt, Staatsarchive Landeszentrale für politische Bildung, Bremen.

Slaves working on the foundations of the bunker.

One of the sections of the Valentin Bunker – still showing some of the damage inflicted by Grand Slam bombs in the final attack by the RAF.

After German capitulation, two British soldiers look at an unfinished Type XXI U-boat. The Valentin Bunker was specially designed for the construction of this revolutionary type of submarine. Reichsminister Albert Speer hoped to assemble one of these 'miracle boats' every 56 hours, but none of them ever left the Valentin pens.

Part of one of the reinforced walls of the Bunker in Farge. 'Gebraut für die Erwigkeit '– 'built for eternity' – the Bunker has far outlived the Reich it was intended to serve.

A wall banner in the 'House of Commemoration' at the Neuengamme camp. The banner lists just some of those who died on one day in April 1945 in the camp complex.

WilliamWarnock was Ireland's Charge d'Affaires in Berlin, 1939-1944. After the war, he returned to Germany as Irish Ambassador to the German Federal Republic. He is seen here, on the left of frame, with a member of the German Foreign Office in Bonn in 1961.

A caricature of de Valera drawn by my father. He detested de Valera's social conservatism – in relation to issues such as divorce, contraception and the censorship of books – but, like many Irishmen serving with the Allied armed forces, supported his policy of Irish neutrality.

The former Cadet Officer, Christopher Ryan, photographed in 2004. Originally from Tramore in County Waterford, Ryan was taken prisoner in January 1941 after his ship, the *Speybank*, was captured by the surface raider *Atlantis*. He spent the next four years as a prisoner of the Germans. He was the last of the Irish merchant seamen to arrive in the Farge labour camp. While there, he was subjected to repeated beatings, contracted typhus and tuberculosis, and lost almost half his body weight. Despite that, he returned to Germany in 1947 to give evidence against some of the camp's SS guards, and manged to live to a ripe old age. (Picture courtesy of Mark McCormick, and *Sunday Life*.)

The wreath laid by the last Irish survivor of the Farge camp, Harry Callan, above five crosses for each of the Irish seamen who died there.

there for the longest and who had managed to accumulate some minor privileges: French prisoners were among the last to arrive, and they recorded one of the highest rates of mortality. Overall, however, there was no ethnic or national group that emerged unscathed from their time in Farge.

According to Christopher Ryan, when anyone was shot by the SS guards 'their bodies were left lying on the ground of the compound for days as a warning to the rest of us.' William English also described seeing injured prisoners being thrown to die on rubbish tips, and salt being rubbed into open wounds as punishment for alleged misdemeanours. Despite the death, disease and cruelty of the camp, the Irish prisoners came to rely upon each other for their existence. They were recognisable as a separate group inside Farge because they had been issued with Khaki uniforms – taken from British soldiers who had died at Dunkirk – while they were in the camp at Milag Nord. 'We always kept together', Harry Callan recalled, 'Even when we went out on working parties, we always marched together at the tail end.' Christopher Ryan was one of the youngest of the Irish contingent and for him, it was the collective will and fortitude of his fellow Irish seamen that kept alive in each of them the hope of survival. 'On a few occasions,' he remembered, 'one or two of us would say that they couldn't bear it anymore, and that they would go and work for the Germans. But the rest of us would encourage them not to give up. We stuck together, and told ourselves that we would not give in to the enemy, and that we would survive.'

Ryan's comments may seem somewhat confusing: he states that the Irish prisoners refused 'to work for the Germans' – yet, clearly, they were employed as slave labourers at the Valentin Bunker. The answer to this apparent contradiction lies in the peculiar mixture of legalism and barbarity that characterised much of Nazi ideology. The upper echelons of the SS contained many individuals who were both highly-qualified lawyers and dedicated National Socialists. For that reason, it was part of their stated policy to insist that all foreign workers should sign legally-binding documents with the SS.

This may seem like a risible formality – certainly, as far as slave workers were concerned – but, as we shall see, it became a crucial part of the defence strategy followed by SS officers in several post-war trials. Throughout the length of their captivity, the Irish prisoners were put under great pressure to sign these work contracts. At times, they were induced to do so with offers of more lenient treatment; at other times, they were threatened and brutalised. 32 Irish merchant seamen consistently refused to sign the contracts: in so doing, they denied the SS the pretence that their imprisonment was legal – even by the shoddy standards of Nazi Germany. As a result, the Irish seamen were forced to work for years as slaves, and to live in appalling conditions. They refused to compromise with the SS, and survived primarily by relying upon each other for sustenance.

There were other factors that helped them to endure – some of which were quite unexpected. Harry Callan had been in Farge for almost 18 months when he fell ill. 'I had awful pains in my neck', he told me, 'and it turned out to be pleurisy'. Harry went to see the doctor who attended the camp: 'Dr. Heidbreder wasn't really the camp doctor – he was the village doctor, but he used to come to the camp because there were always a lot of sick prisoners. Anyway, I saw him and he knocked me off work for a while.' Although Dr. Heidbreder was not based in the camp, his role there was clearly a critical one – and some of the prisoners held very different opinions about that role. Heidbreder could determine, after all, whether or not patients were fit to be sent back to work – and that decision could mean the difference between life and death. Some of the Irish patients believed he was a conscientous and caring physician. Others believed that his treatment of some prisoners – particularly, of Russians and Poles – bordered on outright sadism.

Harry Callan was one of those who grew quite friendly with Dr. Heidbreder during his stay in the camp hospital. 'I don't know why it was called a hospital', he told me, 'There was nothing in it – only beds. There was a Russian prisoner in charge, but there wasn't a single tablet or drug in the whole place. There were just two jars of ointment: one was white, and the other was black. The Russian told me that the difference was that the black ointment was for more serious injuries.' The only bandages available in the hospital were made out of paper. More than half of the Irish prisoners ended up spending time there. 'Men lay in their beds in every condition of disease, and were given no treatment', Christopher Ryan recalled, 'There were even cases when patients were taken out of their beds and beaten. There was a terrible smell but there was also a terrible atmosphere of hopelessness'.

Karl Henssler was a German political prisoner: he was a member of the Social Democratic Party, and had been imprisoned by the Nazis since 1939. When he arrived in Farge, he was assigned to the camp hospital as an orderly, and later gave a graphic description of the dreadful conditions in which the patients were kept; 'The stink was maddening', he testified to a military court, 'They were two to a bed under one blanket. Most of them were suffering from diarrhoea. There was muck and filth in their beds, as the patients were too sick to get up to relieve themselves. There was no soap or hot water in the entire camp – not even in the hospital – and the blankets were never washed.' Hennsler also gave evidence that the camp staff – and the *Kapos* – enjoyed a diet that was 'luxurious' in comparison to that of the prisoners. 'This was on account', he said, 'of them using the prisoners' rations to supplement their own.'

As it happened, it was in the hospital that Harry Callan's knowledge of the German language proved to be of some benefit: 'I used to have a good chat with Dr. Heidbreder every time he came in. At the end of about ten days, he said to me 'you're all right to go back to work now' – which was not what I wanted to hear. Then he said to me, 'How would you like to do some work for me in my garden?' So, of course, I said yes.' Harry thought that the work involved would be relatively light, but he soon discovered that the doctor's garden was very large. 'He told me that he had a big field at the back of his house – and he had. It was about four acres, and he had another acre at the front. His wife had three beds dug up to grow vegetables – carrots, and onions, and stuff like that. She was a very strict woman, and she told me what to do.' It was not unusual for the SS to rent out slave labour, but the prisoners seldom found that the work was as good for their health as this proved to be for Harry. Not only was he working in the fresh air every day: he was even allowed to make his own way through the village to the doctor's house.

The doctor and his wife were not the only members of their family: 'They had three children – no, four', Harry said, 'but the youngest was a new-born girl, and I never saw her. Apart from the baby, there were two young boys and a girl.' The girl in question was close to Harry in age, and a relationship quickly developed between them. At that time, almost all German men of their age had been enlisted in the Wehrmacht. The camp authorities were acutely conscious of the shortage of young males, and the penalty for any foreign worker who tried to establish sexual contact with German women was summary execution. In fact, the prisoners were not allowed to step within several yards of any woman that they passed as they marched to and from work every day. Harry Callan believes that the few months he spent away from hard labour at the Valentin bunker may have helped to save his life. His relationship with the doctor's daughter also taught him a lasting lesson. Until then, he told me, he had begun to think that all Germans were brutes. The kindness of that girl made him change his mind.

Prisoners who died at work were brought back to the camp to be buried. 'The SS never handled a dead body themselves', Christopher Ryan recalled, 'If a dead body was brought into the camp, it was always brought by the prisoners .' That involved carrying the bodies on makeshift stretchers for almost four miles from the Bunker site. From time to time, prisoners would attempt to escape. If they were recaptured, there were given 'terrible beatings', then thrown into the camp's punishment cell. According to testimony from the survivors, they could be beaten in that cell for more than twelve hours at a time, and Ryan estimated that 'they usually died within three or four days.' The Irish seamen endured more than two years of this regime: 'At first, we were terribly shocked by these events', Ryan commented, 'but later we grew callous. We couldn't have sympathy with everyone who suffered. We had to preserve our sanity.'

There had, however, been an important development outside the camp of which the Irish prisoners were, as yet, unaware: the replacement of William Warnock as the Irish Chargé d'Affaires in Berlin. Before they were moved to Farge, the Irish seamen had written a number of letters to Warnock. He may not have received these letters – from Stalag X B and Milag Nord – seeking his assistance. At any rate, he never responded to any of them. As the war began to turn against Germany, Dr. Eduard Hempel, the German Minister in Dublin, complained that the Irish Government's attitude had also changed: becoming 'unhelpful and evasive'. In this context, Warnock's apparent sympathy for Hitler's regime may have come to be viewed as potentially damaging to Irish interests – but in any case the strain of his assignment had already become too much for him, and he had formally requested home leave. Warnock was replaced in late 1943 by another Irish diplomat – a young Kerryman named Con Cremin.

Cremin had visited Munich in 1932 to learn German, and had come away with the impression that Hitler was 'a tremendous demagogue'. The Berlin posting was his first as a head of mission. From 1937, he had served in France – first, in Paris, and then in Vichy. He was chosen, in part, for his new assignment because he 'had no sympathy for Hitler or National Socialism'. Cremin's time in France after its fall in 1940 had shown him at first hand the grim realities of Nazi Occupation. According to Niall Keogh, his work in Vichy had 'further reinforced his abhorrence of National Socialism, and [he distanced] the Irish Legation in Vichy (…) from all unnecessary contact with the Germans.' Cremin had first been posted to Berlin in the late summer of 1942, when William Warnock had been involved in a minor accident. He arrived to replace him on a permanent basis as Charge d'Affaires in late 1943. However, the complete hand-over was disrupted by the destruction of the Irish Legation in an Allied air-raid.

Warnock finally left for Ireland in February 1944 – after what Cremin believed was a 'difficult and lonely time in Berlin'. For the remainder of the war, Cremin sent back to Dublin a series of shrewd and objective assessments of the war as it progressed. It is clear that he tried repeatedly to break through the various deceptions that served to obscure the Jewish Holocaust from the outside world. However, Cremin was also well aware that the reports that he was sending back to Dublin were being read by the Nazis – who had cracked the Irish cypher, *dearg*, at the very outset of the war. In Dermot Keogh's words, Cremin 'continued to confront the German authorities about the deportation of the Jews, and bore witness to the Holocaust, even in the last stages of the Third Reich.'

Apart from sending dispatches to Dublin, there was relatively little for Cremin to do in his new posting. He processed several claims against the Germans for attacks on Irish merchant ships, and he dealt with the mail that arrived periodically from Ireland. Cremin also discovered that there were three Irish citizens awaiting execution in Gestapo prisons for espionage on behalf of the Allies. He managed to secure the release of two of them – the third died during an Allied air raid. In August 1944, the Irish Chargé d'Affaires finally managed to visit the merchant seamen in Farge. By that point, they had not had any contact with the world outside the Farge camp for more than a year. Then, an unexpected opportunity for such contact arose. One of the prisoners at Farge, a Swiss national, was permitted to return to his home in Berlin. The Irish prisoners scribbled another letter for their Chargé d'Affaires – describing their situation, and begging for help. The Swiss man agreed to deliver it – a courageous act, since he would undoubtedly have been executed if caught by the Germans. The letter was safely delivered, and, shortly afterwards, Cremin came to the camp.

Christopher Ryan remembered the prisoners' delight – and relief – on the day that Cremin arrived. His presence alone made them believe that they would not all end up in one of the camp's mass graves. 'Mr. Cremin arrived in a black Mercedes', Ryan recalled many years later, 'he was escorted by SS officers, and was allowed to talk to us. He was horrified by the sight of us, and by our [living] conditions.' The driver supplied by the SS later reported that Cremin had stayed at the camp for about two hours, and had distributed cigarettes to the Irish prisoners. According to William English, Cremin told them he was determined that they would be repatriated to Ireland. This was not an unrealistic demand – during the course of the war, POWs were regularly exchanged between the belligerent States, and, in the previous year, more than 100 merchant officers and ratings had been brought from the camp at Milag Nord – first, by train to Portugal, and, from there, on neutral ships to the UK. Cremin argued that the Irish seamen should not even be treated as prisoners of war – let alone as slave workers. While they were waiting to be repatriated, Cremin urged that they should be returned to their former camp at Milag.

By the end of 1944, his campaign for their release appeared to have succeeded. The Irishmen were loaded on to a train, and sent to the port of Flensburg – where they were told they would be sent to Sweden. From there, they were supposed to travel back to Ireland on board a Swedish merchant ship. However, Allied bombing prevented them from reaching Flensburg, and they were returned to the camp at Farge. Despite Cremin's protests, they were not sent back to Milag Nord. His intervention may have resulted in the conditions of their captivity being eased somewhat – it appears that their food rations were marginally improved – but the merchant seamen were still forced to work as slaves in the Valentin Bunker.

Not all of the prisoners took as positive a view of Cremin's attempts to release them from the Farge camp as Christopher Ryan. Some of them pointed out that they received no consular assistance until several months after the D-Day landings – when the looming defeat of Nazi Germany was obvious. According to one report, Cremin was confronted in Dublin many years later by one of the Irish prisoners who had been held in Farge. He asked Cremin why Irish diplomats had not done more – and at an earlier stage – to get him and the other seamen out of the camp. In reply, Cremin claimed that the Irish Government did not know of their whereabouts until the middle of 1944. It is impossible to say if Cremin believed this to be accurate information, but it seems hard to credit that the Irish Government was not aware of the illegal imprisonment of Irish citizens at a much earlier date.

As the war entered its final years, the most senior Nazi officials demanded more and more workers in feverish attempts to reverse their slide into defeat. In October 1944, Albert Speer took direct charge of the deployment of concentration camp workers, but by then the camps had become riven by chaos and upheaval. It was clear that the attempt to turn them into functional pools of labour for the armaments and construction industries had failed. The economic exploitation of the camp inmates had been developed inextricably – and in tandem with – the working of prisoners to death. Indeed, these features were, in the words of Jens-Christian Wagner, 'two sides of the same coin.' During the final phase of their existence, work in the camps was often, as Bertrand Perz has rightly claimed, 'a method for the systematic killing of prisoners'.

There were, of course, some prisoners who were of particular use to the Nazi war economy. These captives may have possessed specific skills, or they may have become familiar with specialist tasks after a period of time. In such cases, both the SS, and the business administrators with whom they worked, were anxious to ensure that camp officials treated their prisoners with some degree of restraint. The situation was quite different for unskilled *Bauhaftlinge* - 'construction workers' – such as the Irish seamen employed as labourers at the Valentin Bunker. These captives were considered to be entirely dispensable – since an endless reservoir of labour seemed readily available in the Nazis' huge prison camps. For that reason, both the SS and the business managers of commercial companies were quite prepared to work their prisoners until they dropped down dead. In such circumstances, it would be difficult to speak of the camps' productive value – at least, not in terms of a viable economic system: instead, the productive capacity of the workers was ignored, and mortality rates inside the camps was allowed to climb even higher.

When the Irish seamen had arrived at Farge in 1943, the guards were all SS personnel who had been moved from the 'mother camp' at Neuengamme. By the middle of 1944, however, their services were needed urgently elsewhere, and a few had been replaced by Wehrmacht soldiers – many of whom were no longer fit for combat – as well as by Gestapo officers, and some civilian police. The Irish prisoners welcomed the relative loosening of SS control but the change in personnel did not lead to a reduction in the camp's death rate. Indeed, it continued to rise as long as the Farge camp was in operation.

In the closing stages of the war, a new danger to the prisoner's lives came from Allied bombing: British and American airplanes were pulverising the industrial and military plants of Bremen by day and night, and Bremen was only 25 or so miles to the north of Farge. The merchant naval cadet, Jack Matthews, had stayed in the camp at Milag Nord after the Irish seamen had been taken to Farge. In late 1943, he was taken out of the Milag camp to a civilian hospital, and witnessed the incredible ferocity of the Allied assault: 'It was like daylight there was so much fire,' he recalled, 'and we were 30-40 kilometres away from the city. I'd seen Liverpool bombed but this was much worse.' When I visited Bremen in 2012, the amount of post-war construction in the medieval town centre testified to the searing effects of the Allied bombing raids.

Because of the depth of the concrete used in its construction, the Valentin Bunker seemed invulnerable to such attacks – and the workers from Farge considered themselves safe when they were within its confines. In fact, by 1944, the greatest risk to the prisoners working on the Bunker did not come from Allied bombs, or even from the camp guards – but from epidemic disease. The tens of thousands of those who died from disease in Nazi camps might be said to have died of 'natural causes'. But their deaths were also the inevitable consequences of years of systematic neglect and cruel abuse. Camp society was, in the words of Wolfgang Soksky, 'a society of the sick', and most of the overcrowded and unsanitary camps were periodically ravaged by a variety of epidemics. Along with oedemas from pneumonia, there were regular outbreaks of other diseases that were highly infectious. Dysentery and tuberculosis were both common, but the most lethal was typhus.

When a typhus epidemic broke out in a concentration camp, the guards responded in a variety of ways – most of them savage. Sometimes they simply executed those who had been infected. In the Majdanek camp, for example, anyone who was even suspected of having typhus was either hanged or shot. It was only after some SS personnel contracted the disease that disinfectant and some basic washing facilities were supplied. At other times, prisoners were quarantined – and then left without food or medicine to die on their own. When typhus was detected in a group of Soviet POWs in the main Neuengamme camp in October of 1941, the prisoners were moved to a new compound and left alone, without food or medicine. Almost 500 of them died within a few weeks. When that epidemic continued to spread, the main camp was also closed down, all external work was suspended, and the disease was left unattended to run its course. By the time it had done so, 1,000 more prisoners were dead.

There were two peaks of typhus infection within the camps in Germany. The first of these occurred in the early years of the war – when the Nazi regime was trying to process unprecedented numbers of prisoners, and the administration of many camps was still chaotic and disorganised. By 1943, that situation had substantially improved, but, in the following year, the rapidly deteriorating situation on different military fronts saw the rise of another – and even more serious – peak. Ironically, it was the breaking down of the whole camp system that allowed typhus to rage with renewed and uncontrolled energy during the final stages of the war. This proved especially true of the satellite camps – such as Farge: according to the Austrian historian, Florian Freund, it was in these sub-camps that the highest rates of fatal disease were usually to be found.

The danger of epidemic disease normally increases with the density of population, and the more crowded the camps became, the worse their hygiene conditions grew. In the Neuengamme complex, this injected bacilli into the system and linked the individual camps in a chain of infection. The prisoners in these camps were particularly vulnerable to opportunistic disease. Chronic malnutrition and a lack of basic vitamins had reduced the physical resistance of the inmates. Injury, exhaustion and psychological stress also heightened their disposition to illness. Added to that was a litany of other contributing factors – such as an inadequate supply of water; the lack of proper washing and sewage facilities, filthy clothing and blankets that were changed very infrequently – if ever. All of this combined to create an ideal breeding ground for the clothing louse – the transmitter of typhus. Since the camp regimes were less interested in stemming epidemics than in the relentless exploitation of their captives, measures to combat typhus were seldom enforced with any significant degree of commitment. This was, after all, a society in which tuberculosis was accepted as a normal part of camp life. It was usually only when SS or Gestapo members were affected that any real attempt was made to address typhus as a medical issue – and even then little or nothing was done to address the underlying causes of the epidemics.

The safest way to deal with typhus outbreaks would have involved the mass delousing of prisoners – disinfecting them, their clothes and their accommodation. This practical solution was well-established and well-known to the SS doctors, but the procedure took time, and it meant disruption of the prisoners' external work schedule. In the context of the camps, it was immaterial to the SS whether the inmates lived or died. The SS had no interest in curing their captives; their explicit policy was to reduce food rations for those who were infected, and to deny them any proper medical treatment. All that really mattered for the SS was that their production targets were met.

Against this background, it is hardly surprising that sporadic waves of typhus swept through Farge. It was later established that even the basic procedures of hygiene and disinfection – which were specified by the SS in their own guidelines - were not followed in the camp. 'There was a good few of us who got typhus', Harry Callan told me, 'I was lucky. I didn't. Billy English he got it, and he lived through it. A few others got it, and got through. But a lot of the ones who caught it died. They hadn't got the energy to fight the disease.' The first of the Irish seaman to succumb was Patrick Breen, from County Wexford. He had been on the *Athelfoam* in 1941, when she was sunk in the North Atlantic by the German battleship *Scharnhorst*. He was already 56 years old when his ship went down, and was 58 when he died on 13th May, 1943 – less than three months after he had arrived at Farge. It is not known what happened to his body, but it seems probable that he was buried in a mass grave outside the camp. Next to die was the radio officer from Ballina, County Mayo, Gerald O'Hara. He had been taken prisoner in 1941 by the surface raider, *Komet*, while serving on the *Devon*, off the Galapagos Islands in the eastern Pacific. He survived captivity in Farge for just over a year, and was aged 50, when he died on 15th March, 1944. He left a wife and two young sons at home in Ballina. According to Christopher Ryan, by the time of O'Hara's death, a pattern had been established: 'Just before they died, they were taken away by SS guards, and we never heard of them again'.

Two more Irish seamen died of typhus in the month after O'Hara. The first of these was Thomas Murphy, who had been rescued from the North Atlantic in 1942, when the *Earlston* – part of the doomed Convoy PQ17 – was en route to Soviet Russia. Murphy had been ill for most of his time in Farge. He left a wife in Dublin, and was 53 years old when he died on 27th April, 1944. On the same day, Owen Corr, from Rush in County Dublin, also died. Corr was serving on the

Silver Fir freighter in 1941 when his ship was attacked in the North Atlantic. He was taken prisoner at the same time and by the same ship as Patrick Breen. Corr had been sent to the secret Freisack camp – where the Germans tried to convince him to join in their plans to establish an 'Irish Brigade'. Corr had chosen, instead, to return to his shipmates in Milag Nord. Irish Military Intelligence had wrongly suspected him of Nazi sympathies, but he also died of typhus in the Farge camp. Corr was the youngest of the Irish seamen to die there: he was 29 years old at the time of his death.

The last of the Irish seamen to die was my cousin, William. There is some uncertainty about the immediate cause of his death: it has been attributed to dropsy, to cancer – and to inadequate medical treatment. One of the Irish seamen in Farge later gave a description of how William died: 'He had been ill for about three days, but the doctor said he had nothing to give him'. My cousin's condition worsened, and the doctor came around again. This time, he decided to operate on the sick man: 'We, that is the Irishmen in the hut, all told him that it would be better for him if he submitted to the operation. Knox was lying on a table. He appeared to be in great pain. There was no anaesthetic, so four of us held him down, one at each shoulder and one on each leg.' Dr. Heidbreder then cut into his stomach: 'He inserted a tube in his side, and drained some water from him. Knox gave a kind of jump when the tube was put into him.' The doctor placed some wadding over the wound to plug it, and William was put back in his bunk. 'The doctor came around two days later, and looked at him again, but did nothing. Knox died in the early hours of the following morning. He was groaning a lot, and was still in great pain. His body was kept in one of the other huts, and he was buried six or seven days later.'

William's ship had been sunk in 1940, off the Madagascan coast, by the surface raider, *Pinguin*. He was both the oldest of the remaining Irish prisoners, and the first of them to have been captured. William had spent almost five years in captivity, and was 59 years old when he died - on Tuesday, 2nd of March, 1945. On the same day, US Marines, from the 26th and 28th Divisions, stormed and cleared Hill 362 on Iwo Jima – a turning point in the battle for that Japanese island, and for the whole war in the Pacific. Meanwhile, General Slim had just launched his assault on the strategic town of Myingyan, in an offensive that would soon drive Japan's 33rd Army out of Burma.

In Europe, the end of hostilities was even closer: on the afternoon of the day that William died, hundreds of RAF bombers took part in a daylight raid on Cologne. The raid was reported to have been 'highly destructive', and, four days later, the city surrendered to American forces. On the Eastern front, the Red Army was sweeping through Pomerania, as it made its way towards the German naval base at Gotenhaven: the port which the *Pinguin* had left in June 1940 on its mission to destroy Allied shipping. But the war was not yet over for the Irish seamen in Bremen Farge, and a few weeks after William's death, they were moved again – for the last time.

10

ENDGAME

By the start of 1945, Allied armed forces had begun to overrun Nazi Germany. In January, they turned back the last major German offensive at the Battle of the Bulge. The broken remnants of the Wehrmacht and Waffen-SS divisions re-grouped to defend the east bank of the Rhine, but, by mid-March, the Western Allies had crossed the river at Remagen, and established a new bridgehead. Due to the catastrophic German losses on the Eastern front, Hitler could not reinforce his defences on the Rhine. The Allied front line now stretched from the Netherlands, across 450 miles to the Swiss border, and there were 90 well-armed and supplied Allied divisions poised to strike into the heart of Germany. It had become abundantly clear – even to the most devoted of Nazis – that the '1,000 year Reich' could only survive for a matter of weeks.

In Farge, the Irish seamen had little knowledge of what was happening beyond their camp. They had, after all, been starved of contact with the outside world for the previous two years. "We didn't know what was going on", Harry Callan told me, 'We had got no news or anything like that. We didn't know that the Allies were so close. They were nearly in Bremen by then.' At that time, the number of prisoners in the Neuengamme complex was around 50,000: 12,000 or so were in the main camp and about 38,000 prisoners in its satellites. In the previous year, more than 5,000, of those who are known by name, had died there – and, despite the Allied advance, the death rate was accelerating.

The Kriegsmarine's orders for Type XXI submarines had been formally placed in May, 1944. The first boats had been scheduled to be completed and delivered in October of that year. Delays in construction saw the estimated launch put back until April 1945 – but, on 10th of November, 1944, following a huge Allied air raid on Hamburg, Speer ordered that 'top priority' be given to the completion of the submarine structures. The work, he insisted, must be speeded up 'by any means'. The implications of this order were clear; the tightening of deadlines meant that the pace of work had to be quickened. This could only have fatal consequences for the slave workers on the construction sites – in the first three months of 1945, 6,000 more of them died.

The prisoners at the Neuengamme complex still remained under the administrative control of the SS, and, at the end of March 1945, the SS began to evacuate the satellite camps. Later, in a War Crimes trial, Heinrich Hoyer, the Gestapo's administrative official at Farge, couldn't recall 'who brought the order to evacuate'. However, he could remember that 'it was the day the documents were destroyed'. Before the camps were abandoned, a vast quantity of SS files were burned. It proved to be a wise move on the Nazis' part – since it helped to ensure that many of their number would escape any future retribution. There was, however, one other crucial issue to be addressed: what was to be done with the prisoners. More than 20,000 of those held in the Neuengamme complex were sent to Belsen, Sandbostel and Wobbelin – where many thousands of them would starve to death, die of disease, or be murdered in the last few weeks of the war. Before the Neuengamme camps were evacuated, some of the guards embarked on a final orgy of unrestrained savagery. More than 1,000 prisoners were taken from one of the sub-camps to a barn near Gardelegen, and burned alive by their captors.

In the same week, around 8,000 Jewish prisoners still held in the sub-camps were sent to Belsen for immediate extermination. A few days later – a few weeks before the war ended – the SS executed 58 men and 13 women in Neuengamme. The following week, more than 9,000 remaining prisoners were transported by train to the harbour at Lubeck, where they were loaded on to ships. The intention of the SS was to scuttle them with the prisoners still on board. However, in a ghastly twist, before they could do so, the boats were mistakenly bombed by the Allies. More than 6,500 prisoners were killed on that day.

Just before the Allied advance reached their camp at Farge, the Irish prisoners were summoned by a senior SS officer. According to Christopher Ryan, 'he told us that we were going back to our old POW camp at Milag Nord.' The next day the inmates formed lines, and were marched back to the Milag camp under armed escort. One of the SS guards later gave evidence that he had asked what he was to do with prisoners whose physical weakness, or ill health might prevent them from completing the march. 'Kill them', he was told.

When the Irishmen arrived back at Milag, the other prisoners were shocked by their condition. They had not seen the Irish seamen for several years, and the rumour had circulated that they had all volunteered to work for the Germans. The skeletal appearance of Christopher Ryan demonstrated how wrong the rumours had been. At this stage, Ryan was still in his early 20s. He was 5' 10' tall, and his normal weight was around 13 stone. When he arrived back in Milag Nord, he had survived typhus, but was suffering from TB in both his lungs, and weighed less than 8 stone. 'We had been delivered into the hands of the Gestapo', he commented later, 'in order to be re-educated in the 'work ethic'.' Instead, they had been subjected to a regime of lethal exploitation.

The Milag prisoners were stunned to learn that the Irish prisoners had received no Red Cross parcels for such a long period. According to W.A. Jones, an Australian seaman, anyone who was forced to survive on the 'scanty prison rations' that were on offer in the Milag camp had 'died like flies in the attempt.' In every respect, the regime in Milag was a good deal easier than that in Farge, and the Milag prisoners were shocked by the stories that the Irish seamen had to tell of their captivity. They told how they had witnessed prisoners being buried alive in latrine pits, and three young Polish POWs being strangled by camp guards just a few weeks previously – when an Irish seaman had been forced to make the noose that was used to kill them. In fact, death dominated the entire camp system in the final months of the war, and in most of the camps this was the deadliest period. They were now hopelessly overcrowded – illness and epidemics were rampant – with sick prisoners often shot, or left outside to die. Even though these were the last days of the Neuengamme camps, the nauseating work of death continued unabated to the end.

Terrible as the treatment of the Irish prisoners had been, even worse crimes were committed in other parts of the Neuengamme complex. The SS Doctor, Kurt Heissmeyer, who worked at the main camp, believed that injecting tuberculosis bacilli into living subjects could serve as a vaccine. He assumed that TB could be cured by artificially creating a second centre for infection in the body. Even before he began his experiments, that theory had been thoroughly disproved by previous research. Heissmeyer's first experiments at Neuengamme were conducted on groups of Soviet prisoners. Four weeks after they had been infected with a highly virulent strain of TB, each group of prisoners was hanged and prepared for medical section. By the end of 1944, it was clear to Heissmeyer that he had not produced a vaccine. In fact, as he later acknowledged, far from curing TB his inoculations had only made the illness worse – and, in some cases, had killed his subjects.

Although he knew that his experiments were worthless, Heissmeyer still persisted with them. The final phase of his research was with Jewish children. In his own words, Heissmeyer 'ordered' twenty children to be delivered to him. They came from Auschwitz, and were chosen by his friend and former colleague, Dr. Josef Mengele. He allegedly encouraged the children to volunteer by asking 'Who wants to go and see their mother?'

The 20 children selected by Dr. Mengele came from Poland, France, the Netherlands, Italy and Yugoslavia. On 26th November, 1944, these children, accompanied by four Polish female prisoners and guarded by an SS man, were locked into a separate carriage, which was then attached to a regular passenger train to Hamburg. The yellow stars of the children – which indicated that they were Jews - had been removed, and they were given chocolate and milk to keep them quiet on the journey to Neuengamme. All of the women prisoners who accompanied them were hanged upon arrival. One of them was pregnant and the overall *Kommandant* of the Neuengamme complex, SS *Obersturmbannführer* Max Pauly, asked that she be dissected after her execution: apparently, he was curious to see 'what pregnancy in a woman looked like.'

Over the next few months, the 20 Jewish children were injected with tuberculosis bacilli. When they became ill, Heissmeyer had their ancillary lymph nodes surgically removed for analysis. By April, it became obvious to Heissmeyer and his associates that they could not pursue their research for much longer – so it was decided to get rid of the evidence of their crimes. The children were driven to a disused primary school at Bullenhauser Damm, which had been used as one of Neuengamme's sub-camps, but had been abandoned. When they arrived there, the children were taken down into its basement. According to one of the SS doctors present, they went there 'completely unsuspecting.'

The children were undressed, injected with morphine, taken into an adjoining room one by one, and hanged from a steel hook set into the wall. Some of the children were as young as five years old, and so small that one SS guard had to use his own body weight to pull the nooses tight: literally hugging the children to death in a perversion of adult care. After they had been killed, the SS also hanged 24 Russian prisoners: they were led into a boiler room in groups of four, and hanged from the pipes. Finally, the SS executed four other prisoners: two orderlies from the Dutch Resistance and two doctors from the French, who had witnessed the experiments and the murders. All the bodies of those who were hanged that night were later burned, and their ashes scattered in open fields. The identities of the orderlies and doctors who were murdered in Bullenhusen Damm are known. The identities of 16 of the 20 children who were killed in the basement were discovered in the late 1970s. The identities of all of the 24 Russians who also died there remain unknown.

Heissmeyer managed to escape the Allied advance – and so did the SS *Obersturmführer*, Arnold Stippel, who had supervised the killing of the Jewish children. Stippel was later caught and imprisoned. He was found guilty of being an accessory to murder, but the German court ruled that he had not acted cruelly – as 'the children had not been harmed beyond the extinction of their lives.' Stippel was sentenced to six years of imprisonment. Since he had already served more than that time in custody, he was immediately released, and compensated with 125,000 Deutschmarks. When the war ended, Dr. Heissmeyer had simply returned to his home in what would become the German Democratic Republic. He established under his own name a moderately successful practice as a doctor. His fantasies of becoming a world famous expert in pulmonary illness were never realised. However, he did set up the only private TB clinic in East Germany – where, he later claimed, his patients had benefited from his experiments in Neuengamme. Heissmeyer was eventually arrested, and at his trial in Magdeburg in 1966, he admitted that he had never regarded 'the inmates of the concentration camp, nor the children, as complete human beings.'

At his trial, it also emerged that Heissmeyer lacked basic knowledge in the field of medicine in which he had claimed to specialise. Otto Prokop, a Professor in forensic medicine, testified to Heissmeyer's 'gross and total ignorance', and concluded that his 'experiments were useless for scientific research'. But there were other, more accomplished physicians and surgeons than Heissmeyer who also could not resist the temptation to experiment on live human subjects. Heissmeyer's superior at Neuengamme, Professor Karl Gebhardt, had his patients shot, and then ensured that their wounds became infected – so that he could investigate a cure for gangrene. Heissmeyer's colleague, Dr. Oberhauser, broke the thigh bones of women prisoners in Neuengamme's sub-camps with a ball hammer – so that she could explore a treatment for fractures. Another colleague, Dr. Stumpfegger, transplanted shoulder blades from live inmates to wounded SS personnel. After their bones had been removed, the inmates were murdered.

It also emerged at Heissmeyer's trial that each child he had experimented upon at Neuengamme had been assigned a guinea pig. The children and the rodents were identified by the same numbers, and whenever Heissmeyer came to test the children, he would inject the guinea pigs with the same infiltrates. By this stage, Heissmeyer knew that the human and animal experiments were equally pointless. He was asked at his trial why he had not, therefore, restricted his experiments to the guinea pigs. Heissmeyer replied: 'For me, there was no basic difference between Jews and guinea pigs.'

In fact, there was little difference between the fruitless and pseudo-scientific experiments that Hessmeyer conducted, and the equally absurd and spurious investigations that other sections of the SS carried out. *Reichsführer* Himmler sent numerous expeditions to remote locations to explore his idiotic racial theories and occult fantasies. Nazi researchers travelled to Tibet to look for traces of what Himmler imagined were proto-Aryans; they scoured Europe in pursuit of the Holy Grail; and they dug up medieval graves searching for the bones of King Heinrich I – 'Heinrich the Fowler' - for whom Heinrich Himmler nursed an infantile fixation. Sadly, there proved to be no shortage of well-qualified academics and researchers who were prepared to take seriously notions that were not even half-baked, and to follow them for years in what proved to be nothing but wild-goose chases. Perhaps they did so in order to advance their careers – perhaps, because they also wanted to believe. It may even have been fear that drove them – and Dr. Heissmeyer – to falsify, modify or obscure the results of their findings. Perhaps it is also in this context that the monstrous scale of the Valentin Bunker can best be understood.

For all its agonising labour, the terrible misery, and the human lives that it expended, the Valentin Bunker was still incomplete when the war ended, and no commissioned U-boats ever left its pens. It was attacked by an RAF squadron on 27th of March, 1945 – just over three weeks after my cousin died. There were 20 Avro Lancaster Bombers in the formation: seven of them carried a single, 6-ton, 'Tallboy' bomb; each of the other thirteen planes carried one 10-ton 'Grand Slam' bomb. Both of these were so-called 'earthquake' bombs that had been specially designed to penetrate German bunkers by the celebrated engineer, Barnes Wallis, of 'Dambusters' fame. None of the Tallboys inflicted any serious damage, but two of the Grand Slams managed to hit the Valentin roof at its weakest point – where the cement was only 15 feet thick - and brought down 1,000 tons of debris.

Even then, there was an attempt to continue work at the Bunker, and it was not until 9th of April that construction ceased, and the decision was finally taken to abandon the submarine pens. On 14th of April, the first satellite camp at Neuengamme was freed by the US 9th Army. When the main camp was liberated, a few days later, it was almost empty of prisoners - they had been moved to other concentration camps. Two weeks later, Bremen was captured by the British Army's XXX Corps, after an intense five-day battle.

There were inmates from 28 different nationalities in the complex of camps at Neuengamme. The Nazis' victims in these camps included French, Greek and Italian POWs, Jews, petty criminals, German communists, homosexuals, prostitutes, Gypsies and Jehovah's Witnesses. Many thousands of unknown Soviet and Polish prisoners also perished. Almost 43,000 of those who died in the Neuengamme camps have now been identified by name. Among them are five Irish seamen.

11

AFTERMATH

The camps at Marlag and Milag Nord were liberated on 2nd of May, 1945, by units of the British 11th Armoured Division. The Royal Navy POWs had all been moved from Marlag to other camps in the preceding weeks, but the merchant camp remained hugely over-crowded, and conditions had rapidly deteriorated. By the time of its liberation, some of the inmates were so ill that they died shortly before, or soon after, they were set free. The 27 Irish merchant seamen who were still alive were more fortunate. Within a fortnight, they were all on a ship on their way home to Ireland.

They were still in a sorry condition when they landed, all of them being under-nourished and badly emaciated. Many of them were also seriously ill and in some cases, it would be several years before they were able to recover and work again. Even the youngest seamen were severely affected. Christopher Ryan had nearly died from an outbreak of typhus a few months earlier, and he had also contracted TB. He would spend most of the next 8 years in hospitals in England, and Ireland. Harry Callan was also ill and was blind for six months after his release because of a vitamin deficiency. 'My health was rotten when we got back', he told me, 'It turned out that I had TB, but I didn't know it at the time. I went back to Derry, but I couldn't get the proper treatment there. I had to go up to Belfast to be X-rayed and get penicillin injections. It took me two years to get well.'

There were other shocks in store for the seamen. They soon learned that – unlike Royal Navy prisoners – they were deemed to have left their employment as soon as their ships had been captured or sunk. This meant that were not entitled to receive any back pay for the years they had spent in the Nazi camps. Some of them found other major difficulties in settling back into the Ireland they had left behind. In several important respects, Ireland proved to be a cold house for those who had survived the camps at Sandbostel, Milag Nord and Bremen Farge – and for other Irish soldiers returning from the war. Not only was there minimal recognition from the Irish authorities of the dreadful experiences that many of them had endured – but some who had returned now faced prosecution by the Irish State.

Almost one in eight soldiers had deserted from the regular Irish Army during the World War. In one month alone – August, 1941 - 450 serving members deserted. The Irish Government believed that a large majority of these deserters went on to join one of the Allied armed services. This practice became so widespread that Gardaí in plain clothes and Military Police began boarding trains heading northwards, in order to apprehend suspected deserters. By 1943, their rate of success at recapturing would-be deserters was so high that those wishing to join the Allied forces had to avoid the normal means of entry to Northern Ireland, and make their way across unguarded fields, and other clandestine routes. During the war, it had proved difficult for those soldiers who had deserted to come back to Ireland when they were on leave. If they were recognized, they were liable to be arrested, imprisoned and sentenced to hard labour. In the war's immediate aftermath, many more chose to return. It soon became clear that the Irish Government had decided to take a punitive and a legalistic response to their homecoming.

The first evidence of this involved two Private soldiers: Patrick Shannon and Patrick Kehoe. Both men had been liberated from German POW camps in May 1945, and had immediately travelled back to Ireland. Both were arrested shortly after they came ashore. Kehoe had been serving in the Irish Army's 22nd Infantry Battalion when he deserted. He had joined RAF Bomber Command, wanting 'to have a crack at Germany' because of the distress of his relatives in London during the Luftwaffe's Blitz. Kehoe had flown 22 missions over Germany before being shot down and taken prisoner. Shannon had been serving with the Irish Army's 2nd Infantry Battalion, and claimed that he had deserted primarily for economic reasons – since he could not support his widowed mother on his meagre pay. Shannon had fought in North Africa, Sicily and Italy, and had been captured by the Germans near Florence. He was an only child, and had been on compassionate leave from the British Army, visiting his terminally ill mother in Dundalk when he was arrested.

The two Privates were tried by an Army court martial, and were ably defended by Captain Peader Cowan. He quoted the normal definition of 'desertion' as 'leaving a post of danger for a post of safety', and argued that both men had done precisely the opposite. In his eloquent defence of the two Irish soldiers, Cowan echoed the themes of Pericles' famous oration for the Athenian dead in the Peloponnesian War. The freedom that is intrinsic to democracy, Pericles had argued, made the voluntary decision of Athens' citizens to risk their lives in war more principled that the choice forced upon the soldiers of a militaristic state. He was referring to Sparta, but his words could be applied with equal relevance to Nazi Germany.

Captain Cowan also quoted the Pope's description of Nazism as a 'satanic spectre', and stated his conviction that 'in any civilized country' it would be considered an honour to have taken part in the fight against fascism. Despite Cowan's eloquence, the court determined that both men should be formally dismissed from the Irish Army as deserters. They were stripped of pay and gratuity rights, and each was sentenced to 156 days of imprisonment.

That term of imprisonment was later commuted, since it had become clear that it would not be practical – for both financial and political reasons – to treat the thousands of other deserters in the same way as Kehoe and Shannon. The Irish Government decided, instead, to impose severe penalties through collective punishment. On 8th of August, 1945, Oscar Traynor, the Minister for Defence, introduced Order 362 under the terms of Ireland's Emergency Powers Act. In essence, this constituted a single trial and verdict for all those who were alleged to have deserted, and who were now to be judged, as Robert Widders has observed, 'en masse and in absentia.'

Oscar Traynor was unyielding in the words he used to describe the Irish Army deserters – informing the Dáil that such men were 'worthy of very little consideration.' It was, in some ways, a characteristically Irish solution to an Irish problem – its political pragmatism buried under layers of sanctimonious rhetoric. However, the penalties that were imposed on Army deserters were real, harsh and long-lasting: they were to forfeit all pay and allowances they had gained while in the defence forces; they were to lose their rights to any pensions earned through that service; they were to lose their entitlement to any future unemployment benefits; and, for seven years, they could not be considered for any form of employment that received public funding.

Given that the Irish State was, at that time, the largest employer in Ireland, it is not surprising that Order 362 soon became widely known as the 'Starvation Order'. Speaking in the Dáil, one Fine Gael Deputy, Thomas O'Higgins, characterized the Order as being 'stimulated by malice, (and) seething with hatred' – whose consequences would be to identify the Irish deserters 'as pariah dogs, as outcasts, as untouchables'.

A comprehensive list of alleged deserters was also drawn up, and circulated confidentially to every Government Department – as well as to all state run services, such as post offices, health services, and bus, rail and shipping companies. The Black List had been compiled with such urgency that it included some inexcusable errors. Joseph Mullally, for example, from Moate in County Meath, had deserted the Irish Army, and enlisted in the British. On June 6th, 1944, he had landed in Normandy with the Green Howards – a Yorkshire regiment – as part of the Allies' D-Day invasion force. Private Mullally was shot dead less than an hour after he had set foot on Gold beach, but, in August 1945, he was posthumously court-martialled, and placed on the Government's Black List – along with dozens of other Irishmen who had been killed on active service in the preceding years.

The Black List did not apply exclusively to Irish Army deserters who had joined the Allied armed forces. There were some deserters who had gone to the UK in order to work in Britain's factories. However, the large majority of those who deserted the Irish Army are believed to have become part of the Allied services, and they were the ones who suffered most from the effects of the Black List. Its underlying bias is apparent when one considers that even a leading IRA figure, such as James O'Donovan, was treated more leniently than these deserters.

O'Donovan later boasted that the IRA's 'S-Plan' – the bombing campaign in England, which killed innocent civilians in 1939 – had been entirely his own 'in conception and execution'. He had conspired with German Military Intelligence during the war, and he had been interned by the Irish Government because of his threat to State security. Nonetheless, he was allowed to resume working for the State-run Electricity Supply Board on his release from prison. There was no loss to his pension rights for the two years he had spent as an internee, and some years later he was even awarded compensation by the ESB for the time he had been imprisoned.

In contrast, the Government seemed determined to find new ways in which Irish Army deserters and their families could be punished. In 1941, the Irish Government had passed a Children's Act – which allowed the State to place a vulnerable child in a so-called 'Industrial School', if one of the parents were absent for a protracted period from the family home. This placed the children of deserters from the Irish Army at particular risk. Since their fathers were likely to be arrested if they set foot back in Ireland during the war years, many had not been able to come home on leave. This, in turn, allowed the State to claim that the children of Irish Army deserters had been abandoned by their fathers. The same Act allowed the Irish State to deny petitions from and on behalf of the absent parent. This seems to have been applied with particular vigour in the case of families where the father had deserted to join the British Army.

The Irish Government also secured the agreement of the British Government to have the payment of Family Allowances, to which Irish soldiers in the British Army were entitled, made directly to the Irish State. In effect, this money could then help to finance the incarceration of the soldiers' children in Industrial Schools – where they could be put to work making rosary beads or picking potatoes, without payment. In 2000, following sensational disclosures of rampant sexual and physical abuse by priests, nuns and other religious in these schools, the Irish Government established a Commission of Inquiry. The Commission issued its report in 2009: its conclusion was that such abuse had been 'systematic, pervasive, chronic, excessive, arbitrary (and) endemic.' The verdict of the Commission was that the children held in Irish Industrial Schools had been treated more like slave workers than individuals with legal rights and human potential.

All this begs the question of why Irish Army deserters were treated with such severity. It must, of course, be acknowledged that it is incumbent on any State to treat desertion from its national Army as a most serious offence. However, in this case, there were clearly extenuating circumstances and to condemn close to 5,000 people out-of-hand, without affording them due process of law, conflicts with basic notions of natural justice. It also contrasts with the more tolerant approach followed by some of the belligerent States.

The British Government, for example, was able to announce a general amnesty, within a few years of the war ending, for those in the Army, Royal Navy or RAF who had deserted between September 1939, and August 1945. It was reckoned that around 12,000 men – out of the four million or so who had served during the war – were directly affected by this decision. In order to avail of the amnesty, British deserters did not have to report in person, and those who were awaiting trial for desertion were immediately released from custody. The explicit purpose of the amnesty was identified by the British Government as the desire to 'restore men to family and community life'. Ireland had not been a belligerent power, but – even though any threat to her neutrality had long passed – there was much less acceptance of those who had deserted the Irish Army.

In Ireland, there were, of course, other factors to be considered. In particular, there was the tortured and ambivalent relationship that had existed between Ireland and her nearest neighbour, Great Britain, for several hundred years. Perhaps, the severity of the Irish reaction to its Army deserters can only be understood in the context of this complexity. Although a large measure of political independence had already been achieved when the war began – and Irish neutrality itself bore witness to that autonomy – there were still many in Ireland who retained some sense of attachment to Great Britain. These sentiments were not confined to 'unreconstructed' Protestants or to any others who could be glibly dismissed as 'West Brits'. As far as southern Irish Protestants are concerned, there seems negligible evidence to support the notion that they volunteered to join the British armed forces in numbers that were disproportionate to the overall size of their population. Indeed, Irish Military Intelligence would not have expressed concern about the presence of Protestants in Ireland's own defence forces, if they had not been seeking to join them. Of the 32 southern Irish seamen held in the Farge camp – it seems that only two came from a Protestant background; roughly the same ratio as in the Irish State as a whole.

Of course, that did not prevent some Nationalist ideologues from claiming that southern Protestants constituted some sort of subversive Fifth Column within Ireland. As late as August, 1944, the political journal, *The Leader*, was still urging the Government to take 'corrective action' to ensure that Protestants fully accepted the principle of Irish neutrality. The journal did not elaborate on what precisely the compulsory 'course of instruction' that it advocated would entail.

Irish involvement in the British armed services requires an explanation that avoids familiar stereotypes. Looking through the thousands of names listed in the Irish Government's Black List of deserters, there are precious few – if any – that appear to come from a professional, or affluent background. The overwhelming majority of those named come from Ireland's urban and rural working classes, and their occupations before they joined the Irish Army are typically given as 'farm labourers', 'boiler men', 'shop assistants', 'machinists', and 'messenger boys'.

Financial considerations were, no doubt, factors for some of those who joined the Allied forces, but they are most unlikely to have been the determining ones. Admittedly, the

British Army paid more than the Irish, and unemployment was a serious problem in Ireland. However, nobody ever got rich by serving as an infantry private or a naval rating, and there was a good deal more money to be made by working in the comparative safety of British armaments factories – which, like their German counterparts, were chronically short of labour. No doubt, some Irish Army deserters did work in such factories – but it is beyond doubt that several thousands of them joined the Allied forces.

Ironically, the two groups who tended to attribute purely mercenary motives to the southern Irish volunteers were at opposite ends of the political spectrum in Ireland: the staunchest Unionists in the North, and the most devout Nationalists in the South. For different reasons, both of these groups preferred to view the world through a black-and-white filter – and it suited both of them to simplify, or caricature, the continuing connection between Ireland and Britain.

The real complexity of that relationship often perplexed and frustrated those Germans who had assumed – and hoped – that they could count upon bitter animosity between the two nations. Officers of the Royal Irish Fusiliers recorded some of this confusion in their regimental accounts of the Italian campaign. In 1944, the Fusiliers had taken a number of German troops as prisoners. As Richard Doherty has noted, the Germans 'were bemused by the phenomenon of Irish soldiers fighting, as they saw it, for England.' They received little enlightenment when they asked those soldiers why they had chosen to fight on the side of the British. The answers they received were along the lines of: 'Sure, we took pity on them', or 'We wouldn't want to see them beat.' In general, the attitude of the Irish troops seemed to be that the English might well be bastards, but they were 'our' bastards: 'We don't like to see anyone else fighting them', one Irish soldier is said to have told the bewildered Germans.

Sympathy for the Allied cause did not make these men Unionists, or anything less than fully Irish in their identity. It simply meant that they had maintained certain links to Britain – through education, or through marriage, or through social ties, or through business and financial interests, or through general cultural sympathy that had been generated through centuries of close – often, too close – association.

Almost all of Ireland's export trade was still conducted with Britain, and most of her financial securities were vested in British banks. Irish emigrants to Britain – the tens of thousands of nurses, factory workers, skilled and unskilled labourers – may have been more interested in their jobs than political ideology. But they also constituted an important social – and economic – link between the two populations. On both the British home front and in military combat, the Irish played a significant and substantial role in the Allied war effort and this was reflected in the numerous distinctions and decorations that they received.

There were also some unexpected connections between the Irish Army deserters, and the merchant seamen who had been imprisoned in Farge. One of those was Peter Lydon, from Tralee, in county Kerry. Lydon's brother was Jack Lydon – a Free State soldier who had been killed in an IRA ambush during the Irish Civil War. Jack Lydon's son – also called Peter - had followed in his dead father's footsteps, and enlisted in the Irish Army. However, he had deserted soon after war was declared, and joined the British services. The elder Peter Lydon's ship was sunk in 1942, and he was sent to Milag Nord. Like the other Irish seamen, he had refused to work for Nazi Germany, and was then compelled to become a slave labourer in Bremen Farge. Like the others, Lydon had endured more than two years of unremitting hardship in Farge. Both Lydons returned to Ireland at the same time. However, within a few months of his return, the younger Peter's name had appeared on the Irish Government's Black List.

William Knott was also one of the Irish seamen sent to Farge. He had grown up in a small fisherman's cottage, and was part of a community that was once sizeable, but is now extinct; Dublin's Protestant working class. Knott came from Ringsend – in the heart of Dublin's docklands – which had a long-established reputation of producing merchant seamen. His father, George, was a postman and his mother, Mary Anne, gave birth to ten children – five of whom died in infancy. Knott went to sea when he was still a boy, and was a veteran by the time he was taken prisoner and sent to Farge. He weighed 12 stone when he went into that camp – and 6 stone when he came out.

Knott's youngest brother John had worked as an unskilled labourer, but joined the Irish Army shortly before war was declared. John became one of those who deserted during its course, and joined the Allied forces – and his name also featured on the Black List. When they returned to Ireland, the restrictions on employment usually meant that men like Peter Lydon and John Knott were left with only one option: to leave the country – and that is precisely what both of them did. It seems likely that a large majority of those Irishmen and women who joined the British armed forces did not return to live in Ireland after the war.

The material hardships faced by those who did return were real and damaging, but, in many respects, they were less serious that the psychological turmoil that many of these Irish citizens had undergone – whether in combat, or as prisoners, or both. Most of those who came back to Ireland from the war had been profoundly affected by the experience. The historian Richard Doherty has described one aspect of the type of change they had undergone. He has two photographs of an Irish soldier in his possession; 'One was taken in 1942, not long after he joined up, and it shows a fresh faced lad, little more than a boy: the second was taken in Italy in December 1944 but the man in it has changed by many more than the three years between the two pictures.'

While the war was still in progress, one psychologist has advised the Allied Governments that psychopathy was the predictable response of most healthy individuals to the experience of intense combat. I know the truth of that observation. After my father died, I found a small diary that he had kept on board the troop ship that had carried him and his brother officers on their journey to India, and into war. When I read the diary, I did not recognise the voice that spoke through its pages. My father wrote with tenderness and without constraint of his love for my mother, of his friendship with Pat Kelly, and of his hopes for the future. I could not easily connect the person who wrote so freely in that small diary with the dissociated emotions and the self-destructive impulses of the man I had known all my life.

While he was on active service, my father contracted ringworm, hookworm, dysentery, and two types of malaria. He was wounded by shrapnel from a Japanese mortar, and developed gangrene. He was imprisoned and tortured by the Japanese, and freed by the army of the Kuomintang. He was also shot twice – the second time, his injuries were so serious that he was officially listed as dead. My mother told me that for years after he returned home, he would shout and scream in his sleep: waking up in malarial delirium, terrorised by nightmares of what he had seen and done.

Men like my father needed guidance and support – but there was little help available in Ireland at that time. Instead, these veterans were ignored – or, in some cases, ostracized and punished. For many of those who came back to Ireland, there were long years in which they did not talk about the war. Harry Callan told me that he never spoke about his experiences in Farge: 'My wife and my own family – they never knew what I went through. As far as they were concerned, I was just a prisoner of war', he said, 'I don't know why I didn't tell them. I just didn't like to talk about it.' Then, in 2005 – 60 years after he was freed from the Farge camp - Harry was approached by a German academic: 'There was a lady professor from a German University who came over here. And I said that I'd see her. She said that she wanted to make a documentary. I said if it was for a University, I didn't mind doing it. That was the first time I had ever spoken about it.'

In a short story written in 1945, Samuel Beckett – who had worked for the French Resistance throughout most of its existence – explored the deep internal conflicts which even the process of remembering could entail. 'Memories are killing', he wrote, 'So you must not think of certain things'. At the same time, he recognized that, 'You must think of them, for if you don't, there is the danger of finding them in your mind, little by little'. Beckett concluded that it was necessary to face these disturbing memories 'for a while, a good while, every day, several times a day, until they sink forever in the mud.'

The reluctance to deal with such 'killing memories', that occurred during the world war was not, of course, confined to its Irish survivors. But, in the case of Ireland, there was an accepted narrative about the war that was used, in effect, to silence the voices and to exclude the experiences of many thousands of Irish citizens. In the case of Germany, the situation was clearly very different, but it might also be said to have involved the repression of a part of its recent history.

12

A STATE OF DENIAL

In 1946, the first of the trials for War Crimes committed in the Neuengamme complex of camps took place. Subsequently, eleven SS members were hanged – including several doctors who had participated in lethal medical experiments on their prisoners. The following year, twelve of the Farge personnel were also tried in Hamburg: five of them were charged with multiple murders. Although the crimes had been committed within the US Occupation Zone, the trial was held before a British military court. The court sat for thirty-seven days and heard harrowing evidence of relentless work, prisoners shot or beaten to death, and pitifully inadequate rations.

Four of the witnesses who travelled to Hamburg to give evidence to the military court were Irish seamen. The first to testify was the cadet officer from Waterford, Christopher Ryan, who identified himself to the court as 'a citizen of

Eire'. Apart from the Irish seamen, the only other witnesses who had been inmates of the camp were two German political prisoners. No Russians, Jews or Poles were able to give evidence – in the case of the Jews, this was because they were no longer alive – and, according to several of the witnesses, these ethnic groups had been treated the worst of all the Farge inmates. 'They were in a pitiable condition', Christopher Ryan testified, 'Lousy, starving and living in much worse huts [than us]. Some of them died every day.'

The absence of Russian and Polish prisoners was cited by Dr. Walter Heidbreder – the doctor who had attended the inmates of the camp – as a factor that would imbalance the court's proceedings to the accused's detriment. Dr. Heidbreder claimed that it was not possible to judge the conduct of staff in the prison by the testimony of the witnesses who had been heard – because their standards of correct behaviour were too high. 'They are Irishmen and political prisoners', he argued, 'The other prisoners were of a lower standard socially, and had different standards of cleanliness'. It later emerged that, when Dr. Heidbreder was treating prisoners from Russia or Poland, he was not prepared to touch them, and insisted that they did not come closer to him than 'two paces'.

In his evidence, Dr. Heidbreder admitted that he had made false statements on death certificates. When filling in the certificates of prisoners who had been shot, he had recorded that they had been killed while 'trying to escape'. In the case of prisoners who had been drowned or strangled by SS personnel, the Doctor admitted that he had recorded such deaths as 'accidental', or 'suicides'. Those who had died from malnutrition or exhaustion were reported as having suffered from 'circulation problems'. Dr. Heidbreder was not the only one to conceal the real cause of a prisoner's death. *Kommandant* Walhorn also admitted that he had attributed the death of one 'Dutch or Belgian' prisoner to syphilis, and it was later revealed that he had died from having his rectum kicked in. In his evidence, Walhorn claimed he had been relieved to discover that this murderous assault had been committed by the foreman of a civilian firm working on the Valentin Bunker – and not by any of his camp staff. However, he conceded that he had no idea whether or not that foreman had ever been punished.

Dr. Heidbreder denied that my cousin's death had anything to do with the operation he had performed. He claimed that the camp hospital was full, which was why he had operated in the Irish hut, on a table that had not been sterilised, and without any anaesthetic. He also claimed that he had not sent William to a hospital outside the camp because he thought it unlikely he would be treated there – and besides, he had imagined that my cousin would not want to be separated from his "Irish comrades". Dr. Heidbreder accepted that most prisoners in Farge were liable to die within three to four months of their arrival. He attributed this to the lack of food and to exhaustion – neither of which, he claimed, was his personal responsibility. He blamed the low standards of personal hygiene among the Russian prisoners for the outbreaks of typhus – but admitted that the prescribed disinfecting procedures had not been followed in the camp. Although the Doctor's contract with the Gestapo had specified that he was responsible for disinfecting the prisoners, he claimed that he was unaware of this stipulation – since 'delousing was not my province'.

One of those who gave evidence was William Knott, from Ringsend in Dublin. He told the court that the Irish prisoners had given Dr. Heidbreder the nick-name of 'Goat-skinner'. 'In Ireland', he explained, 'this is a term for the cheapest type of veterinary surgeon.' Two of the other Irish witnesses agreed with Knott's assessment of the doctor, but one gave evidence on his behalf. John Joseph Ryan from Waterford described Dr. Heidbreder as his friend, and said that he had always treated the Irish prisoners fairly and with sympathy. 'He regretted that so many men died', Ryan assured the court, 'and that he could not do more for them'. Ryan believed that Heidbreder could not be held responsible for the, 'constant beatings' that took place in the camp. Harry Callan was ill at the time of the trial, and did not give evidence, but he told me that also regarded Dr. Heidbreder as a fair-minded doctor, who had genuinely tried to help his patients.

The court was inhibited in its deliberations by the complete absence of any medical records from Farge. These had all been burned in the camp's final days – though Dr. Heidbreder claimed that this had been done 'against my will and without my knowledge.' The doctor also claimed never to have been a member of the Nazi Party, the SS, or the Gestapo. He testified that he had been 'conscripted' against his will by the Gestapo in Bremen, and that he would have left his post if it had been legally possible – but he had been restricted by the terms of his contract. He described his role in the camp as a 'thankless task', and believed that it was only 'because I tried to do what is right', that he found himself on trial.

It emerged, however, in the course of the proceedings that the Doctor had volunteered to work in the Farge camp, that he had been well-paid and that his contract with the Gestapo included a clause that allowed him to give one months' notice if he wanted to leave. When this was drawn to his attention, Dr. Heidbreder claimed that he had 'completely forgotten', about that clause. It also emerged that the doctor had joined the *Sturmabteilung* – the Nazis' original paramilitary wing – ten years previously.

There was credible evidence that Dr. Heidbreder had treated Russian prisoners in particular with consistent harshness. Willi Schramm was a member of the Social Democratic Party who had been sent to Farge in 1944, after the failed attempt on Hitler's life. He told the court that he had witnessed Heidbreder allowing Russian prisoners to die slowly of starvation. On one occasion, he claimed that he had drawn the doctor's attention to a Russian who had developed gangrenous sores. Schramm told the court that Heidbreder had refused him any treatment – saying that they had 'enough' Russians in the camp.

The Prosecution contended that Dr. Heidbreder was responsible for the 'deaths, undernourishment, killings, starvation, insufficiency of clothing and overwork', that occurred in Farge. All of this was, 'a matter of Gestapo policy' – which, it was claimed, had been implemented ruthlessly by the Doctor. Several letters were produced which Heidbreder had written, in which he sternly warned his colleagues against 'too soft' treatment of the prisoners because of the danger that might pose to camp discipline. Heidbreder assured the court that those remarks did not reflect his real opinions, and that he regretted his involvement in the Farge camp. If he were in the same situation again, the Doctor said, he would tell the Gestapo: 'Do with me what you like, but I will not work in such a camp.'

The military court also heard evidence from several senior Gestapo officers – some of whom were also highly-qualified lawyers – as well as from a number of SS guards, a member of the civilian police, and one *Kapo*. There were varying levels of skill and expertise with which these individuals defended themselves against the accusation of war crimes. However, their collective position was greatly aided by the fact that so much of the camp's documentation had been destroyed. The SS had kept detailed records of what had gone on in all of its camps and they were equally careful to ensure that no traces of their crimes would fall into Allied hands. After the main camp at Neuengamme had been evacuated, a last work detail of some 750 prisoners was kept behind for two weeks simply to clean up. The files for the whole Neuengamme complex were burned, and the flogging trestles, the gallows and other instruments of torture were systematically dismantled and destroyed.

Given the lack of documentary evidence, the defence offered by all the SS personnel on trial was fundamentally similar to that of Dr. Heidbreder: while they acknowledged that crimes had been committed, they argued that none of these were their personal responsibility. From the most senior Gestapo officer to the lowest ranking SS guard, they consigned the blame, in the words of the Prosecution, 'to people who are not before the court'. In particular, blame was attributed to two absent individuals: one of these was Dr. Erwin Dornte – Head of the Gestapo in Bremen until January, 1945 – the other was one of the camp *Kommandants*, Heinrich Schauwacker. The latter had only served in Farge for a few months, but his 'evil influence' was cited repeatedly to explain the criminal actions of those on trial.

Schauwacker and Dornte were unable to answer any of these charges against them – since they had managed to evade capture by the Allies – but they were both alleged to have exerted extraordinary power over their subordinates. One SS guard admitted that he had choked a prisoner to death by shoving a raw potato down his throat with a broom handle, but insisted that he had been ordered to do so by *Kommandant* Schauwacker, and was too afraid to disobey. Another SS guard told the court that one night, Schauwacker had entered his room, and ordered him to accompany his *Kommandant*. The guard was led to the administration block where two Polish prisoners were waiting for them. Then, the guard claimed, 'Schauwacker gave me the order to shoot the prisoners. I told him I had no weapon. He put his gun in my hand, and the firing started.' The guard maintained he did not know if he had hit either of the prisoners, but they both ended up dead, and, 'Schauwacker gave me the order to have the corpses carried away' - an order which, once again, he meekly obeyed.

Evidence was also given to the military court by Dr. Alfred Schweder. He was a senior Nazi lawyer who had been appointed to the Gestapo's Regional Office in Bremen to replace Dr. Dornte. Soon after his arrival, Schweder had been asked to investigate the camp at Farge – since reports of irregularities in the way it was being run by Schauwacker had filtered back to Gestapo Headquarters. Dr. Schweder told the court that the camp had been designed for *freie Arbeiter* from occupied territories – who had signed legal contracts with the Gestapo. They were not prisoners of war, he insisted, and therefore, were 'not within the protection of the Geneva Convention.' He claimed that they were workers who had broken their contracts with the Reich – by not working hard enough – and, therefore, deserved to be punished. Since the Soviet Union was not party to the Geneva Convention, he argued that Russian POWs could legitimately be used as part of the same work force. Schweder claimed that, since Poland no longer existed as a political entity, the Polish prisoners were stateless and could also not be protected by the Geneva protocols. As far as Jews were concerned, they had no civil rights under German law, and, therefore, Jewish prisoners could be treated without any legal obligations.

There was a certain twisted logic to this position, but Dr. Schweder found it harder to explain the presence of 32 Irish merchant seamen in the Farge camp. 'I do not know what they were doing at Bremen-Farge', he admitted, 'They should have been protected by the Geneva Convention. It was not my responsibility that they were sent there. It was by arrangement with the military – not the SS. I wanted to get them to an internment camp.' Schweder conceded that murder had been committed in the camp by SS personnel, but insisted that this had not been properly authorised. He blamed his predecessor, Dr. Dornte, for allowing such a brutal regime to develop. According to Schweder, Dornte had taken the *Führerprinzip* to extreme lengths, and nobody was prepared to contradict him or go against his orders. Schweder made it clear to the court that he was only personally responsible for Departments I and II of the Bremen Gestapo: any deaths that occurred in German concentration camps, he stated, were entirely 'a matter for Department IV.'

Dr. Walter Albath was another senior Gestapo officer, and a *Standartenführer* in the SS. He maintained that a 'labour correction camp', like the camp at Farge, was, strictly speaking, 'not a Gestapo organisation'. He told the court that it was 'an independent body, with a channel of communication through its camp *Kommandant* to the Chief of the Gestapo in Bremen'. Since the Gestapo was 'run on the lines that you must not bypass your superiors', he had been powerless to intervene in the harsh decisions that Dr. Dornte had made. Like Dr. Schweder, he disputed on legal grounds that the prisoners were really slaves. 'I know the expression 'forced labour', but these workers were not slaves', he explained to the court, 'They volunteered at

Labour Offices in the occupied territories because they found conditions in Germany better than in their own countries.'

Dr. Albath acknowledged that the workers had received no payment, but pointed out that 'accommodation and feeding was provided [free] for them'. Under cross-examination, however, he conceded that he now accepted that only a 'small proportion of foreign workers came to Germany voluntarily'. He also accepted that the, 'compulsion of workers', was illegal. He agreed that it was also illegal to use punishment cells in a labour camp and he admitted that he was aware that the practice of *Sonderbehandlung* - 'special treatment' – was applied to some prisoners in the camp. When asked what this, 'special treatment' involved, Dr. Albath answered: 'Shooting or hanging'. Dr. Arbath was not the only SS member to claim that he believed all the slaves in Farge had volunteered to work for Germany. 'It was only after capitulation', one of his colleagues told the court, 'that I learnt otherwise.' However, Albath never abandoned his central defence that it was the sole responsibility of Dr. Dornte to 'take further steps' if he suspected that anything illegal was taking place in the Farge camp.

Hans Albert Hasse had joined the Nazi Party in 1929, and the Gestapo in 1938. During the war, he became an SS *Sturmbannführer*, and served on the Eastern front from 1942-1944. He was attached to the Farge camp as its *Kriminalrat* – or Criminal Commissar. He was also the head of Department IV of the Bremen Gestapo – to which

Dr. Schweder had referred – and one of his functions in that role was to determine which prisoners, and how many of them should be sent to work in Farge. Like Dr. Schweder, he claimed that he 'never got to know what the Irishmen were there for'. He also claimed that he had no responsibility for them being 'forced to work', and that he 'could do nothing' to help them without direct orders from Dr. Dornte.

Like Dr. Schweder, he denied that it was the SS or the Gestapo who had brought the Irishmen to Farge, and claimed that even 'Dr. Dornte was not responsible for the Irishmen being sent there'. Hasse believed that there was concrete proof that the SS was not to blame for the Irish seamen's plight: he claimed that it was 'not possible that the SS could have been responsible for them being sent [to Farge] - because they had allowed the Irish Consul to visit them'. Hasse claimed that the SS would never have permitted such a visit if they had wanted to keep the Irish prisoners in the camp. Hasse also claimed that he had arranged the transport and accommodation of Con Cremin, and had accompanied him when he visited the Farge camp. He maintained that Dornte had told him 'that the Irish were neutral civilian internees, and therefore not liable to work.' Despite that, Hasse accepted that the Irish seamen had been compelled to join the labour force at Farge, but insisted this was not his responsibility: 'It was the camp *Kommandant*', he said, 'who ordered them to work'.

Some of the excuses offered by the accused camp personnel lacked basic credibility. *Kommandant* Walhorn agreed with the Prosecution that 'hot water is absolutely essential for hygiene', but argued that it did not follow that the 'lack of hot water will produce disease'. Friedrich Gärtner, a member of the *Schutzpolitzei* – the civilian police – was in charge of the issue of clothing within the camp. He admitted to beating prisoners with a stick or club but blamed the inmates for not doing more to avoid his physical assaults. He assured the court that they could easily have lessened the violence of his assaults 'by bending their bodies in the same direction as the blows'.

Other SS guards admitted to killing prisoners who were 'trying to escape', but insisted they had only intended to wound them. As the Prosecution pointed out, it seemed remarkable that all of those prisoners alleged to have been escaping from the camp had been shot dead, and not wounded. It also seemed strange that the bullets which killed them had all been fired from the front, and at close range.

Underlying much of the evidence given by the accused was a sense that they believed that they had no case to answer. For the SS *Strumbannführer*, Hans Hasse, it seemed entirely straightforward: 'With the possible exception of the Irishmen', he believed that the workers at Farge 'had agreed to work for Germany', and, therefore, 'Germany was entitled to deal with them' if they broke that agreement. The last *Kommandant* at Farge, Helmut Schrader, an *Obersturmführer* in the SS, even claimed that the soaring death rate in the camp was outside human control: he believed it could be explained by climatic factors, which were typical of the region. 'The weather was bad', he informed the court, 'Wet and cold. Nothing could be done about it. The condition of the civilian population was bad too.'

He admitted that the prisoners' mattresses were filthy and infested with lice – but that was simply because many of the prisoners were 'very dirty in their habits'. He had ordered the infested mattresses to be burned, but – through no fault of his own – could not obtain any new bedding. As a result, the prisoners were obliged to sleep on bare boards and tables. *Kommandant* Walhorn insisted that the Irish had been accepted into the camp without proper documentation – which was not his personal responsibility. He told the court that he 'fully accepted that they did not belong in a labour correction camp.' He claimed to have raised the issue with Dr. Dornte, but said that that he had been instructed to mind his own business. As an obedient German officer, he had, of course, accepted and followed that order.

One of the SS Guards was a Dutchman called Daniel Van der Veen. He had joined the SS in 1940, and had seen action on the Eastern Front in the *Standarte Westland* – a Waffen-SS division that was largely composed of volunteers from the Netherlands. Van der Veen had already been tried in Holland – and sentenced to 10 years – before he appeared in front of the military court in Hamburg. He disputed Christopher Ryan's description of him as a 'fanatical Nazi', and claimed to have become disillusioned with the ideals of National Socialism by the time he was sent to Farge.

However, the views that he expressed before the court seemed to suggest that his disillusion was still incomplete. 'Beating is not ill-treatment', he claimed, 'if is used for corrective purposes'. He also maintained that, left to their own devices, 'Russians and Poles just won't work'. They had grown up in countries where 'education is carried out by beating', he maintained, and that was all they could understand. Like the others, Van der Veen declared that he did not know why the Irishmen had been sent to the camp at Farge. He said that it was only after the war was over that he had been told it was because 'they had refused to join the German merchant marine'.

Half of those of those on trial in Hamburg were found guilty, but Dr. Heidbreder , Van der Veen, and Gartner were all acquitted. The only senior officers to receive custodial sentences were the former *Kommandant* of the camp, Karl Walhorn – who received 4 years for ill-treatment of his prisoners – and the camp's *Kriminalrat*, Hans Hasse, who received 5 years for a similar offence. One of Farge's *Kommandants* – Sebastian Schipper – had already been hanged by the British, but that was for crimes committed in another camp. The longest sentence handed out at this trial in Hamburg was to one of the SS guards, who had admitted killing prisoners who were not trying to escape and who was given 7 years.

All of the defendants were helped by the wholesale destruction of the camp's files, and by the lack of other corroborating evidence. One of the witnesses in another war crimes trial described some of the practical difficulties of camp inmates testifying against their former guards. Anita Wallfisch had been asked in cross-examination what day of the week certain murders had taken place and at what time;

'In the camp you had neither a watch nor a calendar, nor would you have been the slightest bit interested whether it was a Monday or a Tuesday', she wrote later, 'That you simply could not answer such a question was enough to make you feel you were not telling the truth'.

The Irish seamen were subject, at times, to similar difficulties, but their testimony to the military court was of critical importance. Gestapo officers had tried to cover their criminal activities with the shroud of legal authority. The presence of 32 Irish seamen in Farge – all of whom had refused to sign contracts with the SS – exposed the fraudulent nature of such claims. In fact, one of the most remarkable features of the trial in Hamburg was that all of the SS personnel who gave evidence – and who laid such emphasis upon the legality of the Farge camp – admitted that they had never read, or even set eyes on the contracts that were supposed to have established its legal basis.

Given that no Polish and Russian prisoners were able to attend and that the two German political prisoners who testified had only been in the camp for relatively short periods, the evidence provided by the Irishmen was of particular significance. The sentences that were passed on the SS personnel from the Farge camp may now seem unduly lenient, but, at the very least, they were made to answer for their crimes, and to pay some judicial penalty. The determination of the Irish seamen to go to Hamburg to bear witness to the crimes that were committed in Farge was not, however, matched by the actions, or attitudes of their Government at home in Ireland.

De Valera had visited Dr. Hempel, the German Minister in Dublin, following Hitler's suicide in order to express his condolences. Characteristically, he later sought to justify this visit in moral terms – and as evidence of his own integrity. He could, he suggested, have feigned a diplomatic illness in order to avoid the demands of protocol, but that would have constituted an 'unpardonable discourtesy'. The discourtesy – or gross insult – that his gesture offered to the countless victims of Hitler's racist aggression was, it would seem, of rather less importance. De Valera did not call to express similar condolences when Roosevelt died because the American MInister had indicated he was not welcome. Furthermore, by the time that de Valera called on Dr. Hempel, there was no longer any threat to Ireland from Germany. Other neutral countries – such as Sweden and Switzerland - did not even consider conveying similar messages of sympathy. Apart from Ireland, the only States that did so were the fascist dictatorships of Spain and Portugal. It is clear that de Valera respected, and, perhaps, felt a degree of affinity with Dr. Hempel – who was something of a pedant about diplomatic niceties – and that feeling appears to have been reciprocal.

Dr. Hempel remained in Ireland for some years after the war – and attempted, bizarrely, to open a confectionary shop. In those years, he remained in contact with de Valera – whom he encouraged to resist Allied demands for the handover of German agents. In a letter written to de Valera on 5th of October, 1946, Hempel also requested him to intervene on behalf of the senior Nazis sentenced to death at the Nuremberg trials. Dr. Hempel expressed concern at the impact that he believed these executions would have on public opinion in Germany, and he asked de Valera to take any 'appropriate measures' he could in order 'to avert disaster'. The Taoiseach was quick to respond to Hempel's request, and civil servants in the Department of External Affairs were instructed to prepare a position paper that condemned the trials at Nuremberg.

They did so with unusual alacrity: within three days, a draft paper issued by the Department characterised these trials as illegal and described them as 'an instrument of the victorious Allies established to punish individuals, [and] citizens of a defeated Axis state, Germany'. This document questioned the Allies' right to try military and political leaders for war crimes – since, it was claimed, there was no statute in law at the time those crimes were committed. A more detailed draft, issued a few days later, dismissed the whole concept of war crimes, and drew an explicit comparison between the Nuremberg trials, and Britain's historic use of the judicial system in Ireland to punish Irish Nationalists.

De Valera summoned the UK's senior representative in Ireland, Sir John Maffey, to inform him of his belief that the execution of any senior Nazis would be a 'tragic mistake'. He urged the UK Government to withdraw its support for the death sentences that had been imposed at Nuremberg. Given that de Valera had approved the execution of six IRA men in Ireland during the war for the crime of murder, it seems curious that he should be opposed in principle to the execution of Nazis for their crimes of mass-murder. The British Government responded in frosty tones to his request: assuring him that the sentences had only been passed after 'prolonged deliberation and [a] scrupulously careful trial'.

The defendants from the Farge camp were fortunate not to have been tried at Nuremberg – or immediately after the war, when sentences had tended to be a good deal more severe. Even by 1947, there was something of a reaction against the prosecution of war criminals. The great set-pieces at Nuremberg seemed to have sated the Allies' appetite for justice. There were other factors which may have led the Allies to side-line efforts to bring those involved in the Nazis use of slave labour to book. To help the recovery of the German economy after the war, it was tacitly agreed by the British and Americans that certain categories among the victims of Nazism would be excluded, in effect, from compensation by the new West German Government. Perhaps inevitably, those who were denied such compensation tended to be precisely those groups with the least amount of political leverage – such as the hapless victims of forced labour.

While the West German State was formally committed to the principle of *Vergangenheitsbewältigung* – the process of coming to terms with its past – all too often that seemed to involve an evasion of its most difficult features. Following the drawing down of what Churchill had termed 'an iron curtain' across Europe, Dr. Konrad Adenauer – as Chancellor of the German Federal Republic – had even demanded the 'pardoning of war criminals and the termination of the defaming of German soldiers', when he negotiated his country's contribution to the military defence of Western Europe.

As early as 1952, a member of the Federal German Parliament, Joachim von Merkatz, had proposed an amnesty for what he termed the 'so-called 'war criminals'' of Nazi Germany. Von Merkatz later became Minister of Justice in the West German State. Dr. Hans Globke served as Director of the Federal Chancellory of West Germany in the same Government as von Merkatz. In an earlier incarnation, Dr. Globke had helped to draft the legislation that had first given Hitler dictatorial power. It was also Dr. Globke who wrote the ordinance that compelled all Jews in Germany to adopt the first names of 'Sarah' or 'Israel'. Dr. Globke had drafted the *Gesetz zum Schutze des deutschen Blutes und der deutschen Ehre* - the law for the Protection of German Blood and German Honour – which prohibited marriage and extramarital sexual intercourse between Jews and so-called ethnic Germans. Dr. Globke had also served as chief legal advisor to the office of Jewish Affairs that was headed by the mass-murderer, Adolf Eichmann. In the 1950s, he had chosen to withhold the alias that Eichmann had used when escaping from Germany – so that his former boss could continue to evade arrest by the Israeli authorities.

When this personal history emerged in the 1950s, Globke was vigorously defended by other leading Ministers in the West German Government. They dismissed any criticism of their colleague's previous role in the Nazi regime as the product of 'Communist propaganda.'

In some respects, this episode is characteristic of the reluctance of important segments of post-war German society to come to terms with the legacy of their country's history. In fact, there was often fierce local resistance even to the presence of memorials that were intended to honour those who had suffered at the hands of the Nazis. Dachau was the first concentration camp to be established by Hitler's regime in Germany. It is reckoned that, by the time the war ended, around 35,000 prisoners had died there and in its sub-camps. The American troops that liberated Dachau had ordered the local authorities to erect a memorial to mark these deaths, but several years passed without any monument being erected, and it seemed that the proposal had been discreetly shelved.

In 1948, the Bavarian Federal parliament petitioned the US Military Government to transfer the camp back to the local authorities, so that it could be used 'for the re-education of the work-shy element' – its original purpose when it was first established by the Nazis. In 1950, a small exhibition was opened in the crematorium at Dachau to commemorate its thousands of victims. However, in 1953, the Bavarian Ministry of Finance had the exhibition removed – in response to public hostility to the commemoration. In 1955, the Dachau county Governor introduced a Bill into the State parliament to have the crematorium itself torn down. After widespread protests from the camp's survivors, an international competition to design of a new memorial in the camp was held in 1958: it took a further ten years for this to be completed.

The history of memorials for the camps at Neuengamme provides further evidence of the reluctance of both local communities in Germany, and their elected representatives to confront the recent past. In 1953, pressure from French survivors of the Neuengamme camps, supported by British Occupation officials, compelled the city of Hamburg to dedicate their first memorial. It was a 7 metre high metal cylinder which carried the barest of inscriptions: 'To the Victims 1939-1945.' For obvious reasons, this did not satisfy the camp survivors – who formed an International Association in 1958. They proposed a more elaborate and – in their eyes – a much more appropriate memorial. Once again, the Hamburg authorities attempted to pre-empt their plan: a new rectangular stone was erected, along with another brief inscription. On this occasion, the number of those who had died in the Neuengamme camps was inscribed on the memorial as 5,500 and not 55,000 –as it should have been. The sheer carelessness of this error indicates a degree of callous indifference, or perhaps – as Harold Marcuse has suggested – it merely demonstrates the 'level of misconception about how bad conditions in the Nazi camps had been.' After a good deal more lobbying, the Hamburg authorities finally agreed to add a small 'document house' in 1981. In 1995, this was turned into a 'House of Commemoration', hung with banners which listed the names of Neuengamme's victims.

The impulse to self-delusion about their complicity in Nazi crimes seems to have extended to every level of German society. In the mid-1980s, the Mercedez-Benz company commissioned a number of professional historians to conduct a survey which they believed confidently would prove that their company had been coerced by the Nazis into using concentration camp prisoners as part of their work force. However – and to the credit of those historians – the findings of their research disappointed their employers. The historians found that private companies, including Mercedez Benz, had colluded enthusiastically in the exploitation of such labour.

It was simply not the case that the Nazi party – or even the SS - held absolute power and that private industry could do nothing to oppose their plans. Until the end of 1941, sub-camps had not been set up outside production plants, or construction sites. But that changed radically in the course of 1942 and 1943. From then on, the growing demand for slave labour came primarily from private companies, and the role of the SS was largely limited to deciding whether prisoners should or should not be assigned to them.

In the case of the Valentin Bunker, the SS lent their captives to private companies in exchange for a 'prisoner's fee'. That fee was discounted in the minority of cases where the company was owned by the SS. Needless to say, the prisoners did not receive a red cent of this money. The costs charged by the SS included the feeding, clothing, accommodation and guarding of their captives – which, not surprisingly, combined to account for the entire amount paid in fees. However, the private firms were held liable for the cost of other 'additional' expenses – such as transport, or any medical expenses the prisoners might incur. In other words, a considerable share of the responsibility for the conditions of the camp inmates was borne by private companies, and it was those companies that often determined the living and working conditions of the slave workers – which means that they played a central role in helping to determine the chances of anyone surviving.

The private companies paid a flat daily rate for the prisoners' services – regardless of the lengths of their shifts – and for the camp prisoners that could have fatal consequences. As Jens-Christan Wagner has pointed out, the productivity of the weak and under-nourished captives was usually significantly lower than that of healthier civilian workers. Indeed, according to statistics produced in September 1944 by the building group Gebhardt and Konig, prisoner labour only became more lucrative than the employment of free workers if the inmates produced more than 50% of the regular output. Only by extending their working hours could the use of slave labour become profitable for the private firms. For that reason, most private companies did their utmost to increase the prisoners' working hours – often to the point of death.

In the years that followed the war, many German companies who had relied upon the use of slave workers showed themselves to be extremely reluctant – to say the least – to acknowledge their exploitation of such labour, or to pay compensation to those from whose slavery they had profited. Benjamin Ferencz has provided one telling illustration of their attempt to obstruct proper restitution for the victims of the Nazis' foreign labour policy. In

September 1944, two civilians arrived for the morning roll call at the camp at Auschwitz. They demanded that all metal workers step forward. One of those who did so was a young German Jew called Adolf Diament. He – along with hundreds of other workers – was sent to the main camp at Neuengamme, and assigned to work in the manufacture of army trucks for the Büssing company. Diament was liberated in April, 1945. Twelve years later, he wrote to his former employers – seeking payment for the work he had done for their company.

Büssing replied with the standard letter that they had dispatched as a matter of routine to all those who had looked for similar payment. In the letter, the firm expressed some sympathy for Diament's situation, but claimed that they had already paid the SS in full for his services. Diament was also warned that, if he decided to sue Büssing, he ran the risk of paying a very heavy price – since the company would seek to recoup their full legal costs from him.

They had misjudged their man. Diament was undeterred by their threats, and proceeded with his action against the company. In response, Büssing became more aggressive. The firm's lawyers questioned Diament's true identity. They claimed to have no records of anyone called Diament who had ever worked for them. They suggested that he was really a communist agitator, planted by the East German *Stasi*. They even cited a Nazi law to argue that, since Diament now held Israeli citizenship, he should not be treated in the same way by a German court as a German citizen.

Diament persisted with his case, and it eventually came to a hearing. In court, it was revealed that Büssing had in its possession a complete list of all those slave labourers who had worked for their company, and knew that Diament's name was on the list. The payment that the company had made to the SS was also found to be null and void – since the court ruled that no-one had the right to sell the labour of someone who had been deprived of his freedom. The court, therefore, found in Diament's favour, and he was awarded compensation. However, this was calculated on the basis of the money that Büssing had originally paid the SS for his labour. Diament may have won the case, but he came away with an award of just $44.45.

Büssing is now part of the Volkswagen Group – the largest auto-manufacturer in Europe. The Volkswagen brand was established in 1937 by the *Deutsche Arbeitsfront* - the Nazi trades' union. For decades, Volkswagen denied ever having used forced labour. Then, in 1998, the company was compelled by a court order to admit that more than 80% of its work force during World War Two had consisted of slave labourers. Volkswagen set up a voluntary restitution fund, but, in the course of the following year, the German Government agreed upon its own scheme for compensation. In 1999, the Forced Labour Compensation Programme was established – with Volkswagen as one of its leading contributors. By then, less than 2 million out of more than 10 million slave workers employed by the Nazis were still living. In fact, it was not until 2004 – fifty-nine years after his liberation - that the only Irish survivor of the Farge camp who was still alive received any money from this fund.

There may be a perception that the SS personnel who worked in the Nazis' concentration and slave labour camps were, more or less, a collection of psychopaths and misfits: representing, in short, the scum of German society. That perception is far from the truth. The historian Karin Orth has demonstrated that even the majority of camp guards did not come from the fringes of society. In fact, most SS officers were recruited from middle ranking managers and civil servants. There has also been a belief that there was a world of difference between the SS camp personnel and those who fought in more conventional military units of the Waffen-SS. In reality, the combat units of the SS, which had been deployed alongside the Wehrmacht, were combined in 1940 under the generic name of Waffen-SS. This process integrated the *Totenkopf* camp guard division – so that all SS guards were also part of the Waffen-SS. That connection was reinforced through the regular rotation of SS personnel between the *Totenkopf* and military units. This meant that, by the time the war ended, more than 60,000 members of the SS had served in the camps.

The Valentin Bunker was constructed under the aegis of the *Verwaltung und Wirstschaft Hauptamt* – the Administration and Business Main Office – which had been established, in April of 1940, to determine all industrial policy, and to run the various businesses owned by the SS. The new Office had recruited young, and professional managers to run these concerns, and they combined modern management techniques, with the pitiless exploitation of the enormous pool of slave labour that was available to them. These new managers were typical of a new wave of recruits to the SS, and this new generation of leaders came from the upper echelons of German society. One study of 221 individuals holding senior positions in the *Veraltung und Wirtschaft Hauptamt* has revealed that two thirds of them had been awarded university degrees, and 50% of those graduates also held doctorates.

As Adrian Weale has observed, such men actively wanted to work, 'in an organisation that was in the ideological vanguard of National Socialism because they were firmly committed to that ideology.' The popular stereotypes of SS personnel may be of brutes or bureaucrats, but, as Weale has pointed out, the reality is that many of its officers were, 'highly educated, creative, technically accomplished members of Germany's intellectual elite.' These doctors, lawyers, architects, engineers and academics were the men who staffed the SS as it expanded throughout the 1930s.

Such SS men were highly ambitious for their organisation, and constantly tried to extend and develop its areas of operation. Over the years, the commercial activities of the SS came to include a bewildering range of ventures: including the management of forests; the running of fish-processing plants and bakeries; the production of organic and herbal medicines, ceremonial sword-making; and the design and manufacture of so-called 'Germanic' furniture. The SS even marketed its own mineral health drink – with the unimaginative brand name of '*Trink-O*'.

When the time came for the cadres, who ran these and other enterprises, to adapt industrial production to the business of genocide and mass murder, they remained, in the words of Adrien Weale, 'unflinching in their dedication both to both the party leadership and the project itself'. These privileged children of Nazi Germany were quite prepared to track down, with remorseless commitment, all those of an undesirable ethnicity, race, religion, politics or sexual orientation. They joined enthusiastically in a political system that accounted such people as deviant, and liable, as such, to the most severe of punishments. Some of the SS cadres who committed such horrendous crimes were punished in the aftermath of the war: the vast majority were not.

Between 1939 and 1945, more than 4,500 SS personnel served in the Neuengamme complex. Over the same period, more than 55,000 prisoners died there. The total number of SS personnel from Neuengamme who were convicted of war crimes was less than 100: in other words, more than 97% of the SS personnel who served in Neuengamme escaped any penalties. What is more, in 1951, the West German Government determined that all SS personnel who had served in concentration or labour camps could claim full pension rights for the time they had spent in them: an opportunity that Frau Schauwacker – the alleged widow of the *Kommandant* at Farge – was quick to exploit. SS personnel were also deemed to be eligible to seek compensation for any time when they had been detained as prisoners of the Allies. This generosity contrasts with the difficulties and obstruction that Adolf Diament was made to encounter when he sought payment from the Büssing Company, and with the meagre compensation that he – and others – finally received.

It is, of course, quite understandable that many Germans found it extremely difficult to face the implications of their recent past. Millions of German lives had been lost in the war, their cities had been ravaged, their armies had been crushed in the field, and their country had been occupied and divided by its enemies. What is more, the Nazi cause for which so much blood had been shed was thoroughly disgraced and discredited. Hitler's delusions – of building a Reich that would last for a millennium – now stood exposed and pitiful.

Against this background, it is hardly surprising that the early attempts to effect *Vergangenheitsbewaltigung* met with a good deal of popular resistance. Even in academic terms, there was virtually no research for several decades into the operation of Nazi concentration camps, labour camps, prisoner of war camps and other detention centres run by the police and judiciary. It was only when a new generation of historians began to emerge in the 1980s that a more systematic and analytical approach was taken to the role of these camps in the Nazi regime. The initial focus tended to fall on the most extreme forms of Nazi depravity: the death camps, such as Auschwitz and Treblinka. In more recent years, critical attention has widened to include the labour camps and sub-camps – including those found in the Neuengamme complex.

In order to progress beyond the traumatic experience of Nazism, it was necessary for German society to seek to understand it. A somewhat similar – though much less critical – need may still exist in Ireland. Popular understanding of the war – and its impact on Irish society - has been inhibited by years of neglect, denial and repression. Ironically, in the years that followed the Second World War, most European nations tended to exaggerate the extent of their contribution to the struggle against fascism. In this respect, Ireland is exceptional. Successive Irish Governments tried to minimise the role that Irish citizens had played in that epic conflict.

Not only did tens of thousands of Irish men and women fight against fascism – but they had all volunteered to do so. That might have been treated as a cause for pride and celebration. Instead, the Irish volunteers were marginalized – with almost 90% of them choosing to leave, or not to return to Ireland in the post-war years. The policy of neutrality was allowed to assume an explicit and unjustified moral dimension. Indeed, it has sometimes been treated as if it were an article of faith in the Irish Republic. Of course, such widely-held ideological beliefs are seldom produced by any one individual. However, in the case of Ireland, a central role in the formation of this historical narrative was undoubtedly played by the man who was Taoiseach throughout all of the war years, Eamon de Valera.

13

A STATE OF NEUTRALITY

In appearance and manner, Eamon de Valera gave the impression of being a rather austere, and aloof individual. It may seem unlikely that such a person could lead – for so long, and so effectively – a party such as Fianna Fáil, that was based upon its catch-all populist appeal, and which became a by-word in Ireland for what might loosely be described as political pragmatism. On the other hand, the sense of a somewhat forbidding distance that characterised much of de Valera's public life also imbued him with a certain gravitas and an air of moral authority. He tended to stamp even the most mundane of his political utterances with the sense that they had been inspired by high-minded ideals. De Valera was a source of some fascination for my father – who detested and respected him in roughly equal measure. I think he considered him to be a sort of Irish Robespierre;

burdened with a fanatic heart, but also incorruptible. Perhaps, my father was right - and wrong – on both counts.

De Valera may have conveyed a slightly other-worldly quality, but he was also an extremely shrewd and skilful political operator. David Gray, the US Minister in Dublin during the war was – to put it mildly – no friend to de Valera and strongly opposed his policy of neutrality, but he still regarded him as 'probably the most adroit politician in Europe'. Gray also believed that 'no-one can outwit, frighten or blandish him. He is not pro-German nor anti-British, but only pro-de Valera.' Gray concluded that de Valera presented the Allies with stark alternatives; 'He will do business on his own terms, or must be overcome by force.'

De Valera had indicated Ireland's future neutrality in the years leading up to the outbreak of hostilities. He had expressed a degree of sympathy with all of the major belligerents. In the 1930s, he was critical of the reparations that Germany was compelled to pay by the terms of the Treaty of Versailles – comparing them to Ireland's annuity payments to Britain that had been agreed in the Anglo-Irish Treaty. He also found examples in Germany's position that could be used to stress the evils of Partition in Ireland: in Robert Fisk's words, 'the German speakers of the Sudetanland were metamorphosed by de Valera into the Catholics of Northern Ireland.'

By 1939, Fianna Fáil had been in power for the previous six years, but was still in the final throes of shedding its role as, in the words of one future Taoiseach, a 'slightly constitutional party'. The IRA was an illegal organisation, but many of the Irish Cabinet had personal acquaintance with its leaders. Seán Russell, the IRA's Chief-of-Staff, had fought alongside Frank Aiken, the Minister for Co-ordination of Defensive Measures, during Ireland's Civil War. He had met de Valera in 1935 to discuss the possibility of 'co-operation' between the IRA and Fianna Fáil in relation to Northern Ireland. Joseph McGarrity, the chief fund-raiser for the IRA in the USA, had also been a former associate of de Valera, while James O'Donovan – who acted as a key link between the IRA and the *Abwehr* – had been under Frank Aiken's command during the Civil War.

The apparent closeness of these relationships may have led the German Intelligence services to overestimate what they thought the IRA and the Irish Government held in common. In 1939, Dr. Ernst Woermann, the Director of the Political Department in the German Foreign Ministry, sent a confidential memorandum to his Minister, von Ribbentrop, in which he outlined his understanding of the differences between the IRA and the Irish Government. According to Woermann, such differences were essentially tactical. 'The difference between the Government and the IRA lies mainly in the method', he wrote, "The Government hopes to attain its objectives by legal political means, while the IRA tries to achieve success by terrorist means.'

Woermann concluded with the observation that 'most of the members of the present Irish Government formerly belonged also to the IRA'. The superficial nature of such an analysis was not confined to Germany's Foreign Ministry; it may also help to explain the fundamental ineptitude of the *Abwehr's* operations in Ireland. In the early years of his Fianna Fáil Government, De Valera may have made some conciliatory gestures to the IRA, but his underlying commitment had been to democratic politics.

Dr. Hempel, the German Minister in Dublin, was made forcefully aware of the strength of that commitment at a meeting with Joseph Walshe, the Secretary of the Department of External Affairs, on 18th of July, 1940. Hempel had complained to Walshe that 'a certain number of people who were 'known to be friendly to Germany' had recently been imprisoned by the Irish Government. He was referring to IRA members, and Walshe's response was clear and unambiguous. Hempel was informed that the people he had referred to were not in prison because they were friends of Germany, but because they had been 'plotting to overthrow the existing State set up by the majority of the Irish people.' Walshe assured him that 'in putting these men in prison' the Irish Government was 'only carrying out its primary duty of defending the State', which he added, was 'the only bulwark between the people and chaos'.

Hempel took Walshe's words to heart, and later he was taken aback at the low quality of the *Abwehr's* intelligence and the utter incompetence of most of its agents – the majority of whom were apprehended by the Irish police within a few days of arriving in Ireland. Hermann Görtz – who had, at least, some personal experience of Ireland, and had been advised by Seán Russell and Francis Stuart – also lost his faith in the IRA's ability to act on Germany's behalf. By 1939, the connections between the Irish Government and the IRA were largely historical. When it came to the crunch, de Valera and his Cabinet colleagues had no difficulty in exercising their lawful authority - with devastating consequences for the IRA. There may well have been contradictions in the Irish Government's security policy, but de Valera and his Cabinet colleagues handled any such conflicts with great dexterity.

The Government made sure, for example, that the Irish public was aware of its strenuous opposition to the introduction of conscription in Northern Ireland. De Valera was also seen to protest at the stationing of US troops in the North. The Irish Government's opposition to the internment and imprisonment of Republicans in Northern Ireland was widely publicized. In fact, de Valera objected to any repressive measures introduced north of the border – including the execution of Tom Williams, an IRA man who had been sentenced to death for his role in the killing of a northern policeman.

While the Irish Government allowed campaigns for Williams' reprieve to receive considerable press exposure, there was no comparable publicity permitted for similar campaigns in the South. Williams was the only IRA member to be executed in Northern Ireland in the history of that State. In the course of the war, the Dublin Government not only interned without trial around 1,000 Republicans, it also sanctioned the execution of six IRA men, and was prepared to allow three more to die on hunger strikes.

Due to the extensive use of official censorship, the effects of these measures were largely concealed from the Irish public.

In other words, the Irish Government promoted a high level of public awareness of the oppression of the Catholic minority in Northern Ireland, and the continuing 'Evil of Partition.' At the same time, the existence of repressive legislation in the southern State was effectively obscured, and the closeness of Irish links with Britain – in terms of commercial trade and military intelligence – were also hidden. The extent of the Irish Government's concerns about Northern Ireland were therefore exaggerated – while the real connections between Ireland and Britain were minimized. The overall effect was to vindicate the policy of neutrality – by suggesting that it was driven by principled objections to British repression in Ireland.

The reality was somewhat different. General Dan McKenna, the Chief-of-Staff of the Irish Army, was of the opinion that only British help could defeat a German landing in Ireland, and de Valera had issued a press release early in 1939, in which he had unambiguously acknowledged that reality: 'Should attack come from a power other than Great Britain', he had stated, 'Great Britain (…) must help us repel it.'

In May, 1940, the Irish Department of External Affairs and Irish Army Intelligence, had entered direct discussions with British officials about military co-operation in the event of a German invasion of Ireland. The Germans did develop plans for just such an operation – although it transpired that these were based on inflated and unrealistic estimates of the IRA's military potential. De Valera also gave his personal support to the Irish Army's Intelligence section in its measures against German spies and against the *Abwehr's* attempts to mobilise the IRA on the side of Germany. Captured RAF aircrews were tacitly allowed by de Valera's Government to cross the border into Northern Ireland – while Luftwaffe prisoners were not allowed the same leeway.

As the war progressed, the issue of Partition became a growing factor in the rationale for Irish neutrality. In its early years, that policy had clearly been determined by the most immediate and practical of concerns. These were spelled out by de Valera on the day that war was declared: 'It is only natural,' he told the Dáil, 'that our people should look at their own country first, and should consider (…) what its interests are.' In other words, de Valera was acknowledging that Irish policy would be determined by precisely the same material criteria as those of the belligerent States.

Over the next few years, there were various attempts by the British to suggest that the abandonment of Irish neutrality could lead to the ending of Partition. For understandable reasons, the Irish Government were sceptical of such suggestions: they could, perhaps, remember that somewhat similar undertakings had been given to John Redmond – leader of the Irish Parliamentary Party at Westminster – during the First World War, and these had not been honoured by the British once that war was over. Nonetheless, it is quite clear that the preservation of neutrality – in the twenty-six counties of Eire - was treated as a more urgent priority by the Irish Government than the possibility of the territorial unity of the island.

As the balance of the conflict shifted – the USA had entered the war, and the likelihood of being invaded by either Britain or Germany gradually diminished – the reasons for Irish neutrality began to find an even sharper focus on Ireland's continuing Partition. This shift in emphasis might be said to have reached its defining moment in a key radio address given by de Valera, soon after the war in Europe had ended. His speech was in response to one that had been made by the British Prime Minister, Winston Churchill to mark VE Day. In this broadcast, Churchill had accused the Irish Government of having 'frolicked' with the Axis powers, and praised Britain for having resisted the temptation to invade the southern Irish State – which, Churchill claimed, would have been both an 'easy', and a 'natural' course of action. Although Churchill also praised the individual contributions of many Irish men and women to the Allied cause, his words seemed to express an attitude of swaggering condescension, and they generated a good deal of resentment in Ireland.

De Valera's response – delivered with his usual air of careful deliberation – was widely considered to have combined dignity and restraint in what was, nonetheless, an emphatic rebuke to the British leader. In this speech, de Valera identified Partition as the fundamental reason for Irish neutrality. He conjured up an elaborate – if somewhat far-fetched scenario – in which England had been conquered, occupied and partitioned by Germany, and wondered aloud how Churchill would react in that situation. This focus on the iniquity of Partition not only represented a significant change in argument, it also implied that Irish neutrality had been determined all along by underlying moral principles, rather than by the mundane considerations of *realpolitik*. De Valera ended his broadcast on a note of unabashed defiance: describing Ireland as, 'a small nation that could never be got to accept defeat and has never surrendered her soul'.

The impact of his words was immediate and profound. When he left the Radio Éireann studio in O'Connell Street, crowds had already gathered to cheer him. He was received with enthusiastic acclaim from all Parties – including those with whom he had fought a civil war – when he entered the Dáil the next day, and his secretary recorded that his office was inundated with telegrams and letters of support for many weeks to come.

It could be argued that the groundwork for this change had been laid over a period of years. In another famous broadcast by de Valera – this one delivered on St. Patrick's Day, 1943 – he had outlined his vision of Ireland in the future. It was an pastoral vision with a distinctly Irish colouration; a land where the people lived frugally, but in the way that God had intended – or, at least, as de Valera was certain He intended – with cosy homesteads, athletic youths and comely maidens. This view of Ireland's future was subjected to sustained ridicule in the boom years of Ireland's Tiger economy. But in the Ireland of the 1940s, strict Catholic sexual morality and an idealized notion of the Catholic family were seen as the front line in a looming confrontation with the secular materialism of the UK and the USA.

De Valera was not a pacifist – as his personal history demonstrates – and it had always been the intention of his Government to defend Ireland's neutrality by force of arms, should that prove necessary. However, as fears of an invasion of Ireland lessened, the distinction between neutrality and pacifism seemed to grow somewhat hazy. Official censorship had been lifted on 11th of May, 1945. This finally allowed the real horrors of the Nazis' concentration camps to be reported through the Irish media, but the reactions they produced in Ireland were rather confused. Perhaps, the monumental scale and loathsome character of Nazi atrocities made them seem incomprehensible to the Irish public. As Conor Cruise O'Brien observed, 'The idea that Nazism differed from all previously known imperialisms as AIDs differs from the common cold was quite a new idea, and unassimilable in our culture.'

This may help to explain why the fate of 32 Irish merchant seamen who had been imprisoned illegally and subjected to great brutality for over two years in a Nazi labour camp, attracted so little press attention and was forgotten so quickly after their return. Even when uncensored newsreels that contained shocking footage shot in Nazi death camps were screened in Irish cinemas, the response of Irish reviewers remained decidedly cautious. Perhaps, it was just too difficult for some to admit that the Allied cause had been just, or that the reporting of the Jewish genocide had underestimated its true dimensions. Instead, Irish newspapers gave space to commentary from what may have been the first of the Holocaust Deniers.

An editorial in the *Irish Press* – the daily newspaper that was controlled by the de Valera family – accused the 'Anglo-Irish' of 'grovelling' in front of 'atrocity stories', and 'fawning round the knees of the victors'. There were disparaging references to the 'one-sided condemnations of brutality'. The *Irish Press* even printed an article by Liam MacGabhann, entitled 'Buchenwald becomes Box Office', which accused those who had filmed at that infamous camp of deceiving and manipulating their viewers. MacGabhann claimed that the bodies of concentration camp victims had been knowingly placed and filmed in those 'positions which are most likely to arouse the emotions.' He also questioned whether or not the deaths had occurred as a result of 'deliberate cruelty' – or from some other unforeseen circumstances. Another journalist observed that similar depravity 'could be found anywhere, at any time, in any nation.' He also piously urged his readers to consider that, 'the man who genuinely feels neutral for the weary burden of humanity will always be neutral about horrors and stories of horrors, for neutrality (means) a genuine compassion for all suffering'.

Since it strains credulity to believe that the Irish Government had been ignorant of what was happening in the Nazi camps, it is equally difficult to avoid the charge, suggested by Clair Willis, that Ireland had chosen to remain silent during the war about the mass murders being committed throughout Europe 'in order to keep Germany sweet'. In this context, it may be worth remembering that, according to Frank Gallagher, Director of the Government Information Bureau, de Valera had turned to him, late in 1941, 'with a rueful smile', and said: 'I wish there was some way of knowing who would win this war. It would make decisions much easier.'

The novelist, Elizabeth Bowen, was one of the first to detect the current of self-satisfaction that attributed some spiritual dimension to Ireland's policy of political neutrality. 'The most disagreeable aspect of this official 'spirituality' is its smugness', she wrote, 'I have heard it said (and have heard of it constantly being said) that 'the bombing is a punishment on England for her materialism'.' Viewed from the perspective that Bowen describes, the World War was understood merely as a conflict of rival materialisms. The two opposing sides were equally unspiritual – and, therefore, 'each as bad as the other'. Gerald Boland, the Irish Minister for Justice, claimed to be astonished at 'the cheek' of the Allied powers daring to try anyone for war crimes, when these were the same people who had 'murdered the cream of the Polish Army' at Katyn, and who had bombed 'undefended' Dresden.

Throughout the war years, de Valera consistently – and, perhaps, unconsciously – identified the interests of the Irish State with those of his own political party. In so-doing, he helped to establish a form of political hegemony that was unique in Europe. Following the end of the Emergency,

Fianna Fáil stayed in government for almost all of the next fifty years. Over that period, the policy of neutrality began to assume the attributes of a superior moral condition. Although de Valera had explicitly connected Irish neutrality with the 'evil of Partition', it was a policy that had worked, in several respects, to entrench the internal division of the island. In the course of the war, Northern Ireland had aimed to maintain and strengthen her constitutional links with Britain – and Churchill paid a generous tribute to those efforts in his VE Day broadcast. But that development had been paralleled by a move in exactly in the opposite direction south of the border – where neutrality was, in Padraig Murphy's words, 'the greatest test of the effective assertion of sovereignty that the then relatively new state had faced.' The Irish State could fairly be said to have passed that test, and, if the Irish Government did not follow a path of neutrality entirely because of high moral principles, then it did not differ greatly from the practice of any other European country.

It could be argued that Ireland's neutrality had technically been breached by German action during the course of the war. Article 2 of the Irish Constitution – drawn up by de Valera and ratified through a public referendum in 1937 – claimed that the national territory formed a single entity, which was the 'whole island of Ireland'. Seen in that light, the Luftwaffe's air raids on Belfast in 1941 were assaults on a city that all Irish Nationalists claimed as their own. As John P. Duggan has pointed out, the Belfast air raids can only have shattered any illusion held by the Irish

Government that, 'the Germans had been respecting the integrity of the 32 Counties in refraining from bombing the Six Counties.'

The Luftwaffe's attacks on Belfast were deliberate and sustained: the raid on 15th of April, 1941, had involved more than 200 heavy bombers. The previous year, de Valera's Government had lodged the strongest diplomatic protests when the Luftwaffe had accidentally dropped bombs on the North Strand in Dublin. After the bombing of Belfast, de Valera expressed his regret at the carnage in the North – 'their sorrows are our sorrows', he told a public meeting in Carlow – but there would be no similar diplomatic protests.

Ironically, it may have been the Partition of Ireland that helped to guarantee Irish neutrality. The British did not have access to the ports of southern Ireland, but they were able to operate strategic bases in Northern Ireland – notably, out of Derry – and it was from these bases that they mounted their counter-assaults on the German U-boats that were operating in the North Atlantic. If those bases in Northern Ireland had not been available, then it is clear that the incentive for the British to seize the ports of southern Ireland – or to starve the Irish State into submission – would have grown, and those options might have proved irresistible for Churchill.

In this context, it could also be argued that the Emergency helped to create an unintended sense of what might be termed '26 county nationalism' in southern Ireland. No doubt, the very notion of such a development would have been viewed by many Irish Nationalists as utterly abhorrent, particularly, by some of those who helped to create such a sentiment. No doubt it also involved profound ideological contradictions – but many southern Irish people seemed quite happy to accept and accommodate such contradictions. Comprehensive censorship had helped to ensure that, in reality, the preservation of the integrity of a 26 county State had become the primary national goal. It enjoyed widespread popular support – even if, at a formal level, there was still an insistence that the most important objective of Irish policy was the political re-unification of the island.

For my father, the First Battalion of the Inniskilling Fusiliers in which he served came to represent an alternative paradigm. He was fond of reminding my mother's northern relatives that the majority of those Irishmen who volunteered to fight for the Allies came from southern Ireland. Before the war, my father had taken a generally unsympathetic view of northern Unionists. He had gotten to know some of them in Burma for the first time, and they had apparently won his respect. They formed just one component in his battalion – which he liked to believe represented every major tradition on the island of Ireland.

He once showed me a series of photos of St. Patrick's Day celebrations that had been taken during the Burmese campaign. The pictures were not of good quality, but he was very fond of them. At the time, I was dismissive of what I considered to be his uncharacteristic sentimentality, but, in retrospect, I understand that they represented for him genuine evidence of a type of national unity. I believe that my father glimpsed in those blurry images something that he would have liked to find on his return to Ireland. Perhaps, there could have been some way to use this shared experience to change perceptions within Ireland when Irish soldiers from both parts of Ireland went back to their respective homes. If there were, it did not materialise – by the end of the world war, the two Irelands seemed further apart than ever.

It is possible to acknowledge that neutrality during the war was the best option open to the Irish government – but still to question some of the legacy that has been passed on to succeeding generations. For some, there are obvious difficulties in reconciling Irish neutrality with the catalogue of heinous crimes committed by the Nazis. It can seem as if Ireland stood aside from participating in a war that had involved the defeat of a genuinely evil ideology. Far from being motivated by any high ideals, Irish neutrality may be viewed as the product, in the words of Robert Fisk, of 'a narrow, constrained morality'. What is beyond doubt is that the policy of neutrality played a formative role in shaping the type of Irish society that emerged in the post-war years. Through the collective experience of the Emergency, political neutrality became deeply embedded as a central element in an Irish view of the world.

An alternative – and critical – view of the morality of that world-view came in the early 1960s from what must have seemed like a most unexpected source. In 1963, the *Irish Press* – which was still under the control of the de Valera family – had published the memoirs of Dr. Eduard

Hempel, the former German Minister in Dublin. Their publication led his son, Andreas, who had grown up in Ireland during the war years, to write to the *Irish Times*. In this letter, he told of his 'dismay' at reading his father's memoirs. The real background to that story, he wrote, was not furnished by diplomatic protocol, but 'by firing squads and concentration camps'.

For Andreas Hempel, the picture that emerged from his father's account was one of time spent 'ignoring the great moral issue of those terrible years'. He believed that the 'only justification' for publishing these memoirs lay in the light they shed on Ireland's policy of neutrality. He suggested that it had never been shown 'beyond reasonable doubt' that this was 'the right policy for Ireland, or the only one'. The publication of his father's memoirs, he concluded, 'can only revive those doubts'.

Neutrality may not originally have been conceived as a moral issue, but the temptation to accord it that status seems to have proved irresistible. The exemplary belief that Ireland should retain the right to choose its own path in world affairs could sometimes become fused – and confused – with an acceptance that there was fundamentally little to differentiate in ethical terms between the two sets of belligerents in the World War. This underlying attitude may help to explain some of the enthusiasm with which the work of one writer was embraced in Ireland – a writer whose most celebrated fiction seemed to raise the concept of neutrality beyond conventional ethics into a form of artistic obligation.

14

RADIO WAVES

Shortly before the Irish merchant seamen arrived at the Farge labour camp, a new voice was heard for the first time on German radio. It belonged to the Irish writer, Francis Stuart, and his broadcasts were not intended for German, but for Irish listeners. When he arrived in Berlin in 1940, Stuart had been given a spacious apartment on Nikolsburger Platz, and immediate financial assistance. He also received a warm welcome from the Irish Legation. Soon after his arrival, William Warnock, the Irish Charge d'Affaires, helped him to organise a party to celebrate St. Patrick's Day. Stuart later claimed that, when he arrived in Berlin, he was already convinced that Germany would lose the war. His decision to come to Germany under those circumstances was presented as if it were an act of ascetic sacrifice, driven by Stuart's desire to bear witness, as a writer, to the cataclysm that was about to engulf Europe – and Germany, in particular.

It is, of course, impossible to determine Stuart's motives with certainty. However, he would have needed to be very far-sighted, at the start of 1940, to predict with any degree of confidence that the war would be lost by Germany. Hitler had, after all, just expanded German territory to include much of what had been lost in the Treaty of Versailles – and had encountered minimal opposition. Almost two years would pass before he would declare war on the two States that would prove to be his most formidable opponents: the USA and the USSR. In early 1940, in the eyes of most Germans – and many Irishmen – the war was about to be won by Hitler, and it is difficult to understand on what basis Stuart might have thought otherwise.

It may also be worth mentioning that, when the going got really tough, and it was clear that Nazi Germany had indeed lost the war, Stuart abandoned Berlin and headed south to the Austrian border with Switzerland. He made strenuous attempts to find sanctuary in that neutral State, and, when he failed to do so, Stuart was careful to surrender to the Western Allies, whose democracies he professed to despise – and not to Soviet forces, whose regime he professed to admire.

Apart from the lectures that he gave at Berlin University, Stuart found other ways to keep himself occupied in wartime Germany. Within weeks of his arrival, he had written some scripts for William Joyce – 'Lord Haw-Haw' – a fellow Irishman, a fervent anti-Semite, and a dedicated fascist. Stuart's work for Lord Haw-haw did not last for long - he did not share Joyce's taste for colourful invective and they had very different priorities. By the end of 1942, however, he had begun to make weekly broadcasts on his own – for *Irland-Redaktion*, a radio service aimed at an Irish audience. Although Stuart insisted that he was not engaged in partisan broadcasting, he was working for a radio service that came under the authority of Joseph Goebbels' Ministry for Propaganda, and Dr. Goebbels had little doubt about the ultimate purpose of any of the media that he controlled. In 1933, soon after the Nazis came to power, he had identified radio as one of their most powerful weapons: 'it would not have been possible', he wrote, 'for us to take power, or to use it in the ways we have without radio.' As the war progressed, the importance of radio broadcasts increased – not just for Germany, but for all of the belligerent powers: its immediacy and widespread availability was of obvious importance.

From the start, Stuart used his broadcasts to make his political position clear. On 8th October, 1942, he spoke with open admiration of Hitler, whom he compared favourably with Lincoln, Ghandi and Parnell. He assured his Irish listeners that Germany had become 'an inspired nation', and that 'the source of that inspiration [was] rooted in one man: Hitler.' In his broadcast of 16th of December, 1942, Stuart told his listeners that, when he first found out about Hitler, he was 'completely fired by enthusiasm.'

Stuart praised the 'vision and courage', with which the Führer had defied international 'financiers and bankers' – clearly recognisable, in this context, as Jews – and boasted that 'the word dictator' did not frighten him. It was, he went on, 'preferable to be ruled by one man whose sincerity for the welfare of his people could not be doubted than by a gang whose only concern was for the market price of various commodities'. As both Brendan Barrington and Fintan O'Toole have pointed out, these references – to a gang of financiers who control the world's markets – convey an implicit appeal to the notion of an age-old Jewish conspiracy: an appeal that is entirely compatible with the poisonous anti-Semitic forgery: *The Protocols of the Elders of Zion.*

The years leading up the outbreak of war had seen a relative growth in anti-Semitic, and fascistic sentiments within extreme nationalist groups in Ireland – such as Ailtirí na hAiséirghe ('Architects of the Resurrection'). This development was evident in Stuart's own family background: his mother-in-law, Maud Gonne MacBride – an English woman who held extreme Irish Nationalist views - had written an article in 1938 entitled 'Fascism, Communism and Ireland', in which she argued that Ireland had much to learn from the totalitarian regimes in both Germany and the Soviet Union. She claimed that the Reformation had freed England from the moral restraints of the Catholic Church. Since then, she believed, England's 'alliance with the Jewish money powers and her proficiency in the unholy science of usury [has] enabled her to make London the centre of the banking system'. Clearly, Madame MacBride – as she liked to be known – had never forgiven Oliver Cromwell: apart from his depredations in Ireland, he had, after all, allowed Jews to settle freely in England.

It must be acknowledged that Madame MacBride's son-in-law avoided such crudely racist commentary, and he frequently protested on air that he was not in 'the ranks of the propagandists'. Nonetheless, his broadcasts are replete with the sort of rhetorical flourishes that are characteristic of Nazi ideology. He marvelled at 'the perfection of the German war machine'; he endorsed Hitler's view that Germany 'had too little living space for her population'; and he argued that 'arms [are] the most effective means left to mankind to revolt against the god of money.' Stuart even hailed the German defeat at Stalingrad as an existential "triumph of flesh and blood.' He claimed that German soldiers 'can overcome all human limitations', with their innate 'qualities of endurance and tenacity' which were 'not yet realised by their enemies.' When the Allies invaded Italy, Stuart predicted their imminent defeat: Italians, he claimed, would prove to be 'much better soldiers than the American mercenaries' because they were defending the glories of European civilisation.

Stuart praised the work of the Indian nationalist, Subhas Chandra Bose, and his Free India Legion – which had been founded in Berlin in 1942, and which, by 1943, had formally become part of the Waffen-SS. Bose had imagined that this force would spearhead a German invasion of India, but Hitler did not share Stuart's high opinion of the Legion – describing it as 'a joke', and suggesting that Indians were better suited to 'turning prayer wheels', than fighting. Stuart also congratulated the Burmese people on having overthrown British colonialism, and establishing their political independence. British colonialism may have been detested by the Burmese people, but in 1943, the puppet government that had been installed in Rangoon was entirely controlled by the Imperial Army of Japan.

In contrast, Stuart expressed nothing but contempt and derision for the Allied cause – and for democracy in general. He consistently identified President Roosevelt as 'warmonger number one,' and predicted that an Allied victory would usher in an era 'that would be far worse than any previous dark age in history'. For Stuart, the USA was merely an 'international gangster' that was hell-bent on 'imposing its ideas on the rest of the world'. He condemned its actions, and added, without a trace of irony, that if Germany were ever to behave in a similar manner, then he 'would say the same'. He expressed outrage at the presence of Allied troops in Northern Ireland, and described them as 'Chicago and Manchester corner boys' who did not know 'the difference between Ulster and Uruguay.'

At times, he indulged in an insipidly Irish version of the Nazi themes of *Heimat* – the love of 'Homeland' - with formulaic and sentimental references to Ireland's 'sacred soil' that had been ravished by the mere presence of American soldiers. In his broadcast of 1st of January, 1943, for example, he imagined the 'dark ruin of Shane O'Neill's castle … under the shadow of Cave Hill' becoming polluted as 'the latest Broadway and Holywood melodies whine over the water, [and] conscripts from the … money-mad American cities swarm ashore, ... singing their metallic, foreign-sounding songs [in] the sad, haunted land of Ulster.' There is a good deal more of what has been described – aptly – as 'lugubrious mish-mash' in his other broadcasts.

While William Warnock was Ireland's Chargé d'Affaires in Berlin, Stuart seems to have remained on cordial terms with him, and they liked to play golf together. In 1942, Warnock invited the entire *Irland-Redaktion* team to attend the Irish Legation's St. Patrick's Day celebrations. The Irish Government did not always welcome the German broadcasts, but that did not deter Warnock from inviting the programme staff around for some festive drinks. Warnock also allowed Stuart to listen to Radio Éireann programmes on the Legation's radio set, and he asked his secretary, Eileen Walsh, to deliver Irish newspapers directly to Stuart so that he could follow events in Ireland. As Gerry Mullins has pointed out, in so-doing, he was 'wittingly or otherwise, helping [Stuart] to keep his talks up to date with events back home.' He certainly displayed a good deal more interest in Stuart and his radio work than he appeared to take in the fate of any of the Irish citizens held prisoner by the SS in Germany.

Robert Fisk has suggested that it is to Warnock's credit that he eventually chose to distance himself from Stuart, and believes this is evident in Warnock's refusal to issue him with a new Irish passport. However, the decision not to issue a passport to Stuart was taken in Dublin, and was related to the advice that Stuart had given to his Irish listeners on how to vote in an impending Irish election.

The Irish Government may not have chosen to complain to the German authorities about the persecution of Europe's Jews, but clearly there were some issues on which they were prepared to make a stand. Stuart eventually stopped broadcasting from Germany at the beginning of 1944. According to his own account, this was because he had refused to follow the official line of anti-Soviet propaganda. His refusal has sometimes been cited as evidence that Stuart was not really sympathetic to Nazism – and was, rather, something of a political naive whose views were not coherent, let alone doctrinaire. However, it may be worth pointing out that Stuart never resigned his teaching position at Berlin University: he only stopped working there when the Nazis closed it down – along with all of Germany's other third-level institutions. It could also be argued that Stuart's reluctance to criticise Soviet Russia only reveals his liking for 'strong men' such as Hitler and Stalin – and his instinctive preference for a totalitarian regime.

As it happens, that was much the same position taken by his mother-in-law, Maud Gonne MacBride, in the article that she had published a few years earlier. For Stuart, the policy of neutrality seemed to offer an opportunity for Ireland to exercise its true spiritual vocation. He appeared able to persuade himself that this neutrality could be equated with a traditional concept of romantic creativity, and an openness to the sufferings of the world. In this, he might be said to have anticipated some of the future significance which the concept of neutrality would acquire in Ireland.

Following a brief spell of internment in France and a
few years spent living in London, Stuart returned to Ireland
and resumed his writing career. It is, perhaps, from this
period that his image – as the archetypal 'outsider' of Irish
literature – dates. It could, however, be argued that, in several
respects, Stuart was actually a consummate 'insider'. He
had, after all, been born into a well-established and affluent
family. He had attended Rugby – one of the leading public
schools in England. His literary career had been launched
and promoted by the Irish Senator and Nobel Laureate,
W.B. Yeats. He had been invited to become a member of
Yeats's prestigious Irish Academy of Letters when he was
just 22. He had married the daughter of Maud Gonne -
the famous beauty, muse, widow and political activist. He
lived for many years in his own castle. His children were
sent to exclusive fee-paying private schools. His brother-
in-law became a senior Government Minister. Given that
background, one might be forgiven for thinking that there
are outsiders and outsiders.

In the years following his return to Ireland, Stuart
became a respected figure in Irish literary circles. Indeed, he
was often treated with a degree of sensitivity and deference
that might have seemed more appropriate to extend to the
victims of the Nazis. His biographer and friend, Kevin
Kiely, has described his first meeting with Stuart in 1977.
Stuart was giving a talk to young writers, and taking part in
a public debate on 'The Writer and the Politician'. Before
the workshop took place, its moderator, the respected poet
and critic, Anthony Cronin, suggested that those present

should not 'rile [Stuart] with awkward questions'. Cronin even warned those present not to mention the name of the poet Yeats in Stuart's presence – since it might stir up some unpleasant memories.

The publication of Stuart's most important work – *Black List, Section H* – had sealed his reputation in the eyes of many influential figures in the Irish literary world. The book was written in Ireland in the early 1960s, but Stuart had difficulty in finding a publisher, and it did not appear in print until 1971. For many Irish readers, it established Stuart's status, in the words of Sylvie Mikowski, as a 'heroic arch-dissident'. Stuart had described his life as a 'living fiction', and his book combines elements of a conventional autobiography with those of a novel. This central ambiguity permits Stuart, simultaneously, to expose and to conceal himself. The book follows the major incidents in Stuart's life – including his decision to go to Berlin at the outbreak of the World War. Every character in the work is identified by their actual name – except for Stuart, and his mistress – and the narrative is built around real historical events. What is, perhaps, most striking about the book is that Stuart does not ask pardon or apologise for his association with Nazi Germany. Indeed, he comes close at times to inviting the condemnation of his readers.

The central character in Stuart's book believes that he belongs in Germany 'in the company of the guilty' because of his 'peculiar [and] flawed' imagination. Since the book is presented as a novel, it allows Stuart the freedom to manoeuvre, with considerable skill, between identifying the central character as himself – and treating him as a purely fictional creation. It could be argued that the book misrepresents Stuart's actual opinions and his real activities during the war – and that the most controversial features of both have been excised – but since the book does not claim to be an autobiography, that can be dismissed by Stuart's defenders as an irrelevant criticism. Throughout the work, the priorities of the central character are those of an archetypal Romantic artist – which, by Stuart's definition, situates him fundamentally at odds with conventional society. The victory of the Allies is, therefore, perceived as being 'not just over the Nazis', but over all 'personal modes of thought' that run counter to a popular consensus.

Although Stuart's book is currently out-of-print, it was well received throughout the English-speaking world when it first appeared: Lawrence Durrell, for example, thought it was 'a book of the finest imaginative distinction.' However, Stuart's work has received its most extravagant praise from Irish reviewers – many of whom were and are distinguished novelists and critics in their own right. Colm Tóibín believed that it evoked 'a sense of absolute truth and total honesty'. John Broderick believed it offered 'a journey into the interior of the spirit'. It was praised for its 'honesty and courage', its 'spiritual wisdom', and the challenge it posed to 'the metonymic degradation that individuality undergoes in Irish life-writing'. Antony Cronin considered that it proved Stuart to be 'after James Joyce, the greatest Irish novelist of the twentieth century'.

For me, all of this represents a grossly inflated assessment of the book's merits. For me, Stuart is no James Joyce – whose greatest novel includes a highly sophisticated exploration of Jewish identity in Ireland. Neither is he the Irish equivalent of P.G. Wodehouse – a naïve man, who did not deliberately chose to spend the war in Nazi Germany, and whose broadcasts from that State were genuinely devoid of political intent.

Stuart may not have been a Nazi – but he was, without question, a collaborator with the Nazis' political system: he admired Hitler; he gave expression to anti-Semitic feelings; and he broadcast, for a radio service run by Dr. Goebbels' Ministry of Propaganda, extreme anti-British and anti-American sentiments at a time when the Allied powers were at war with Nazi Germany. Much of this personal history remained unscrutinised following the publication of *Black List, Section H*, and Stuart's sanitised accounts of his time in Germany were largely taken at face value. This raises the obvious question of why he was not more closely questioned about his past – and why his book seemed to appeal so strongly to Ireland's literary intelligentsia.

I met Stuart on just one occasion, but witnessed the personal charisma that he could exert. I can also acknowledge that *Black List* has obvious literary qualities – although, as Antony Cronin has noted, the writing is not 'formally beautiful, grand, rich or exalted.' However, I would suggest that what Cronin terms the 'painfully exact' nature of Stuart's prose projects a disarming – but misleading - sense of its author's candour. Like Stuart, the central character broadcasts radio talks to Ireland, hoping that his Irish listeners will 'dissociate themselves' from the victors of the war, and 'forego participation in the celebrations' of peace. For me, this relativist view of both sets of belligerents only serves to mask the underlying passive-aggressive nature of Stuart's writing. It also manages to connect, at another level, with an Irish experience of political neutrality: re-affirming the comforting notion that Ireland's neutrality during the war had been determined by underlying moral principles. This may help to explain why Nuala O'Faolain, a writer whom I knew and liked, felt compelled to question the motives of those who queried Stuart's history: expressing her 'amazement' that his critics, 'were comfortable with their own righteousness'. Other writers echoed that condescending view – implying that Stuart's detractors were motivated and excited by the frisson of their own piety.

In the years that immediately followed the Allied victory, Stuart had, indeed, paid a price for his activities during the war – although, in comparison to the hardships encountered by many Irishmen who had fought against German or Japanese fascism, that price cannot be regarded as exceptionally high. He was shunned by some of his contemporaries, and he was also obliged, for the first time in his life, to seek out regular, waged employment. Once he returned to Ireland, however, the rehabilitation of his reputation began in earnest, and the poet Anthony Cronin was to play a central role in that process.

In 1981, Cronin was acting as a cultural advisor to the Irish Taoiseach, Charles J. Haughey: a notoriously vain politician, who styled himself as a patron of the arts in the manner of a Renaissance prince – at the same time that he led de Valera's sea-green Party into the mire of financial corruption. In 1981, Stuart and his wife were invited by Haughey to attend the official opening in Dublin Castle of the celebrations that were designed to mark the centenary of the birth of James Joyce. Stuart managed to overcome his long-standing antipathy to Joyce – he had once dismissed *Ulysses* as the product of masturbation fantasies – to attend the lavish gala event as an honoured guest.

In 1981, Cronin also persuaded Haughey to establish a new Academy of the Arts in Ireland – the *Aosdana*. Cronin helped to ensure that Stuart was chosen to be one of the first members of *Aosdana*, and in receipt of a yearly stipend from Ireland's national Arts' Council. Then, in 1996, Cronin also played a role in ensuring that Stuart was elected a *Saoi* – a 'wise one' – the highest accolade possible in the Irish Arts' world. Previous *Saoi* had included the Nobel Prize winner Samuel Beckett, who had been a friend of Paul Léon and who worked with the French Resistance during the War. Stuart was presented with a gold-plated *Torc* – a symbol of the ancient Celtic bards – as a mark of the State's recognition and esteem. Only one of *Aosdana's* 200 members resigned in protest at Stuart's election. That was the Irish-language poet Máire Mhac an tSaoi. Her stance had a very particular historical resonance: her father, Seán MacEntee, had fought in the 1916 Rising; he had been a founding member of Fianna Fáil; he had served in de Valera's Government during the war; and he had been central to the formulation and implementation of Ireland's policy of neutrality. In that respect, Máire Mhac an tSaoi's resignation not only reflected her opposition to the decision to honour Stuart, but also passed an implicit judgement on the political and ideological legacy of a preceding generation.

Writing in Ireland's *Sunday Independent* newspaper to justify Stuart's election as a *Saoi,* the novelist and critic, Colm Tóibín stated categorically that Stuart had no connection with 'politics, or anti-Semitism, or fascism, or Nazism.' It seemed that he accepted Stuart's own accounts of his time in Germany, and his evaluation of himself as an ostracized writer, writing for other ostracized people.

It did not seem to have occurred to Tóibín, or to a number of other highly intelligent individuals, that Stuart might have lied about his past life – for fairly obvious reasons of self-interest. Stuart had stated, for example, that the broadcasts he made for *Irland-Redaktion* had little to do with politics. Instead, he claimed that his broadcasts 'dealt very often with literature, both English and Irish, and ... with other literature.' He also suggested that 'when they were political, [his broadcasts] concentrated on the internal situation in Ireland.' He claimed that he had criticized de Valera's Government for executing IRA prisoners, and had advised his listeners not to support de Valera's Party, Fianna Fáil, in the Irish General Election of 1943.

As Brendan Barrington has established, Stuart's claims were 'wildly inaccurate' in almost every detail. His broadcasts 'hardly ever made reference to literature', and the actual advice he gave to Irish voters in the 1943

General Election was not to support Fine Gael – which was the principal opposition to de Valera's Fianna Fáil. When Barrington published *The Wartime Broadcasts of Francis Stuart,* it proved beyond doubt that the bulk of Stuart's broadcasts were not only explicitly political in nature, but that they articulated views and attitudes that were quite 'consistent with the broad thrust of German propaganda'. The broadcasts have been characterized – in my opinion, accurately – by Eunan O'Halpin as being a poisonous mix of 'apocalyptic nihilism, anti-British rants and cryptic anti-Semitism'. It is clear that Stuart tried to conceal and misrepresent his actual involvement with Nazism – either by direct denial, or through obfuscation and intellectual sophistry.

In fact, even Stuart's own account of his time in Nazi Germany varied considerably over the years. In a magazine article published in 1950, Stuart described himself and Frank Ryan as being 'close friends'. In 1989, Stuart gave a very different version: he claimed 'never to have liked Ryan', and that Ryan had boasted he would be a Minister in an Irish Government following Germany's victory in the war. In 1950, Stuart claimed that he did not meet Ryan in 1941: in 1989, he claimed to have attended a Kurstendamm nightclub with him in that year – in the company of several senior Nazis.

Stuart's defenders had sometimes challenged his critics to produce some concrete evidence – even one sentence from his work – that could establish any trace of anti-Semitism. Such evidence was produced by Barrington. In the 1920s, for example, he revealed that Stuart published a pamphlet which argued that Ireland should be purged of British influence in the same way that Austria had been freed of Jewish control. In December of 1938, he wrote a letter to the *Irish Times* opposing any plans that might be afoot to offer Jewish refugees sanctuary in Ireland. His letter came just one month after *Kristallnacht* – when German Jews were murdered, their businesses ransacked, and their synagogues destroyed with the active connivance of the Nazi State.

Stuart's later broadcasts were not so explicit, but they still made use of the accepted codes – such as references to 'international financiers and bankers' – that were commonly used in Nazi Germany to designate Jews. It was, in its own way, a remarkable achievement on Stuart's part that he was able to sidestep all of this history, and re-invent himself as someone who had never been much interested in politics. The Irish seamen who died in Farge may not have possessed Stuart's creative skills, and they were certainly not as well-connected with leading figures in Ireland's literary and political circles - but they proved unflinching in their refusal to collaborate with the Nazis, and the price that some of them paid makes whatever hardship Stuart may have endured pale in comparison.

In 2001, Colm Tóibín looked back, in the *London Review of Books,* upon his decision to support the honouring of Stuart: 'No one in Aosdana, as far as I am aware, had lost family in the War', he wrote, 'All of us were part of the legacy of Irish neutrality, and all of us, debating the issue of

Francis Stuart, were living in a sort of backwater, protected from the terrible pain and anger suffered by the families of those killed by the Nazis.' Tóibín went on to raise a fundamental question: 'I believed and still believe that the honour was justified, but I'm not sure I would believe this if I had lost friends or family.' This last statement strikes me as problematic – especially when it comes from such a perceptive and imaginative writer as Tóibín. Does one really need to have friends or family who suffered at the hands of the Nazis to be able to apprehend their monstrous crimes – or Stuart's acquiescence in their depravity?

It might be argued that ignorance of the immense suffering inflicted by the Nazis was possible in the immediate aftermath of the war. However, even at that time, the notion that Ireland could be immune 'in its conscience and heart' from the pain and horror of the war was rejected by the novelist Kate O'Brien. She argued that – despite the censorship and the cultural isolation – the imagination of Irish citizens could not be entirely cut off from the war that was raging abroad, and the issues that were at stake for the whole of Europe.

Ireland may not have been a belligerent State, but the country was still deeply affected by the war – and continues to be. There are no precise figures available, but, in 1944, the British recorded that more than 140,000 serving members of their armed services had given Irish addresses for their next-of-kin. The Irish Government's own assessment – according to a confidential memorandum, written by Joseph Walshe, the Secretary for the Department of External Affairs - was that around 150,000 Irish men had gone 'to British forces'. That seems like a considerable over-estimate, but apart from Irish soldiers, sailors and airmen, tens of thousands of Irish workers were also employed in Britain's wartime factories, and the British estimated that about 1 million Irish residents had relatives who were either in the Allied armed services, or working in the UK. It is reckoned that at least 9,000 southern Irishmen were killed in action while serving with Allied forces.

The exact numbers of those Irish men and women who fought and died in Allied uniforms, or worked in British factories, will probably never be known for certain – and, in a sense, it is irrelevant. There were five European states that remained neutral throughout the war: apart from Ireland, these were Sweden, Spain, Portugal, and Switzerland. What is clear is that none of the last four countries supplied volunteers to fight for any of the belligerent States on anything remotely approaching the same scale as Ireland. The Irish State may not have been part of the war, but the war was a reality for a very large number of Irish citizens.

It would be a mistake to lose some sense of proportion about Francis Stuart's contribution as a broadcaster in Nazi Germany. He played, at most, a very minor role in the output of Nazi propaganda, and does not even seem to have had much influence on his audience – which is hardly surprising, since the scripts of his broadcasts make for very dull reading. Stuart might be considered fortunate to have escaped any severe penalty from the victorious Allies – whereas his former colleague, William Joyce, was hanged.

In fairness, Stuart did not share Joyce's rabid anti-Semitism, or his long-standing commitment to the cause of fascism, and, of course, he had also not achieved the same popular impact – even in Ireland.

Writing about Stuart in the *London Review of Books*, Colm Tóibín rejected the naïve belief that 'writers should be good people'. Of course, that doesn't mean that, as human beings, we don't still *want* them to be good – which may help to explain why Tóibín had once seemed at pains to establish that Stuart was not a bad person. It should go without saying that I share Tóibín's belief that writers – or artists of any kind, for that matter – needn't necessarily be good. If the history of Nazi Germany teaches us anything, it is that highly educated, creative and intelligent people can prove unable to resist the impulse to engage in the most despicable of crimes against their fellow human beings. We may not expect our writers, musicians, lawyers, or doctors to be saints. However, I don't believe that this should exempt any State from an obligation to scrutinise the criteria by which it decides which of its citizens it will celebrate, and which it will ignore.

When Stuart died in 2000, he was, according to Mary Kenny, afforded 'the honour due to a venerable bard'. When Mary Robinson, as President of Ireland, spoke about Stuart at the time he was awarded his Golden Torc, she described his role in contemporary Irish culture as 'awkward.' In reality, I believe that the history of some of the Nazis' Irish victims raises issues which have proved to be much more awkward for the Irish State to address.

Another Irish writer left the safety of Ireland for the dangers of continental Europe during the war years – and he also recorded a radio broadcast from Europe to an Irish audience. In some quarters, Samuel Beckett has the reputation of being an introverted, cerebral and detached artist. However, he engaged directly with the reality of Nazism – and in a very different way to Stuart. Beckett returned to France from Ireland soon after war had been declared, and lived in Paris for the first few years of the German Occupation. He saw the effects of that Occupation at first hand, and witnessed the persecution of some of his Jewish friends – including his former Trinity College classmate, Alfred Peron, as well as the friend of James Joyce, Paul Léon. Beckett's response to such injustice was characteristically understated: 'You simply couldn't stand by', he later wrote, 'with your arms folded.'

Instead, Beckett joined a French Resistance cell, and became involved in passing information to British Intelligence. When that cell was betrayed in August 1942, by a Catholic priest who was secretly working for the Gestapo, Beckett fled to the Vaucluse, in southern France, with his partner, Suzanne Dechevaux-Dumesmil. They lived there in hiding for the rest of the war, but continued to assist the Resistance – aware that, if they were caught or betrayed again, the penalty would be death. After the war, Beckett was awarded the *Croix de Guerre*, and the *Médaille de la Résistance*, but typically, he shrugged off his role in the struggle against German fascism as mere 'boy-scout stuff'.

In the summer of 1945, Beckett returned to Ireland. His visit came at a turning point in his development as an artist, and he felt uncomfortable and uneasy at the degree of self-satisfaction which he encountered in his native country: 'My friends (in France) eat saw-dust and turnips', he wrote, 'while all of Ireland safely gorges'. His feelings resembled those of the writer, Seán O'Faolain, who believed that the cultural isolation produced in Ireland by six years of neutrality, had led to 'the prolonged suppression of our natural sympathy with tortured humanity'.

Beckett soon went back to France, along with other Irish volunteers, to work for the Red Cross, at a hospital in Saint-Lo, in Brittany. While he was there, Beckett recorded a broadcast for Radio Éireann about the relief work that was being done. Money for the hospital had been raised in Ireland, but there had been some complaints from Irish sources that the French were not sufficiently grateful for the help they had received. In his radio broadcast, Beckett responded by saying that the Irish volunteers who were in Saint-Lo 'will come home realising that they got at least as good as they gave.' He believed that what they would bring home was 'a vision and sense of a time-honoured concept of humanity in ruins'. They might even, he suggested, bring back to Ireland 'an inkling of the terms in which our condition is to be thought again'.

In 1945, there were few who could have argued with Beckett that the very concept of a common humanity lay in ruins. When set against the extent of the depravity, heartache, and devastation that the war had brought to the world, the cultural pretensions of European civilisation could only seem risible and absurd. In the years that followed, Beckett used drama – with exceptional boldness, rigour and integrity – to examine just how the human condition might, indeed, be 'thought again'.

15

WHAT WAR?

The Irish seamen who were sent to the camp at Farge were there for two principal reasons: the first was the German war industries' insatiable demand for labour – the second was their nationality. The merchant seamen were all non-combatants from a neutral State – which should have been their ticket home. Instead, they were singled out for especially harsh treatment because they were Irish. But that was not what kept them in Farge. They remained in the slave abour camp for other reasons. The first of these was because they consistently refused to work voluntarily for the Germans as *freie Arbeiter* – despite years of brutal and degrading treatment. The second reason – and, for me, the more critical – was the apparent indifference of their own Government, and its representatives in Dublin and Berlin. Such prolonged neglect stands in uncomfortable contrast to the efforts made by other European countries – both neutrals and belligerents – to ensure the health and welfare of those of their citizens who were being held captive in Nazi Germany.

It might be argued that the Irish Government and its representatives did not know that Irish citizens were being held in German POW, internment, and slave labour camps. That seems most unlikely. It did not require much specialist intelligence to be aware that many Irish seamen were to be found in the Allied merchant fleets. Given the lack of a comparable Irish marine, it seems fairly obvious that Ireland's sea ports would help to provide seamen for Britain's merchant navy. They had, after all, been doing just that for several hundred years. Looking through a random selection of crew lists from the war years, it is quite unusual to come across any British merchant ship that does not appear to have had some Irish crew members. In any case, not all of the Irish merchant seamen in the Farge camp had been serving on British ships - they were also captured on Norwegian, New Zealand, Australian and Dutch freighters.

The Irish Government was well aware of the war of attrition that Germany was waging against Allied merchant shipping. They knew that thousands of ships had been sunk and others captured, along with their crews. Against that background, it would seem reasonable for any interested party to conclude that there were probably some Irish seamen among those who had been taken prisoner.

Despite that, it would appear that no attempt was made to ascertain whether any Irish citizens were being held illegally in German camps. What makes this failure more dismal is that very little effort would have been needed to establish what had happened to these merchant seamen. When they were taken prisoner, they had filled in their *Kriegsgefangenen Postkarte* – their POW postcards – which were forwarded to the Allied authorities. When the Irish seamen were in the Sandbostel and Milad Nord camps, they had received visits from the Protecting Power and the Red Cross – who had also passed on their details to the relevant authorities.

The seamen sent letters and postcards back to Ireland informing their families that they were still alive, and were being held captive. While they were in the camp at Milag Nord, they also wrote a number of times to William Warnock, the Irish Charge d'Affaires in Berlin, seeking his assistance. It is, admittedly, possible that he never received their letters. However, it seems surprising that correspondence from a naval internment camp in northern Germany could be safely received in Ireland, but was not able to reach a much closer destination that was within the German Reich. There is also the unchallenged testimony of *Kommandant* Karl Walhorn before the military court in Hamburg, in which he claimed that details and photographs of the Irish seamen had been sent to the Legation in Berlin on two separate occasions in the course of 1943.

Even if one accepts that the seamen's letters to Warnock all went astray – and that *Kommandant* Walhorn, for his own reasons, was not telling the truth when he claimed to have sent details of the Farge prisoners to the Irish Legation – it still leaves an underlying question unanswered. Why did the

Irish authorities display such little interest in finding out what was happening to its own citizens? It is hard to escape the conclusion that their attention was focused on other issues, and that they felt they had other priorities to address.

Some of these may well have seemed more urgent – others appear less so. The death of James Joyce, for example, merited the personal attention of Joseph Walshe, the Secretary to the Department of External Affairs. Within hours of the news of Joyce's death reaching Dublin, he had sent a confidential 'blue code' telegram to Francis Cremins, the Irish Envoy in Geneva, asking him 'to find out if [Joyce] died a Catholic'. This suggests that – despite his scandalous and subversive reputation – Joyce remained, in both intellectual and social terms, someone with whom the Irish governing class could identify more easily than with the rag-tag bunch of seamen who were locked up in a German prison camp.

The Irish seamen were selected to be sent to the Farge camp because they were Irish, but their suffering has been largely ignored in their own country. In 1947, the first attempts were made to erect a National Memorial that would mark the sacrifices of Ireland's merchant seamen. However, after thirty years of endeavour, the project had gotten nowhere. In 1977, a new Committee was established, and after years of further lobbying - and half a century after the war ended - a memorial was finally unveiled in 1991 to the seamen from Ireland who were lost at sea during the Second World War. It lists the names of more than 150 Irishmen who died, primarily as a result of German naval action. According to Paddy Launders, the Chairman of the organizing Committee, these Irishmen had been 'forgotten by their fellow countrymen'. He believed that these seamen were only remembered 'by the loved ones who mourned their loss, and the comrades who remember them'. It may seem strange that the deaths of these Irish victims should not have been acknowledged in their own country for so long. Perhaps their fate raised too many disagreeable questions about the precise role that Ireland had played in six years of global warfare.

The granite monument in Dublin's docklands represents a handsome tribute to Ireland's seamen, but it does not bear the name of my cousin William, or Thomas Murphy, or Gerald O'Hara or any of the other Irishmen who were used as slave workers in Bremen Farge, and who perished in the Nazi terror. The reason given for this omission was that they were not serving on Irish-registered merchant ships when they were captured. Three of the five Irishmen who died in Farge were from County Dublin, one was from Mayo and another from Wexford. The Germans could identify 32 merchant seamen as Irish – even though they didn't sail beneath an Irish flag, but under those of Norway, the Netherlands or Britain. It would appear that some of their fellow countrymen have not been so sure.

The Ireland to which my father and others returned was not inclined to celebrate the actions of its citizens who had fought against fascism in Europe, and in Asia. In November of 1945, the Irish Government banned an Armistice Day parade by Irish veterans of the World War.

Instead, the veterans had to make their way to Dublin's War Memorial at Islandbridge individually, wearing their medals underneath their coats – as if they were a cause of shame. The reluctance to recognise the role that Irish men and women had played in the defeat of fascism continued in the following decades. The current 'Volunteers Project', based in University College, Cork, has interviewed many Irish veterans of the Second World War. Most of them considered that they were fighting for the defence of Ireland as well as Britain, and that was certainly the view of my own father. According to Brian Girvan, many veterans complained that their sacrifices were never recognized by the Irish State, and that they faced hostility from the public when they returned home. I remember my mother was indignant that US military personnel were allowed to wear their uniforms in the towns and villages of southern Ireland – while Irish men and women who had served in British forces were not accorded the same right.

As recently as 1983, Fianna Fáil criticized the presence of Irish Army representatives at a Remembrance Day ceremony in Dublin. At that time, the Party was in opposition, and led by Charles J. Haughey. As a student at University College Dublin, Haughey had marked VE Day – and the collapse of the Nazi regime – by burning a Union Jack in front of Trinity College. His action was allegedly in response to provocative behaviour by some Trinity students, but Haughey remained proud of this juvenile escapade for the rest of his life. Ireland's first National Day of Commemoration was held in 1986 – to mark the sacrifices both of those who fought for Irish Independence, and those who fought for other causes. It represented a small but significant shift in the political culture of the Irish Republic: once again, Charles J. Haughey chose not to attend the ceremony.

It later emerged that, while Haughey was striking a pose of principled opposition to honouring the memory of those who had fought against Hitler, he was also secretly trousering millions in cash from his wealthy supporters: money that allowed him to maintain a lifestyle of conspicuous extravagance – living in a large Georgian mansion, riding to hounds, and holidaying on his own private island. It was, to say the least, a far cry from the abstemious habits of his Party's founders.

The most extreme assault on the memory of the Irish who had fought in the Allied forces took place in the year that followed Ireland's first National Day of Commemoration. Ten civilians and one policeman were killed in Enniskillen, County Fermanagh, on 8th of November 1987, in what came to be known as the Poppy Day Massacre. A twelfth victim died later. They had been attending a religious service to mark Armistice Day, and the bomb is believed to have been planted by units of the IRA that were operating on both sides of the border. On the same day, the IRA placed a much larger device at another Armistice event in the nearby village of Tullyhommon. That commemoration was made up of children from the local Boys' and Girls' Brigades – scouting organisations associated with the Presbyterian Church in Ireland – but, thankfully, the IRA's bomb failed to explode.

Among those buried by the Enniskillen explosion was a local shop-keeper, Gordon Wilson, and his daughter, Marie, a young nurse. They had somehow managed to join hands under the rubble, and Marie was able to speak to her father just before she lost consciousness. 'Daddy', she said, 'I love you very much.' She died in hospital a few hours later. I drove to Enniskillen the day after the bombing to film an interview with Gordon Wilson. He had already expressed forgiveness for her daughter's killers: 'I will pray for them tonight', he said, 'and every night.' I did not share Gordon Wilson's religious convictions, but I was humbled by them, and I was not alone. The brazenly sectarian nature of the Enniskillen atrocity disgusted many Irish men and women who came from a Nationalist or Republican background, and many were also moved by the humanity of Gordon Wilson's response. His forgiveness of his daughter's killers may have helped to accelerate the development of greater respect for differing traditions within Ireland. That process was already under way before the Enniskillen bomb. It had been championed by a number of popular journalists as well as by some leading academic historians. As such, it clearly represented a greater willingness to recognise the real diversity of Ireland's modern history.

Such recognition was of great importance to the Irish citizens who had fought for the Allies during World War Two – and it remained so long after hostilities had ceased. In 1995, my father took part in one of the last major parades that were designed to mark the fiftieth anniversary of the end of the Second World War. He carried the standard of the Irish section of the Burma Star Association through the centre of London, along a route that was packed with large crowds. It was clear that the experience was cathartic for him – allowing him to express his pride both in being Irish, and in having fought in the war against fascism. 'The crowds clapped and cheered us all the way', he wrote later, 'A good few of them could see the Republic's standard, and I could hear Irish voices shouting out 'Good Old Dublin!' as we went past'. He described the occasion as deeply emotional for him. 'As we marched along', he wrote, 'all I could think of were those young men that didn't come home, and who were left on the battle fields of Europe, Africa and Asia, so many years ago'.

Later, when my father was dying and in the intensive care ward of a Dun Laoghaire hospital, an X-ray was taken of his chest. The following morning, a young doctor approached me, with a sheepish grin. He told me that the X-ray had shown that there were fragments of metal in my father's chest. He wondered if I could offer any explanation. I told him that they probably came from a mortar bomb. He looked blankly back at me. 'From the war', I added. 'What war?' he said. His response was not entirely surprising – it has only been in recent years that the role played by Irish citizens, and by the Irish State, in World War Two has begun to attract popular attention, and the treatment of Irish veterans has been questioned.

Such questions do not seem to have troubled the mind of Charles J. Haughey – and he was not the only one whose career prospered after the war was over. William Warnock, who had served as the Irish Chargé d'Affaires in Berlin from 1939 to 1944, returned to Germany – this time as a fully credited Ambassador to the Federal Republic. Before his distinguished career ended, Warnock would also be appointed as Ireland's Ambassador to Washington – usually considered the top posting in Ireland's diplomatic service. He did not chose to spend his retirement in Ireland, but in Canada – content, one presumes, to end his life in a country whose Head of State was the British Queen. Any previous sympathy he held for the Nazis was now dismissed as the product of 'youthful enthusiasm': Paul Léon might have taken a somewhat different – and, perhaps, a harsher view. William Warnock was certainly not a Nazi, but he proved to be a timid and ineffectual representative of his country during the tumultuous years of the Second World War. He was not prepared to make an attempt to save the life of Paul Léon, or any other Jews – even when he was asked to do so by the Irish Government – and his weakness may also have contributed to the suffering of some of the Nazis' Irish victims.

Francis Stuart was involved in one last controversy before his death in 2000. In October, 1997, he had appeared in a TV programme on the UK's Channel 4. In the course of an interview, Stuart compared 'the Jew' to 'the worm that got into the rose and sickened it'. When I saw the interview on air, I assumed that Stuart was alluding to William Blake's poem, 'The Sick Rose', in which Blake suggests that the 'dark secret love' of the 'invisible worm', that 'flies in the night' is destructive: corrupting the rose's beauty and ending its life. However, Stuart insisted that he regarded the metaphor as praise: 'all those so-called healthy roses", he elaborated, 'they need exposing – many of them are sick'. This interpretation was enthusiastically endorsed by several leading literary figures in Ireland – such as the poet, Paul Durcan, who suggested that Stuart's metaphor constituted a 'profound spiritual affirmation'. Kevin Myers was one of the few journalists who challenged that opinion: writing in the *Irish Times* soon after the programme was broadcast, he claimed Stuart had allied himself with the 'most bestial enemy of civilization that Europe has ever known', and suggested that he held anti-Semitic views.

Stuart sued for libel, and, two years later, the case was settled out of court when the *Irish Times* agreed to pay damages, and issued an abject apology. Stuart's supporters were jubilant. Writing in the *Irish Independent*, it seemed that Anthony Cronin could hardly contain his delight. He believed that the apology marked 'a complete vindication' of Stuart's account of his role in Germany during the war. He re-affirmed the widely accepted view of Stuart as a 'political innocent', and questioned the motives of those who had accused him of being anything else. To understand Stuart's actions 'requires an act of the historical imagination', Cronin wrote, and it seemed to him that 'some alleged historians are incapable of making it.' The following year, Brendan Barrington published the transcripts of Stuart's broadcasts, and effectively demolished any notion that Stuart had been as politically naïve as he – and Cronin – had claimed. Shortly before he died, Stuart spoke for one last time about his wartime role. He had always refused to say that he regretted his actions, but now he said that he felt 'intensely sorry for the hurt [he] had caused so many people' by 'appearing' to have supported the Nazi regime. It was clearly a qualified expression of remorse, but it was the closest that Francis Stuart would ever come to an apology.

The German spy, Herman Görtz - who had been briefed by Stuart, and who had stayed at his castle in Wicklow – was buried in Dean's Grange cemetery in 1947, with a Nazi flag covering his coffin. He had swallowed a vial of poison at the Aliens' Office in Dublin, after he had been told that he was going to be deported to Germany. It seems that he feared he was about to be handed over to the British authorities. Swastika badges were worn by many in the large crowd at his funeral, and a young woman stepped to the graveside after the burial to give the Nazi salute.

Görtz's funeral was attended by the long-serving Fianna Fáil Deputy, Dan Breen – whose study walls were still adorned with portraits of Adolf Hitler. James O'Donovan, the IRA leader who had conspired with the Nazis, was also present to pay his last respects. O'Donovan kept his permanent and pensionable job in the Electricity Supply Board until he reached retirement age. Towards the end of his life, he wrote a memoir in which he noted with obvious satisfaction that, thanks to his careful instructions, there had been 'no fatalities' as a result of the IRA's bombing campaign in England in 1939. Given that a number of civilians were killed during that campaign, O'Donovan's comments may seem puzzling. However, he was referring exclusively to any casualties that IRA members might have inflicted upon themselves: for O'Donovan, the deaths of innocent civilians do not seem – literally – to have been worth counting.

As a Nazi Party member, and an NCO in the *Abwehr*, Helmut Clissmann was interned for three years after the war by the British authorities in Germany. On his release in 1948, his wife approached Seán MacBride, the Minister for External Affairs in the Irish Government, requesting a visa for him to come to Ireland. MacBride – who was the son of Madame MacBride, the brother-in-law of Francis Stuart, and a former Chief-of-Staff of the IRA – quickly expedited the visa, and Clissmann was able to settle in Dublin with his family. He became a very successful businessman, representing various German firms in Ireland, including the giant Schering pharmaceutical company. Schering admitted in 1999 that they had used forced labour in their factories during the war, and had not agreed to pay any compensation to those workers. Schering was also the company that had supplied the warning agent for the production of Zyklon B, used to gas Jews and other prisoners in Auschwitz and similar death camps. Ironically for someone who had been a member of an organisation that imprisoned, tortured and murdered its political opponents, Clissmann helped to found the Irish section of Amnesty International.

In 1951, a life-size statue of Seán Russell – the IRA's Chief of Staff in 1940, who died of natural causes on his way to Ireland in a German submarine – was unveiled in Dublin's Fairview Park. In contrast to Ireland's World War veterans, 5,000 people were permitted to march to the Park from the centre of Dublin. The parade was accompanied by the Transport Workers' Union band, and was attended by several members of Dublin Corporation. After the eulogy to Russell had been given, a squad of six masked IRA members fired three volleys of gun shots.

Russell may not have been a National Socialist, but like Francis Stuart, he accepted the hospitality and association of those who were. He did not question their anti-Semitic and anti-democratic beliefs, and he was happy to co-operate with the Nazis. As Kevin Myers has pointed out, Russell is the 'only Irish victim of the Second World War to have a statue in his honour in Dublin', and Dublin may be the 'only capital in the EU with a statue to a Nazi collaborator'. Perhaps, on this occasion at least, Myers was too kind to Russell's memory: I do not regard him as a 'victim' of the Nazis. Russell's statue has been damaged repeatedly over the years. The current version was re-commissioned in 2009. It is made of bronze, and it is said to have been fitted with sensory alarms to protect it from further attacks.

In sharp contrast, the fate of Ireland's merchant seamen has been largely ignored for most of the decades that have passed since the war ended. Of course, any State is likely to have some features of its history which – for a variety of reasons – have been buried or repressed. It could be argued, for example, that the important tradition of constitutional nationalism in Ireland – as exemplified by Daniel O'Connell, William O'Brien or John Redmond - has been seriously neglected in the teaching of Irish history in Irish schools.

It is clichéd to claim that history is written by the victors, but in the case of Ireland, the victors represented two different factions within the same political tradition of physical force. For decades, the dominance of that tradition was reinforced through Ireland's educational system. It has only been in relatively recent times that this historical narrative has come under sustained scrutiny. In the case of those surviving Irish veterans of the Second World War, this process has allowed them to speak more openly about their experiences.

When I first met Harry Callan, he showed me a poster advertising a talk that he had given at University College, Dublin, about his imprisonment during the war. He was clearly delighted that he had been given the opportunity to speak openly about his ordeal – without his identity or integrity as an Irishman being questioned. For me, Harry was not only the last surviving Irish seaman from the labour camp at Farge: he was also the last person alive who had spoken to my lost cousin, William Hutchinson Knox. He described William to me as 'a quiet man. Reserved, but well spoken. You could tell that he had been educated.' Harry was surprised that his rank was only that of an AB seaman. He would have expected a more senior post – perhaps, as a 'donkeyman' in charge of the engines. I wondered what else he could tell me. Harry paused for a moment – then, he leaned forward towards me and said quietly: 'You have his voice'.

I suppose it was an obvious enough connection, but it was not one that I had anticipated. For an instant, I seemed to feel the presence of William beside us; abruptly summoned from that fearful camp in Germany to Harry's cosy living room. Then Harry reminded me of something else about the way my cousin spoke – something more fundamental than the depth or tone of his voice, but which I had forgotten. William had a severe stutter.

For much of the last century, stuttering was viewed as a major disability. It was also an impediment that could effectively bar stutterers from a wide range of occupations. Stuttering has been observed in human speech for more than 2,500 years, but there is still no agreed explanation for its cause. It has been attributed to a variety of psychological considerations – such as childhood trauma, sibling rivalry, suppressed anger, or sexual fixation. However, it has also been connected with purely physiological factors – such as deformation of the tongue, lips, jaw or larynx. Sometimes, a child's parents have been blamed – at other times, it has been chemical imbalances that have been held responsible.

Despite such confusion about its origins, there has seldom been any shortage of cures on offer. These have involved hypnosis, electric shocks, faith healing, and psychoanalysis. Sometimes, stutterers have been fed with nauseous potions and snake-oil medicines in the forlorn hope that their nervous systems would respond. On occasion, even more outlandish forms of treatment have been followed. One of these entailed the insertion of a battery at the back of the throat - which was intended to keep the soft palate 'distended like a sail'. Mechanical appliances have also been constructed, and furnished with a range of springs, wires, clamps and screws. Face masks have been designed to prevent the teeth from being clenched: others have kept the breathing passages open with an elaborate system of metal tubes.

By the time that William was born, the focus had moved to what were then considered to be more scientific procedures. A variety of surgical operations – such as the removal of the adenoids, widening of the dental arch, and reduction, notching or slitting of the tongue – had become more frequent. But stuttering was also associated with personality disorders – and even, in some cases, with mental retardation, or handicap. In J.M. Synge's classic drama, *The Playboy of the Western World*, the father of the eponymous hero, dismisses his own son with contempt as a 'stuttering lout'. His cruel judgement, at first, seems to be validated by the son, who has admitted that he is 'slow at learning'. However, Synge had his own bitter experience of being treated as 'the fool of the family' – the original title of his play – and before the curtain has fallen, the nature of the father's prejudice has been exposed, and the human potential of his son begun to be realised.

In fact, recent studies suggest that stutterers tend to be of above average intelligence. In this and other respects, the condition remains something of an enigma – although contemporary research suggests that it is inherited, and can probably be traced to a neurological defect in brain function. What is not in dispute is the crippling effect that stuttering can often have upon those who suffer from the impediment. The American novelist, John Updike, who experienced bouts of intense stuttering, described his own physical symptoms as 'repulsive'. For obvious reasons, stuttering can lead to feelings of low self-esteem and social awkwardness. When King George VI – whose chronic stutter has become famous as a result of the movie *The King's Speech* – wished to propose to his future wife, he did so by handing her a letter. The English writer, Margaret Drabble, believed that her pronounced stutter led to great loneliness as a child, since it meant she grew up 'virtually friendless'.

This feeling of isolation can extend well beyond childhood, and become deeply ingrained in an individual personality. Sometimes, stutterers can seek refuge in forms of employment where they do not have to interact much with members of the public, or where they can work entirely on their own. William's father, as a doctor, can only have been acutely aware of his son's condition. As a leading surgeon, he would also have known of the new procedures, and supposed advances in the latest forms of medical treatment. I do not know what – if any – of these alleged remedies were tested by him on his son: all I know is that – if they were – they were found wanting. I wonder if William's persistent stutter delivered an unspoken, but implicit rebuke to his father's professional pride: reminding him constantly that he was a physician who could not heal his own offspring.

There were other factors that may have contributed to William's sense of isolation within his family. He was the youngest of three boys. The eldest – another Francis Blake Knox – was almost twelve years older. This son was, by all accounts, the sort of character that used to be described as a 'man's man'. Francis left home in Kingstown while he was still young to join the British Army. Apparently, it was just the sort of career that he relished, and he became a Major when he was still only 22. Nine years passed between his birth and the arrival of a second son. This one was named after his uncle Harry, but soon became known as 'Hal' – like Shakespeare's young Prince. He seems to have been a very different character to his elder brother – and soon played a different role. Hal was the white-headed boy, and the darling of the family. Two years later, a third son came along. William seemed to be defined by what he lacked: he didn't have the no-nonsense energy of his brother, Francis – or the unassuming charm and good looks of his brother, Hal. Instead, he might have been considered to be the runt of the litter; with protruding ears and a stubborn speech impediment that would not – or could not - be cured.

Francis, the eldest brother, had left the family home while William was still a young child – so he grew up alongside Hal. Given the severity of his speech impediment, the closeness of that relationship may have been of heightened importance to William: he had a brother close to him in age – whom he might depend upon not to make fun of his difficulties. As they grew older, Hal could have played a crucial role in helping William to integrate into the social life of Kingstown and Dublin. But, when William was 10 years old, that possibility was closed forever when Hal died, unexpectedly and suddenly. I had been told that his death was due to some sort of generic 'fever' – a spectre of disease arising from an era when antibiotics were unknown. Perhaps I am being unfair, but I can imagine William's father donning a black silk hat, and stepping into the carriage that would bring him to Dean's Grange cemetery to bury his beloved son: coming back to find that the child with a knotted tongue was still in the house.

William did not even share a surname with the rest of his family. Instead, he bore a dead man's name. The 'William Hutchinson' who had been the Master of Kingstown for almost 60 years, and whose legacy and memory were still to be found all around the town. Even to-day, the patrol boat of Dun Laoghaire's Harbour Authority is named after him. According to one tribute, the Master had acted throughout his life with, "outstanding moral as well as physical courage', and with 'decisiveness, foresight, efficiency and imagination'. Not the easiest act for a stuttering boy to follow. Perhaps, that was why William felt he needed to escape, not to anywhere in particular – just from one port to another, from one voyage to the next. Perhaps, the destination was immaterial, and it was always the journey that mattered. William never married, or settled on board one ship, or assumed a position of responsibility, or stayed on the same sea route, or even identified a next-of-kin. Gradually, he seems to have loosened the bonds that had joined him to his family, and to Ireland.

Yet, in the last years of his life, William was pulled back by his own history. It was his place of birth that sealed his fate and brought him on his final journey to the camp at Farge. I would like to think that while he was there William found some reserves of moral and physical strength that were comparable to those of his namesake. He managed to survive for almost five years as a captive of the Nazis – including more than two years when he worked as one of their slaves. He was able to hold his nerve during all of that time – he did not compromise with his captors, and he kept faith with his fellow Irish prisoners.

One of them had told me the story of William's confrontation in Farge with an SS officer on two separate occasions. The first time, Harry Callan merely described the incident. The second time, he acted it out – complete with my cousin's stutter. 'You work for the British – why won't you work for us?', the officer had said. 'I can still see Knox standing there', Harry told me, 'in front of that SS man, and holding out his hand and telling him, with that stutter of his: 'I don't b-b-b-believe in b-b-biting the hand that has f-f-f-fed me.' Harry shook his head: 'I'll never forget that.' He was concerned that I might be offended he had imitated my cousin's speech, but I thought it only gave the words an additional resonance to know that William needed a special sort of courage to speak them.

16

FARGE

Farge is a small inland port that nestles on the River Weser in the state of Bremen in northern Germany. I drove through the village in the spring of 2012, in the company of my son, Jamie, and his partner, Caoimhe Gallagher. We had come here to visit the Valentin Bunker, but at first I thought that the SAT NAV system had led us to the wrong location. This village seemed so pretty in the morning sunshine: like a picture postcard, with its neatly thatched houses, its manicured gardens and its pristine streets. A postwoman in bright yellow overalls waved to us as she cycled down an avenue where the trees were beginning to break into leaf. Groups of laughing children made their way home from the local primary school. The whole atmosphere was redolent of what the Germans call *Gemutlichkeit* - the inner peace that is supposed to accompany a sense of belonging, of being accepted, of feeling completely at home and at ease with oneself. Then, we looked up and saw the Bunker.

It seemed to hang over the village like some sort of giant incubus – a huge swathe of grey concrete that stretched into the middle distance. We got out of our car, and walked gingerly towards it. The point of entry was perhaps thirty or forty yards from the nearest house, but the building was entirely surrounded by high fencing, and entrance was strictly by appointment. No doubt, this was intended to exclude intruders, or vandals – but it also seemed as if it had been designed to contain the monstrous energy of the Bunker itself. The grim functionality of its structure managed to convey some slight sense of Modernist design. This was once, after all, one of the world's largest building projects, and the degree of technological innovation developed here was remarkably advanced. At the same time, the construction of the Bunker was dependent on the back-breaking labour of thousands of slaves and there was a complete absence of architectural features. The Bunker seemed to me to represent, simultaneously, a testament to the creativity of those who planned it – and a proof of their corruption. I was both impressed and repelled by what I saw.

Building work on the Valentin Bunker continued until just a few weeks before the war ended, and is material evidence of Nazi Germany's extraordinary capacity to engage in huge military and industrial projects – even as the Third Reich was crashing down in inglorious defeat. But the Bunker is also a monument to the hubris of the Nazis. The U-boat assembly lines may have been protected by massive concrete walls, but the supply lines to the Bunker – intended to bring manufactured sections of the boats from factories all over Germany – would have remained highly vulnerable to Allied air attack, and so would the finished submarines – if any had been properly completed - as they made their way down the Weser to the North Sea. But, of course, that scenario remains hypothetical because the agonising labour that thousands of slave-workers were forced to expend on Project Valentin was all for nothing. Albert Speer's beloved factory was still incomplete when the war ended. For all the technological bravura of his plans, they proved to be inadequate, and there were persistent and severe quality control problems with the prefabricated sections of the submarines. Although 118 U-boats were formally certified as finished, only four of these were rated as fit for service, and none of them ever left their pens.

The overwhelming size of the Bunker expresses, in its own way, the desire of a fascist regime to bully and intimidate its citizens. It was impossible not to admire the human ingenuity and determination that went into its construction, but equally impossible to ignore the extraordinary human suffering that this entailed. The Bunker was a place where vicious beatings and summary executions were the everyday penalties for those who were judged not to be working hard enough – regardless of their physical abilities. After the war, hundreds of unidentified bodies were found buried in the neighbourhood. My cousin William was not one of them: I am grateful that his grave was marked – so were those of three of the four other Irish seamen who died in Farge. Within a year of the war's end, their bodies had been exhumed and transported to an Allied War Cemetery at Rheinberg – more than 200 miles south west of the Bunker. Their graves are now indistinguishable from the thousands of other white headstones in Rheinberg, laid out in tidy rows, and set in immaculate lawns.

Our guide led us inside the Valentin Bunker. A large party of Germans were already half-way through a tour, and we waited for them to finish. They looked like pensioners from some nearby factory – on a day's outing – but they were not old enough to have been directly involved in the war. We watched them walking around the vast, echoing interior: in silence, for the most part; listening respectfully to their guide; occasionally stopping to gaze up in awe at the towering, lime-streaked walls. After they had left, I asked where they came from. I was told that each had signed up for the visit in one of the public libraries in Bremen: I wondered if they did so in an attempt to understand their parents' generation – or from some other impulse. I could not read from their expressions what they were thinking. Perhaps, their emotions were as conflicted as my own.

The surface area of the Bunker is the size of six football pitches. It is currently divided into five main sections – some of which are closed to the public because of the danger of falling masonry. Those sections are pock-marked with shell holes, and are home to thousands of bats. Thankfully, they were all asleep during our visit, but we were told that, at night, the cavernous space is filled with the noise of their flapping wings. Until recently, one section of the bunker had been used by the *Deutsches Heer* – the current German Army – as a storage depot. It was put up for sale as a commercial warehouse in 2010, but there were no takers. There was a plan to knock the whole place down, but the Bunker had been designed to be indestructible, and '*gebaut für die Ewigkeit*' – built for Eternity. It has far outlived the 1,000 year Reich it was intended to serve, and the cost of destroying it has become so prohibitively expensive that the option has been abandoned.

The Nazis constructed more than 2,000 bunkers in Germany – with more than 100 in Bremen alone. Almost all of these were built by slave workers. For decades after the war, the bunkers were officially designated as civilian shelters – in case of some future enemy attack. That threat has receded so the Federal German authorities decided, in 2007, to de-commission over 200 of them. Since then, around half of these bunkers have been converted for other uses. Some of them are now being used as apartment blocks: others have become rehearsal studios and art galleries. The bunkers are advertised as offering 'cool temperatures in summer', and 'warmth for the winter'. They are apparently regarded as 'hot properties', and their previous history is now described as a 'talking point'.

The Valentin Bunker – by far, the largest in Germany - is no longer on the market. In 2011, the Bremen Regional Authority launched a programme to establish a museum there to help explain to young Germans one aspect of their country's troubled past. Bernd Neuman, the Minister for Culture in the Federal German Government, described the

Valentin Bunker as the centre of 'an inhuman network that exploited human labour' for the goals of National Socialism. Our guide told us that, since the museum opened, it has attracted around 1,000 visitors a month.

She was particularly pleased that some of these had come from the village of Farge itself. 'We threw an Open Day', she said, 'and 500 villagers came to have a look around'. Since the Bunker had been there for most of the previous 70 years, I wondered why none of them had visited before. 'They preferred to ignore it', our guide told us. That must have required some effort – given the colossal dimensions of the Bunker, and its proximity to the village: not so much an elephant in the room as a Tyrannosaurus, reeking of blood. Perhaps, the villagers had learned how to disregard what they didn't want to see during those years when thousands of slaves had filed past their homes – every day and every night - to work and die in the belly of this beast.

The Farge villagers weren't the only ones to delude themselves about the nature of the Bunker. Even as the Third Reich was in its death throes, *Grossadmiral* Karl Dönitz still fantasised about a turn-around in the war through the deployment of the 'miracle boats' that would emerge from Farge. In fact, his 'wolf-pack' tactics of submarine warfare had been rendered obsolete by the superior technology of the Allies, and nothing that was manufactured in the Bunker could have altered that reality. Dönitz could not face this truth, and so he continued to fight for raw materials and supplies for the Bunker long after it had become pointless. He also remained convinced to the end of his life that the slaves who worked there had only got what they deserved. Writing many years after the war was over, Dönitz clung to the view that that '99 per cent' of those sent to work on building sites like the Valentin Bunker were 'habitual criminals'. According to Dönitz, these were the very people whom the democratic Weimar Government – that preceded the Nazi regime – 'had allowed to roam around free until their next murder, sexual offence or serious act of violence'.

It may seem astounding that someone like Dönitz - the man who had ordered his naval commanders to let Allied merchant seamen drown – should express any moral disapproval of arbitrary 'acts of violence'. However, to the end, the last Führer of Nazi Germany believed that the German people could not be 'grateful enough' for the incarceration of the Farge prisoners, and their employment on the Valentin project.

Despite the public commitment to its future as a museum, there is not a great deal at present for the casual visitor to see inside the Bunker. It appears that there have been some political difficulties, and the promised federal funding has not yet arrived. This means that there is still only a relatively small exhibition currently on display. Nonetheless, I was pleased to see that, not only are the Irish prisoners identified as one of the national groups who were used as slave workers but there were large photos of several of them – including Harry Callan. A book has also been published which acknowledges the presence of the Irish merchant seamen in the camp. It is, of course, sadly ironic that the ordeal of these Irishmen is now formally accepted in Germany – but is still not recognised in Ireland.

There are, however, unmistakable signs of change in Irish attitudes towards the war. In January, 2012, Ireland's Minister of Justice, Alan Shatter, paid an eloquent tribute to those Irish men and women who had fought for the Allies: 'For too many years', he said, 'their contribution in preserving European and Irish democracy was ignored'. He also announced that the Irish Government intended to pardon retrospectively the thousands of Irish soldiers who had deserted the Irish Army to join Allied forces in the Second World War, and had been collectively punished by the Irish State. The Irish Government accepted, for the first time, that the State's treatment of these deserters had been unjust and unfair: 'It is untenable', the Minister stated, 'that we [continue] to ignore the manner in which our State treated the living who returned to [Ireland] having fought for freedom and democracy.'

Alan Shatter also criticised Ireland's attitude towards Europe's Jews during the war. 'In the 1930s', he told the *Irish Times*, 'practically all visa requests from German Jews were refused by the Irish authorities.' The Minister believed that the Irish people should 'no longer be in denial that, in the context of the Holocaust, Irish neutrality was a principle of moral bankruptcy'. Shatter thought that this moral bankruptcy was 'compounded by the then Irish Government who after the war only allowed an indefensibly small number who survived the concentration camps to settle permanently in Ireland.' The Minister also reminded the Irish press of the visit that de Valera had paid to the German Minister in Dublin, Dr. Eduard Hempel, to express his condolences on the death of Hitler.

There was little that was new in what Alan Shatter had said. In 1945, in the immediate aftermath of the war, Seán O Faolain had assessed the impact of neutrality on the Irish nation in somewhat similar terms: 'We have suffered by the prolonged suppression of our natural sympathies with tortured humanity', he wrote, 'our admiration for endurance and courage and our moral judgement have been held in abeyance.' What was, perhaps, most significant in Alan Shatter's comments was that they were spoken by a serving Minister in an Irish Government, and that he was not simply expressing abstract sympathy, but was promising specific political action to remedy a long-standing injustice.

As my son, Caoimhe and I came out of the gloom of the Farge Bunker into the warm spring sunlight, we made our way towards a sculpture by the German artist, Fritz Stein, which stands just outside the enclosed site. In some respects, it is a modest piece of work, and might appear dwarfed by the overwhelming size of the Bunker, but - perhaps, because of its intimate scale – it conveys great emotional power. It depicts a group of slave workers being crushed by the weight of a great block of stone. The Nazis called the camp where William and his Irish comrades were held an *Arbeiterszelunglager* – an 'Education through Work' camp. Stein gave his sculpture a more appropriate title: *Vernichtung durch Arbeit* – 'Extermination Through Work'.

As we stood beside it, I saw that a wreath of red poppies had recently been laid at its base. When I looked closer, I could see that it had been put there by Harry Callan on his last visit to the Bunker. The circle of poppies had been garlanded with ribbons of the Irish Republic's national flag: the green, white and orange Tricolour. I was struck by this juxtaposition, and commented to my son that those two powerful symbols of our country's fractured history were seldom seen together. 'Why shouldn't they be?', he asked me, 'Why can't we be proud of both?'

I still don't know why my father told me so little about our cousin's ordeal in the camp at Farge. Perhaps, he felt a little ashamed that William had not died a 'proper' soldier's death. More likely, he was simply too absorbed – or haunted – by the memories of the jungle war he had fought in Burma to think, or care much about his cousin's fate. Be that as it may, William was edged out of our family's story – just as he and the other Irish prisoners held illegally in the Nazis' labour camp were denied a place in Ireland's national narrative. However, I don't believe that our past history – as individuals or nations – is ever static or frozen by the passage of linear time. I agree with the English writer, Jeanette Winterson, that there is a real sense in which we are sometimes able to retrace our steps – to pick up what we dropped, and try to mend what others broke. For a variety of reasons, my cousin William was cut loose from the rest of his family: I am glad to welcome him back.

NOTES

1. SUDDENLY WHILE ABROAD

The brief discussion of the war in Burma in this chapter draws upon an unpublished manuscript written by my father, describing his experiences with the Inniskilling Fusiliers. It also draws upon several conversations I had with him – and with my mother – across a period of years. I have quoted in this chapter from *Defeat Into Victory* (London, 1956), the classic account of the Burma Campaign written by Field Marshall Viscount Slim. The discussion of censorship during the Emergency draws principally upon Donal O Drisceoil's *Censorship in Ireland, 1939-1945: Neutrality, Politics and Society*, (Cork, 1996). Clair Wills has also provided an original and penetrating cultural analysis of Ireland in the war years in *That Neutral Island: A History of Ireland During the Second World War* (London, 2007). Robert Fisk wrote a pioneering narrative of this period in his *In Time of War:*

Ireland, Ulster and the Price of Neutrality, 1939-45 (Dublin, 1983). In an interview for that book with Frank Aiken, Fisk reports that Aiken claimed that the Irish Cabinet had early knowledge of what was happening in the Nazi camps. I have also drawn upon Joseph T. Carroll's *Ireland in the War Years, 1939-45*, (Newton Abbot, 1975), and Ian S. Wood's *Ireland During the Second World War*, (London, 2002). This chapter has also been informed by the collection of essays in *Ireland in World War Two: Neutrality and Survival*, Edited by Dermot Keogh and Mervyn O'Driscoll (Cork, 2004). An unusual, but revealing perspective on Ireland in the war years is given in Martin S. Quigley's memoir *A U.S. Spy in Ireland* (Dublin, 1999). John de Courcy Ireland made an important contribution to the maritime history of Ireland, and, in this instance, I am indebted to his *History of Dun Laoghaire Harbour*, (Dublin, 2001). An overview of the Allied Merchant Navy is provided in Peter Elphick's *Life Line: The Merchant Navy at War, 1939-45*, (Chatham, 1999). Some of the anger felt by Allied seamen on North Atlantic convoys is expressed forcefully in Nicholas Monserrat's famous novel about the war, *The Cruel Sea* - see also *The Real Cruel Sea* by Richard Woodman, (London, 2010). Samuel Beckett was interviewed by Israel Shenker for the *New York Times* in May of 1956.

2. THE GERMAN RAIDER.

This chapter draws upon a number of accounts of the role that the *Hilskreuzers* – or surface raiders – played in the early years of World War Two. J.H. Brennecke's *Ghost Cruiser HK 33*, (London, 1954) provides a vivid account of the first - and, as it turned out, the last – voyage of Ernst-Felix Krüder and the *Pinguin*. I have also drawn upon Robert McQueen's *Hitler's Early Raiders*, (Dunbeith, 2011); on Bernard Edwards' *Beware Raiders! German Surface Raiders in the Second World War* (Barnsley, 2001); on J. D. Waters' *German Raiders in the Pacific (*Wellington, 1947*);* and on James P. Duffy's *Hitler's Secret Pirate Fleet: The Deadliest Ships of World War II,* (Westport, 2001). A more general description of this aspect of the World War can be found in *The War at Sea. 1939-45,* (London, 2005), by S.W. Roskill. A brief, but powerful description of the Battle of the Atlantic is given by Max Hastings in *All Hell Let Loose: The World at War, 1939-45,* (London, 2012).

3. THE IRISH LEGATION

In writing this chapter, I consulted the following files in the National Archives in Dublin: DFA/10/A/36; DFA/10/A/47; DFAS/10/92; DFA/10.P/3; DFA/10/P/81; DFA/4,241/127; and TSCH/3/S14526. Apart from the books by Fisk, Carroll and Wills that have already been cited, I have also drawn upon *Documents on Irish Foreign Policy*, Volumes IV, V, VI and VII, (Dublin, 2004-010), Edited by Catriona Crowe, Ronan Fanning, Michael Kennedy, Dermot Keogh and Eunan O'Halpin. I am also indebted to Dr. Niall Keogh's *Con Cremin: Ireland's Wartime Diplomat*, (Cork, 2006); *Memoir: My Life and Times*

(Dublin, 1999), by Conor Cruise O'Brien; and Andreas Roth's *Mr Bewley in Berlin: Aspects of the Career of an Irish Diplomat, 1933-1939*, (Dublin, 2000). Dermot Keogh provides an illuminating and comprehensive account of Ireland's Jewish community in *Jews in Twentieth-Century Ireland: Refugees, Anti-Semitism and the Holocaust*, (Cork, 1998). See also Richard Ellmann's *James Joyce*, (Oxford, 1965); and Toby Thacker's *Joseph Goebbels: Life and Death*, (New York, 2009). I have also considered comments made by Michael Drury, one of William Warnock's colleagues, in response to an article that I wrote on this subject for the *Dublin Review of Books.*

4. ARMED WITH A POP GUN

In this chapter – and elsewhere – I have drawn extensively upon an interview with Harry Callan, the last surviving Irish inmate of the labour camp in Farge, recorded at his home in Dublin in December, 2011. As well as drawing upon the works of McQueen, Edwards, Waters and Duffy, which I have already cited, I have also made use of *The Raider Kormoran* (London, 1959), a detailed account of the ship's exploits, written by her Captain, Theodor Detmers after he had returned to Germany in 1948. I have also drawn upon *Prisoner of the Kormoran*, as told by the Australian merchant seaman W.A. Jones to James Taylor, (London 1945): Jones was also taken prisoner by Thedor Detmers in 1941, but, unlike the Irish seamen, he was repatriated to England within two years. An unusual insight to the fate of civilian passengers on board merchant ships that were sunk or captured by German surface raiders – such as the *Kormoran*, or the *Atlantis* - can be found in Carolyn Gossage's *The Accidental Captives: The Story of Seven Women Alone in Nazi Germany*, (New York, 2011).

5. THE MINING TOWN

The title of this chapter is taken from a comment made by David James in his book *Prisoner's Progress* (London, 2008). Once again, I have drawn upon my interview with Harry Callan of December, 2011. Gabe Thomas's book *MILAG: Captives of the Kriegsmarine*, (Glamorgan, 1995), provides by far the most detailed account of the history of the Milag merchant navy internment camp. I have also drawn upon general histories of the experience of prisoner of war camps in Nazi Germany, including Adrian Gilbert's *POW: Allied Prisoners in Europe, 1939-45* (London, 2006); and Seán Longden's *Hitler's British Slaves: Allied POWs in Germany, 1939-45* (London, 2005). The details of the investigation into the death of Cadet Officer Walter Skeet can be found in the National Archives at Kew in London (WO 311/159 and C493568.). I have also drawn upon the taped interviews with the Cadet Officer, Jack Matthews, from the *Athelfoam* – the ship that AB Patrick Breen served on – and the Engineering Officer, John Woods, from the *Silver Fir* – on which AB Owen Corr served - which can be found in the Imperial War Museum in London. Ulrich Mohr and Arthur Sellwood tell the story of the ship that captured the

Irish Cadet Officer, Christopher Ryan, in *Atlantis: Story of a German Surface Raider*, (London, 1973). Perhaps, the most illuminating account of this ship's exploits can be found in *The German Raider Atlantis* (New York, 1956), written by her Captain, Bernhard Rogge, with Wolfgang Frank. This book formed the basis of the movie that was made in the 1960s, and which starred Van Heflin as Rogge. The account of Gerald O'Hara's capture and captivity has drawn upon a presentation made by his son, Eamon O'Hara, entitled *From Ballina to Bremen*, to the Euro-Schulen-Organisation in 2007. Paul Lund and Harry Ludlam provide a detailed account of the debacle of the North Atlantic convoy PQ17 – on which AB Patrick Murphy was taken prisoner – in *On PQ17: The Convoy to Hell*, (Slough, 2010).

6. THE ABWEHR'S IRISH FRIENDS

The most detailed account of the German attempt to recruit Irishmen to fight on the side of the Third Reich can be found in Terence O'Reilly's *Hitler's Irishmen*, (Cork, 2008). O'Reilly concludes that only two Irish members of the Allied armed forces ended up on active service with the Waffen-SS. Given that there were probably in excess of 1,000 Irish POWs in Nazi Germany, this figure clearly represents a very small proportion. See also *German Activities with Irish POWs*, (KV 3/345) in the National Archives at Kew, in London. The relationship between the IRA and the *Abwehr* is explored by David O'Donoghue in *The Devil's Deal: The IRA, Nazi Germany and the Double Life of Jim O'Donovan* (Dublin,

2010). The report of Fr. O'Shaughnessy on his visit to the Freisack camp may be found in the National Archives, in the files I have already cited. Reports on the Freisack operation can also be found in the British National Archives in Kew, in London. The perspective of Irish Military Intelligence is provided by Maurice Walsh in *G2: In Defence of Ireland: Irish Military Intelligence*, 1918-45, (Cork, 2002). I have drawn upon the article by Brian Hanley, *Oh Here's To Adolph Hitler: The IRA and the Nazis*, that appeared in *History Ireland* in May/June, 2005. See also David O'Donoghue's *New Evidence of IRA/Nazi Links*, in *History Ireland*, March/April, 2011. Very useful background information can also be found in John P. Duggan's book on Dr. Eduard Hempel, which I have already cited. For further details of Francis Stuart's attempts to translate W. J. Maloney's book about Casement, see *Roger Casement in Death: Or Haunting the Free State*, (Dublin, 2002), by W.J. McCormick. See also Eunan O'Halpin, *Spying in Ireland: British Intelligence and Irish Neutrality During the Second World War*, (Oxford, 1998), and, by the same author, *Defending Ireland: The Irish State and its Enemies since 1922*, (Oxford, 1999). For a more detailed discussion of the Wannsee Conference, see Robert Gerwarth's *Hitlers Hangman: The Life of Heydrich*, (Yale, 2011).

7. THE SS AND CO

This chapter draws upon a number of histories and analyses of the SS. These include Adrian Weale's *The SS:*

A New History, (London, 2012). I have also made use of *Die SS: Eine Warnung der Geschichte* (Munich, 2002) by Guido Knopp. I have drawn upon some recent studies of the concentration camp system, including *Concentration Camps in Nazi Germany: The New Histories*, (Oxford, 2010), Edited by Jane Caplan and Nikolaus Wachsmann; and Wolfgang Sofsky's *The Order of Terror: the Concentration Camp*, (Princeton, 1997). Adam Tooze's *The Wages of Destruction: The Making and Breaking of the Nazi Economy* (London, 2006), and Michael Thad Allen's *Hitler's Slave Lords: The Business of Forced Labour in Occupied Europe*, (North Carolina, 2004). The last two mentioned provide detailed explanations of how the camp system related to Nazi Germany's war economy. Mark Mazower's *Hitler's Empire: Nazi Rule in Occupied Europe* (London, 2008) is also useful in this regard. I am grateful for the assistance I received when I visited the former concentration camp at Neuengamme in May, 2012, and for their rough guide to the camp: *KZ-Gedenkstatte Neuengamme*. In this chapter, I have also drawn upon the interviews given by survivors of the Farge camp to the *Irish Times* when they returned to Ireland in 1945, and upon interviews given by Christopher Ryan to the *Daily Mirror* newspaper in 2000, and to the *Sunday Life* newspaper in 2004.

8. THE BUNKER

Albert Speer's autobiography *Inside the Third Reich*, (London, 1976), provides an account and attempted explanation for his actions during World War Two. A more complex analysis of those actions is given by Gitta Sereny in her remarkable and exhaustive work *Albert Speer: His Battle with Truth*, (New York, 1996). A rather more detached account can be found in Joachim Fest's *Speer: The Final Verdict* (London, 2001). I have also consulted Dan van der Vat's *The Good Nazi: The Life and Lies of Albert Speer*, (London, 1997), and Blaine Taylor's *Hitler's Engineers: Fritz Todt and Albert Speer – Master Builders of the Third Reich*, (Newbury, 2010). See also *U-Boat Bases and Bunkers, 1940-45'*, by Gordon Williamson and Ian Palmer, (Oxford, 2003); *Hortensien in Farge: Uberleben in Bunker Valentin*, (Bremen, 1996), by Raymond Portefaix, Andre Migdal, Klaas Touber and Barbara Johr; *U-Boot Bunker Valentin: Kriegswirtscaft und Zwangsarbeit Bremen-Farge, 1943-45* (Bremen, 1996), by Dieter Schmidt; and *Hitler's U-Boat Bunkers*, (Stroud, 2002), by Jak P. Mallmann Showell. In discussing the Valentin Bunker, I have also made use of Marc Buggeln's excellent *Bunker Valentin: Marinerustung, Zwangsarbeit und Erinnerung*, (Bremen, 2010). Once again, I have drawn upon Adam Tooze's analysis of the German war economy, and on Mark Mazower's work, which I have already cited. Along with my son and his partner, I was able to visit the last remaining Type XXI U-boat, William Bauer, in Bremenhaven in the spring of 2012. I am grateful to the Technikmuseum for their *Kleine Geschichte und Technik der deutschen U-boote*. Once again, I have drawn in this chapter upon the interview which I conducted with Harry Callan in 2011.

9. HEART OF DARKNESS

In writing this chapter, I have drawn upon the transcript of the war crimes trial of SS guards, and others in the Farge camp by a British Military court in Hamburg in 1947. I have also drawn upon my interview with Harry Callan, and with the interview given in 2004 by Christopher Ryan to the *Sunday Life* newspaper in Northern Ireland. This chapter has also been informed by Eugen Kogon's *The Theory and Practice of Hell: The German Concentration camps and the System Behind them* (New York, 1950); Naomi Baumslag's, *Murderous Medicine: Nazi Doctors, Human Experimentation, and Typhus* (Westport, 2005); and *The Nazi Doctors: Medical Killing and the Psychology of Genocide*, (United States, 2000), by Robert Jay Lifton. See also *Masters of Death: The SS Einsatzgruppen and the Invention of the Holocaust*, (New York, 2003), by Richard Rhodes; and *The Last Nazis: SS Werewolf Guerrilla Resistance in Europe, 1944-47*, (London, 2000), by Perry Biddiscombe. I have also drawn again upon Dr. Niall Keogh's book on Con Cremin, which I have already cited.

10. ENDGAME

An overview of this stage of the war in provided by Max Hasting's in the work I have already cited. In this chapter, I have drawn again upon Gabe Thomas's account of the merchant navy internment camp at Milag Nord. I have also drawn upon my interview with Harry Callan, and upon interviews that Christopher Ryan gave to the Irish newspapers that have also already been cited. Gunther Schwarburg provides a harrowing description of the murder of the 20 Jewish children in *The Murders at Bullenhuser Dam The SS Doctor and the Children,* (New York, 1984).

11. AFTERMATH

In writing this chapter, I have consulted the Black List that issued by the Irish Government in 1945, or, to give it its full title: *List of Personnel of the Defence Forces dismissed for desertion in time of National Emergency pursuant to the terms of Emergency Powers (No. 362) Order 1945 (S.R. & O. 1945, No. 198) or of Section 13 of the Defence Forces (Temporary Provisions) Act, 1946 (No. 7/1946).* Robert Widders has also provided a powerful and emotional account of the implications of the Irish Government's actions in *Spitting on a Soldier's Grave,* (Kibworth, 2012). Several journalists – notably, Kevin Myers – have played an important role in bringing this history of the attention of the Irish public. An account of the last days of Belsen is given by Ben Shephard in *After Daybreak: The Liberation of Belsen, 1943-45,* (London, 2006). Jack Harte's *To the Limits of Endurance,* (Dublin, 2007), includes a powerful description of his experience as an Irishman who was a prisoner of the Germans. Stephen Flower gives a detailed description of the man and the process which led to the defences of the Valentin being finally breached , in *Barnes Wallis Bombs: Dam Busters, Tallboys and Grand Slams,* (London, 2010). Samuel Beckett's short story, *The Expelled,* from which I quote in this chapter, was published in his *Texts for Nothing,* (New York, 1967).

12. A STATE OF DENIAL

See Helen Fry, *Denazification: Britain's Enemy Aliens, Nazi War Criminals and other Reconstruction of Post-war Europe*, (Stroud, 2010). Benjamin B. Ferencz provides an account of the Adolf Diament case in *Less than Slaves: Jewish Forced Labor and the Quest for Compensation*, (Indiana, 2002). See also Paul Roland's *The Nuremberg Trials*, (London, 2010); and William J. Bosch's *Judgement on Nuremberg: American Attitudes Towards the Major German War Crimes Trials*, (North Carolina, 1970). The denazification of Germany is further explored by Frederick Taylor in *Exorcising Hitler: the Occupation and Denazification of Germany*, (London, 2011); by Norbert Frei in *Adeneur's Germany and the Nazi Past: The Politics of Amnesty and Integration*, (Columbia, 2002); and by Erik Lommatzch in *Hans Globke: Beamter im Dritten Reich und Staatsseketar Adenauers*, (Frankfurt, 2009). A file devoted to Dr. Heidbreder can be found in the National Archives at Kew, in London, (WO 235/441). It may also be worth pointing out that the British hanged 33 SS personnel from the Neuengamme complex and imprisoned a further 53 in the immediate aftermath of the war. In the decades that followed, the German authorities only imprisoned 11 former SS members, and hanged one.

13. A STATE OF NEUTRALITY

In this chapter, I have again drawn upon the cited works by Wills, Carroll, Fisk and O Drisceoil. The biography of De Valera by the Earl of Longford and Thomas P. O'Neill, *Eamon de Valera*, (London, 1974), is little short of a hagiographic work, but remains a useful text. A more contemporary and balanced assessment of de Valera is provided by Diarmuid Ferriter in *Judging Dev: A Reassessment of the Life and Legacy of Eamon de Valera*, (Dublin, 2007). A much more bizarre offering comes from John J. Turi in *Englands Greatest Spy: Eamon de Valera*, (Dublin, 2009): as its title suggests, Turi argues that de Valera was actually working throughout his life for British Military Intelligence. A pioneering account of the *Abwehr's* activities in Ireland was provided by Enno Stephens in *Spies in Ireland*, (London, 1965). A more recent account comes from Mark. M. Hull in *Irish Secrets: German Espionage in Wartime Ireland, 1939-1945*, (Irish Academic Press, 2004). Although she has sometimes been denounced as a British spy, Elizabeth Bowen's dispatches from Ireland during the war read more like informed journalism. in this chapter, I have also drawn upon John P. Duggan's *Herr Hempel at the Irish Legation in Dublin, 1937-45*, (Dublin, 2003). See also *Returning Home: Irish Ex-Servicemen After the Second World War*, (Dublin, 2012), by Bernard Kelly; and David Egerton's *Britain's War Machine: Weapons, Resources and Experts in the Second World War*, (London, 2011).

14. RADIO WAVES

This chapter draws upon Brendan Barrington's *The Wartime Broadcasts of Francis Stuart, 1942-44* (Dublin 2000) – which reproduces all the existing transcripts of Stuart's broadcasts for the radio service provided by Irland-Redaktion, as well as providing an insightful analysis. The story of Irland-Redaktion is explored in some detail in David O'Donoghue's *Hitler's Irish Voices: The Story of German Radio's Wartime Irish Service*, (Dublin, 1998). Mary Kenny has provided an excellent background to Stuart's broadcasting work in her *Germany Calling: A Personal Biography of William Joyce – Lord Haw-Haw*, (Dublin, 2004). I have also drawn upon Kevin Keily's biography of Stuart: *Francis Stuart: Artist and Outcast*, See also *Subhas Chandra Bose in Nazi Germany: Politics, Intelligence and Propaganda, 1941-43*, (London, 2011). (Dublin, 2007). See Francis Stuart, *Black List, Section H*, (Southern Illinois, 1975).

15. WHAT WAR?

In this chapter, I have drawn upon *Ireland and the Second World War: Politics, Society and Remembrance,* Edited by Brian Girvan and Geoffrey Roberts, (Dublin, 2000). I also found Richard Doherty's *Irish Men and Women in the Second World War*, (Dublin, 1999), to be very useful. I should explain here that the killing agent used in Zyklon B was odourless: for the safety of SS personnel, a warning agent – which exuded a pungent smell – was added to the chemical compound. Following the publication of Brendan Barrington's book, which reproduced the transcripts of Stuart's wartime broadcasts, Kevin Myers was quoted, in the Observer newspaper, as saying that he believed the settlement of Stuart's libel case had been 'a grotesque miscarriage of justice'. According to a file in the National Archives at Kew, in London, Clissmann is identified as having worked 'both for the *Abwehr* and the Janke Bureau, a political intelligence-gathering organization working on behalf of the Nazi Party.' (KV 6/81) The description of the 1995 war veterans parade in London comes from an unpublished manuscript written by my father in that year. Once again, I have drawn upon my interview with Harry Callan that took place in of December. The discussion of stuttering draws primarily upon Benson Bobrick's *Knotted Tongues Stuttering in History and the Quest for a Cure*, (New York, 1995).

16. FARGE.

See *Donitz: The Last Führer*, (London, 1995), by Peter Padfield. See also *The Memoirs of Karl Doenitz: Ten Years and Twenty Days*, Introduction by Jurgen Rohwer, and Foreword by Jak Showell, (London, 2012). The title of Donitz's autobiography is a precise reference to the time he spent in Spandau prison in Berlin, following his conviction for war crimes at Nuremberg.